IMAGES
*of America*

# PITTSBURGH'S SHADYSIDE

*On the cover*: Please see page 117. (Courtesy of the University of Pittsburgh Archives Service Center.)

IMAGES
*of America*

# PITTSBURGH'S SHADYSIDE

Donald Doherty

ARCADIA
PUBLISHING

ISBN 978-0-7385-5701-4

Published by Arcadia Publishing
Charleston, South Carolina

Printed in the United States of America

Library of Congress Catalog Card Number: 2007938996

For all general information contact Arcadia Publishing at:
Telephone 843-853-2070
Fax 843-853-0044
E-mail sales@arcadiapublishing.com
For customer service and orders:
Toll-Free 1-888-313-2665

Visit us on the Internet at www.arcadiapublishing.com

*To Dad, who gave me an appreciation for the built environment.*

# Contents

# ACKNOWLEDGMENTS

A book takes much more than an author to complete, and this book would have never been finished if it were not for the gentle prodding of my editor, Erin Vosgien. I would also like to thank the Shadyside Action Coalition and the Historic Shadyside Committee of the Shadyside Action Coalition for helping to make this book a reality. I especially wish to thank Peggy Atkinson and Suzanne Kardon for helping connect me with images, but Peggy Ott, Carol McGinty, Susan McGinty, and John Barlow also contributed. A very special and warm acknowledgment goes out to Jim Tinnemeyer for generously offering his time to find extraordinary images from the Shadyside Presbyterian Church archives and sharing his substantial knowledge of East End history. Individuals with connections to a historic home or family from Shadyside, and sometimes both, were particularly exciting to connect with while working on this book. Special thanks go to Martha Perego for her McCook family memories and generosity in providing family photographs. It was also a special pleasure to meet Nancy McNary Smith and visit the home that Maj. Joseph F. Denniston built and lived in. She generously provided historic images of the home that she and her husband have lovingly maintained. Finally, archives were essential to this book, and four Pittsburgh archives were particularly important. The University of Pittsburgh Archives Service Center provided a large number of images for this book, and its staff members were a pleasure to work with. In particular, Miriam Meislik energized this project through her support and enthusiasm. Special thanks go to Ed Galloway of the University of Pittsburgh Digital Research Library for providing scanned historic maps. The Library and Archives Division, Senator John Heinz History Center supplied a number of images with the help of its professional staff. I would particularly like to thank Lauren Zabelsky, who is a lot of fun to work with in addition to being a person who goes out of her way to be helpful. Even though I came to the Chatham College Archives late in the development of this book, archivist Jamie Peretich bent over backward to help select beautiful images and to be extraordinarily helpful. I also came late to the Carnegie Mellon University Architecture Archives where Martin Aurand was remarkable at finding images in record time. Thank you to everyone, including Arcadia Publishing, the Athenaeum of Philadelphia, the Georgetown University Library, and all the others who have helped in this endeavor. Finally, thank you to my wife and son, with whom I look forward to spending more time.

# INTRODUCTION

From its inception around 1860, Shadyside has been one of Pittsburgh's most desirable neighborhoods. Before then, the area was farmland owned most notably by the Aiken family, but there were also smaller farms. It was the need for faster travel and shipment of goods from the west to Philadelphia that set the stage for the development of the farming community that became Shadyside. In December 1852, the Pennsylvania Railroad opened a line through the area, the same line that is used today. The Pennsylvania Railroad connected with an existing canal and incline system, known as the Portage Road, that carried passengers and cargo over the Alleghenies. The Portage Road significantly slowed the rate of travel, but it was still much faster than the alternatives. It was not until November 1, 1855, that the Pennsylvania Railroad ran all the way through between Pittsburgh and Philadelphia without the need to move passengers and cargo between trains and canal boats.

Thomas Aiken (1815–1873) is said to have dreamed of a planned suburb with a centrally located church on his land. His land was part of his family's heritage going back to the 1780s when Jacob Castleman owned an estate known as Castlemania. Thomas Aiken's uncle David Aiken had married Jacob Castleman's daughter Rachel Castleman. Thomas Aiken married David and Rachel's daughter and eventually inherited their land. His land included most of what now lies between Aiken Avenue, Neville Street, Fifth Avenue, and the Pennsylvania Railroad tracks. With modern transportation passing through his land, Thomas Aiken recognized an opportunity to provide affluent businessmen in nearby Pittsburgh a place for their families to live in the country while also providing them a relatively rapid and easy commute to work in the city. When his son David Aiken was 21, Thomas Aiken divided the farm between them. Thomas Aiken took the east side from Amberson Avenue to Aiken Avenue, and David took the west side from Amberson Avenue to Neville Street. The Aikens lobbied the railroad to add a stop on their land. Andrew Carnegie, superintendent of the Western Division of the Pennsylvania Railroad, agreed in 1860 to a flag stop at the end of Amberson Avenue. By the early 1860s a station was built and named the Shady Side station.

The Shadyside Presbyterian Church got its start the same year that the Pennsylvania Railroad train began stopping at Shadyside. On Sunday, April 29, 1860, at 4:00 in the afternoon, Thomas and Eliza Aiken with William and Joanna Negley held the first Shadyside Sunday School. Thomas Aiken was superintendent, and the other three were teachers. William Negley and his wife were close friends of the Aikens, and all attended the East Liberty Presbyterian Church. Both families lived in East Liberty until Thomas Aiken inherited his father-in-law's property and moved to the Shady Side farm in 1855. Later William Negley purchased land in Shadyside and moved nearby the Aikens. It took hours to arrive at services in the East Liberty Presbyterian Church by the main modes of mid-19th-century transportation—foot, horseback, or carriage. The Shadyside Sunday School provided neighborhood access for the 40 students in attendance on that first day.

The first Shadyside Presbyterian Church building was completed in July 1867 and formed the nucleus of the growing Shadyside community rooted in the Scottish Presbyterian tradition. Pastor Dr. William Trimble Beatty began preaching on September 9, 1866, in the Shady Side train station, which he did every Sunday night until the church building was completed. The first church building was rapidly outgrown as the community grew, and a second building was completed in 1874. Finally, the church rebuilt again, completing the third and current church building in 1890.

Soon after becoming the first pastor of the Shadyside Presbyterian Church, Beatty led a group of Pittsburghers in making the dream of solid academic training for women a reality. They wanted to provide women with an education comparable to that which men could receive at the time at "colleges of the first class." A similar college had been started downtown by the Methodists in 1854 and was known as the Pittsburgh Female College. The Pennsylvania Female College was chartered on December 11, 1869, and it was decided to purchase the Berry estate, the largest residence in western Pennsylvania at the time, to house the college. The college would grow and become the Pittsburgh College for Women in 1898 and then Chatham College in 1955.

Another academic institution that got its start in Shadyside was the Shady Side Academy. The Shady Side Academy college preparatory school for boys, then known as the Shady Side Classical Academy, held its first classes in September 1883 and began meeting in a one-room brick building at 926 Aiken Avenue that same year. The school's charter was issued on June 6, 1885, with the aim to offer boys of ambition and determination the best facilities to prepare for high-standard college education. As the academy became more popular, a new room was added to the building, but the academy quickly outgrew the space. In September 1885, the Shady Side Academy moved to a new building at Morewood and Ellsworth Avenues.

Today the question of "Where is Shadyside?" or, more precisely, "What land may we say belongs to the Shadyside neighborhood?" is one that people have widely varying opinions about, but there are solid historic answers to the question.

Most concretely, the City of Pittsburgh now considers the 7th Ward to be Shadyside. On the map the 7th Ward encompasses all the land between Penn Avenue to Neville Street and Centre Avenue to Fifth Avenue. There is no correspondence between this map of Shadyside and any particular zip code, and the area encompasses at least three zip codes.

Historically, Shadyside was the East End neighborhood between Aiken Avenue, Neville Street, Fifth Avenue (both sides), and the Pennsylvania Railroad tracks. The area, for instance, between Centre Avenue, Millvale Avenue, and the railroad tracks contained one large estate through much of the 19th century, the Alexander Bradley estate, which was listed as a Shady Side address. Today much of that estate land is officially listed by the city as part of Bloomfield.

William B. Negley owned and developed much of the land between Aiken and Negley Avenues. This neighborhood was often referred to as Shadyside in the historic records and so was the land on the other side of the Pennsylvania Railroad tracts around the Shady Side train station. The former area is where the Walnut Street commercial district is today, and the latter area is the location of the Shadyside Hospital.

Everything east of Negley Avenue was referred to as part of East Liberty or simply the East End. The commercial districts up Highland, Shady, and Ellsworth Avenues were natural extensions of the vibrant East Liberty commercial district. Until the second half of the 20th century there Ellsworth Avenue included a bridge over the Pennsylvania Railroad tracks.

Finally, there is the question of Chatham College and the Woodland Road estates, which to this day consider themselves part of Shadyside. The Shadyside community and, in particular, the first pastor of the Shadyside Presbyterian Church were instrumental in the founding of Chatham College, and so they have always been an integral part of the Shadyside community.

# *One*

# Suburban Estates 1868–1900

The City of Pittsburgh was incorporated in 1758, and Shadyside was annexed by Pittsburgh in 1868. The planned suburb of Shadyside was established and the first Shadyside Presbyterian Church building was opened in July 1867. Among the prominent early citizens of the neighborhood was Judge Marcus Acheson, who lived with his family on Amberson Avenue. The Achesons' daughter Mary Wilson Acheson married Charles Hart Spencer. Judge Acheson gave his daughter and new son-in-law a new house for their wedding present. The Spencer house was, and still is, at the center of the Shadyside neighborhood that Thomas Aiken and his son David Aiken laid out. Charles Spencer was a middle manager in Henry Clay Frick's business concerns but never distinguished himself in business. However, it is fortunate that he was a passionate photography hobbyist. Shadyside was entirely residential during these years with only schools and churches intruding on the domestic quality of the place. It was where family life ran its course in its own way for affluent middle-class residents like the Spencer family or fabulously wealthy residents like the Pitcairn family. Through Charles Spencer's camera especially, one is able to see the 19th-century Shadyside and the people living there. In 1860, when the Pennsylvania Railroad began stopping at the end of Amberson Avenue there were 20 families living in Shadyside. By 1870 the Shadyside area had a population of 2,272 and was already one of the wealthiest wards in the city.

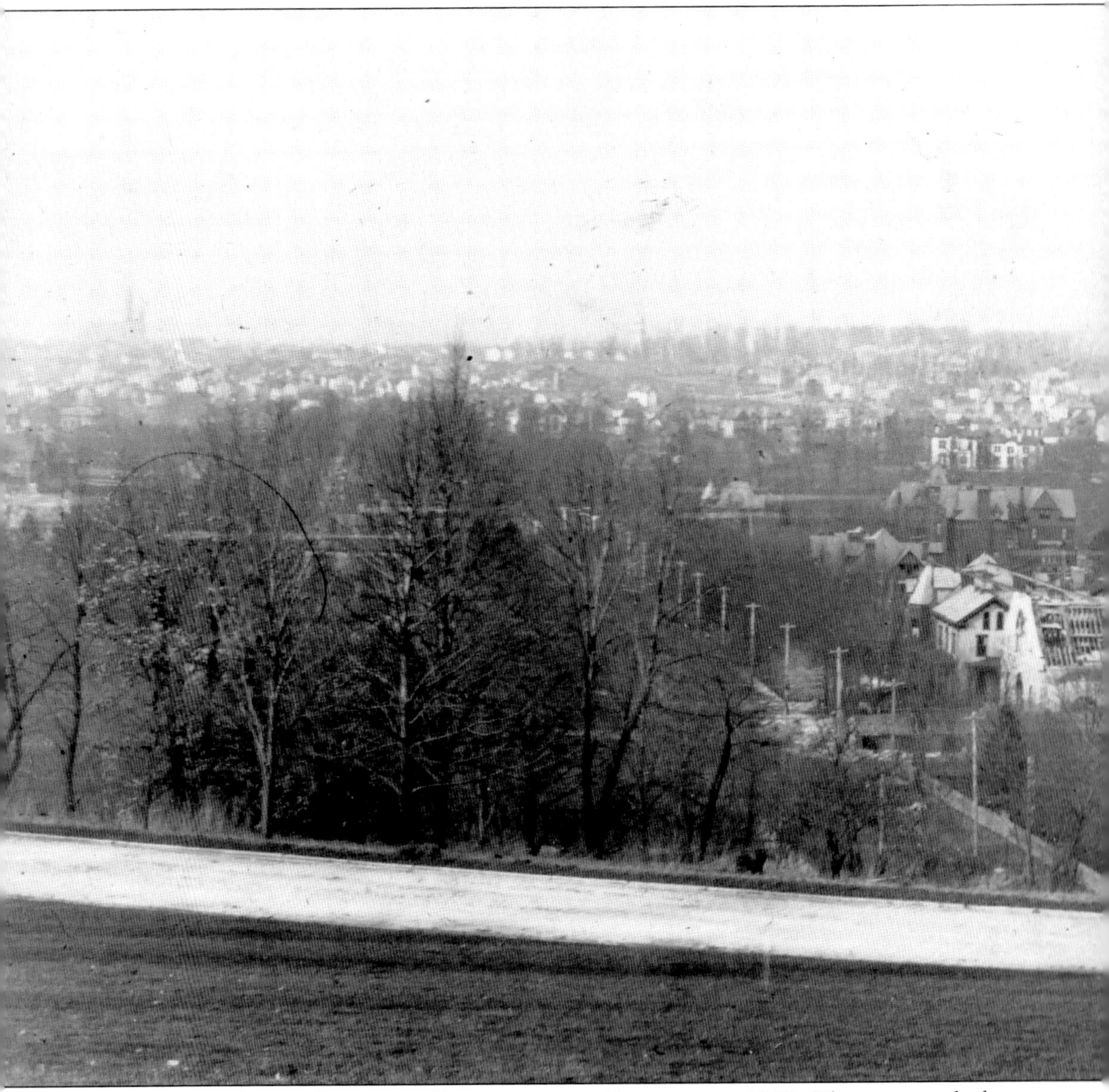

**CONSTRUCTION OF SHADYSIDE PRESBYTERIAN CHURCH, C. 1889.** The center of what was once the Aiken farm is highlighted by the construction of the third church building since the founding of the Shadyside Presbyterian Church in 1866. Shepley, Rutan, and Coolidge of Boston

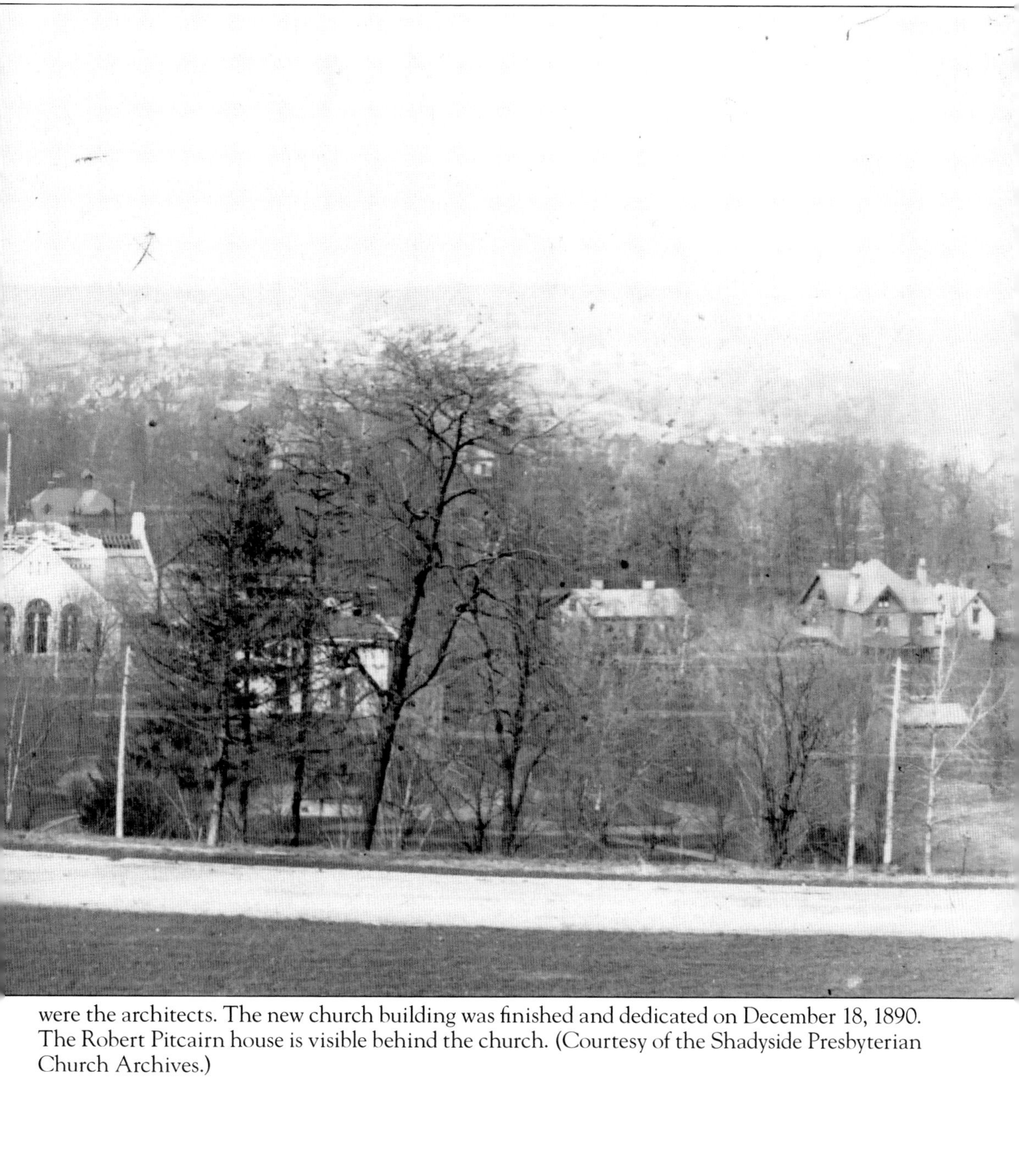

were the architects. The new church building was finished and dedicated on December 18, 1890. The Robert Pitcairn house is visible behind the church. (Courtesy of the Shadyside Presbyterian Church Archives.)

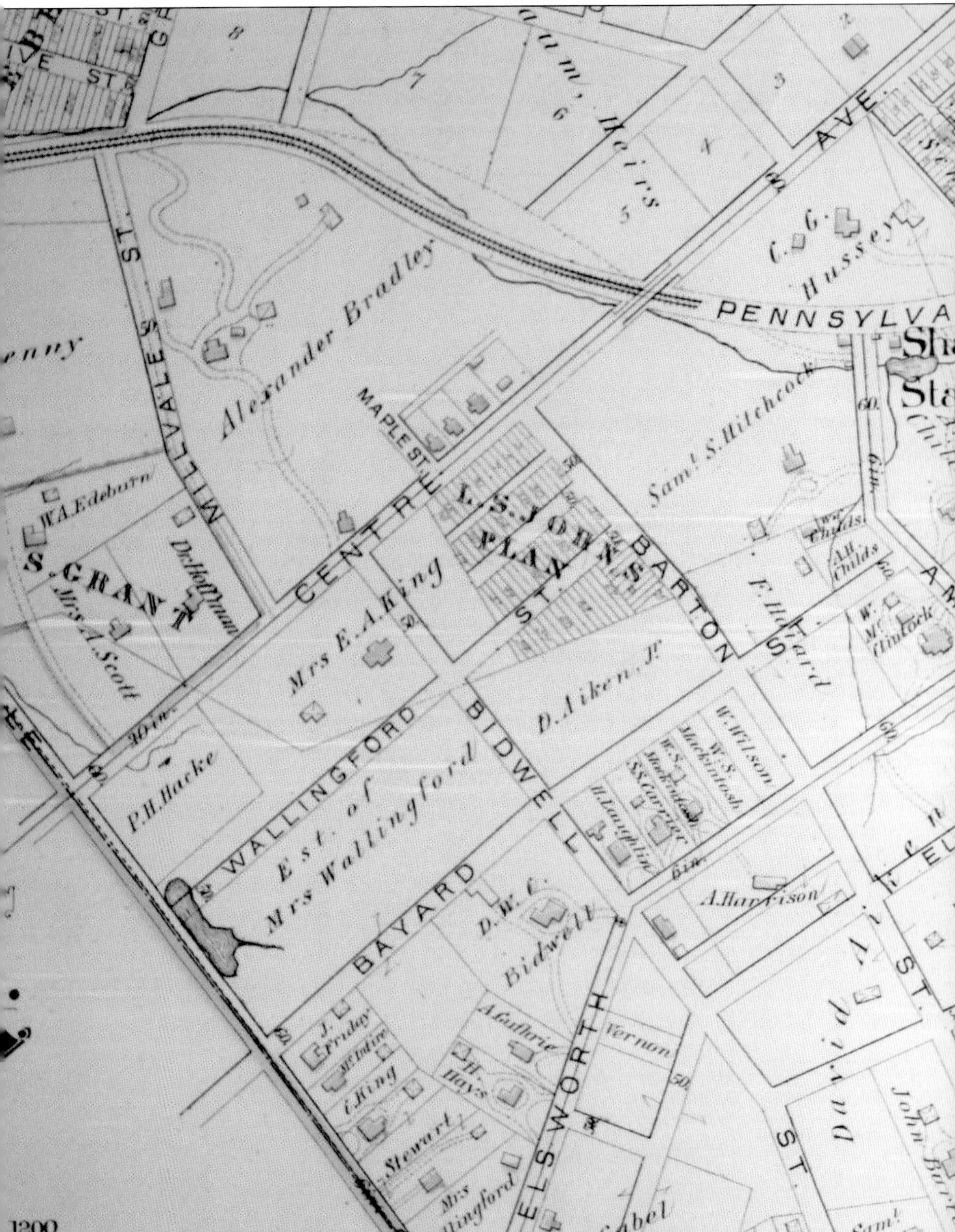

Alexander Bradley
MILLVALE ST.
MAPLE ST.
CENTRE
AVE
BARTON
S. JOHNS PLAN
Sam'l S. Hitchcock
C. G. Hussey
W. A. Edeburn
Mrs A. Scott
Mrs E. A. King
WALLINGFORD
BIDWELL ST.
D. Aiken. Jr
Est. of Mrs Wallingford
P. H. Hacke
BAYARD
D. W. C. Bidwell
A. Harrison
A. H. Childs
W. Wilson
ELSWORTH
Vernon
A. Guthrie
H. Hays
Stewart
Mrs Wallingford
A. Gabel
1200

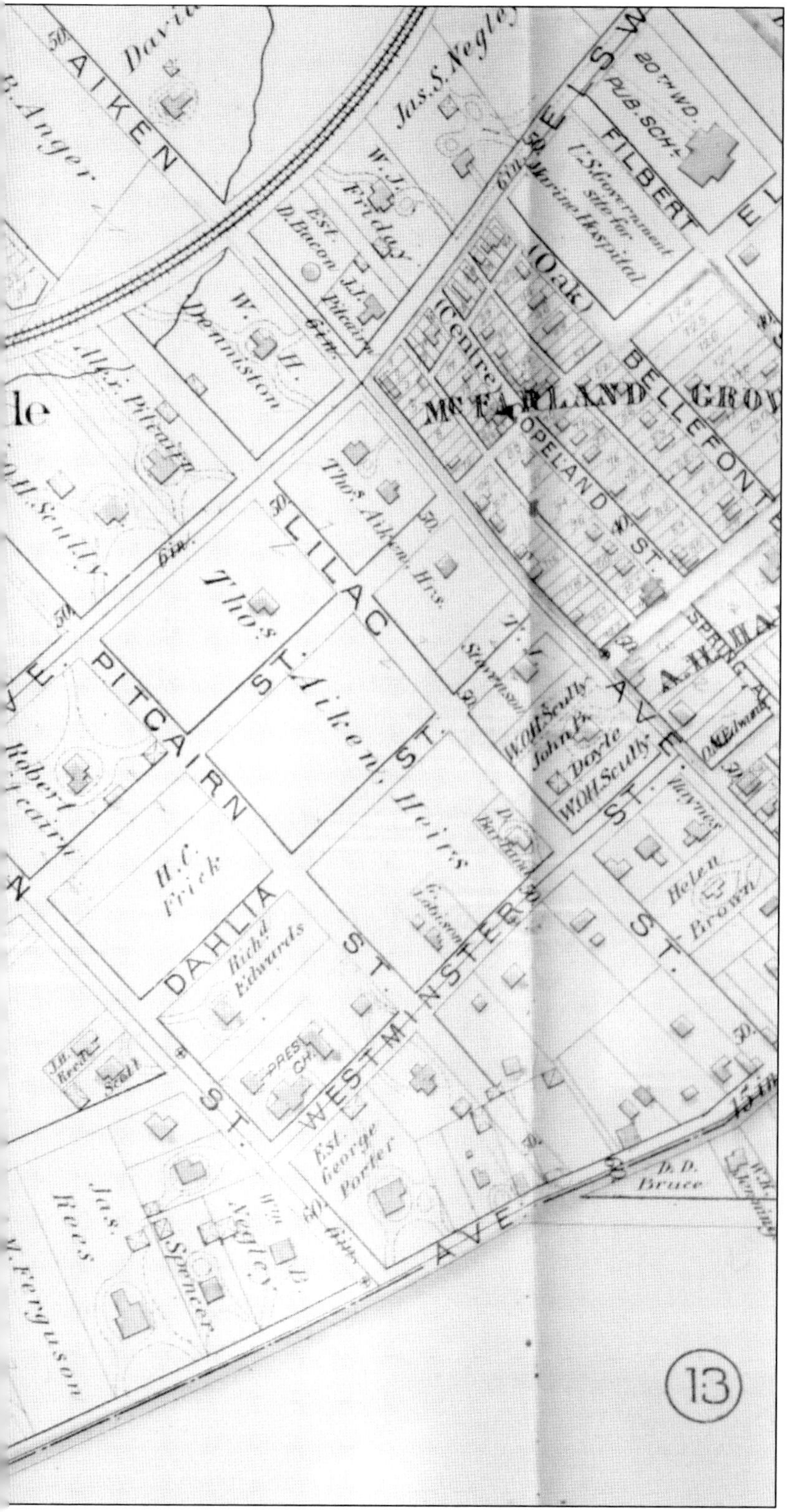


**SHADYSIDE AREA MAP, 1882.** Today Shadyside is recognized by the City of Pittsburgh as encompassing the area from Neville Street to Penn Avenue and Centre Avenue to Fifth Avenue. Historically Shadyside, often spelled as Shady Side, began as the area defined by Neville Street at left, Aiken Avenue at right, Fifth Avenue at bottom, and the Pennsylvania Railroad line at top. The Pennsylvania Railroad was completed in 1852 from Philadelphia to Pittsburgh but still used the canal and incline system over the Allegheny Mountains. Shadyside incorporated into Pittsburgh in 1868. A flag stop was placed at the end of Amberson Avenue as early as 1860 until the Shady Side station was built a couple of years later.

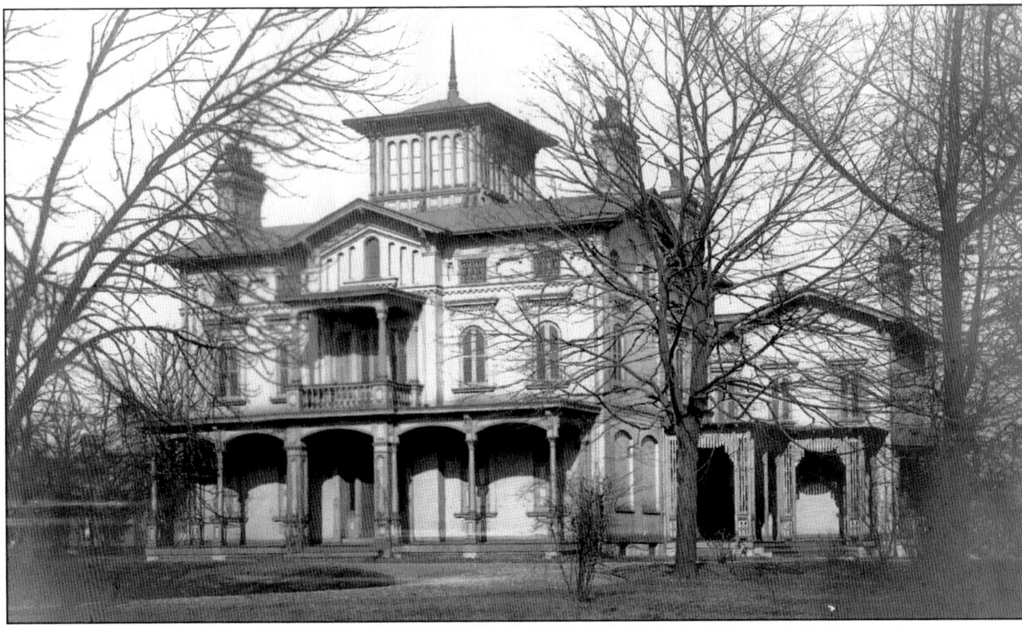

**RESIDENCE OF ALEXANDER BRADLEY, C. 1890.** Bradley owned one of the early estates in Shadyside with a grand wood-structured home typical for the neighborhood during the mid-19th century. The 1886 map shows the large chunk of land the Bradleys lived on next to the Pennsylvania Railroad tracks, bordered by Centre and Millvale Avenues. (Courtesy of the Library and Archives Division, Senator John Heinz History Center.)

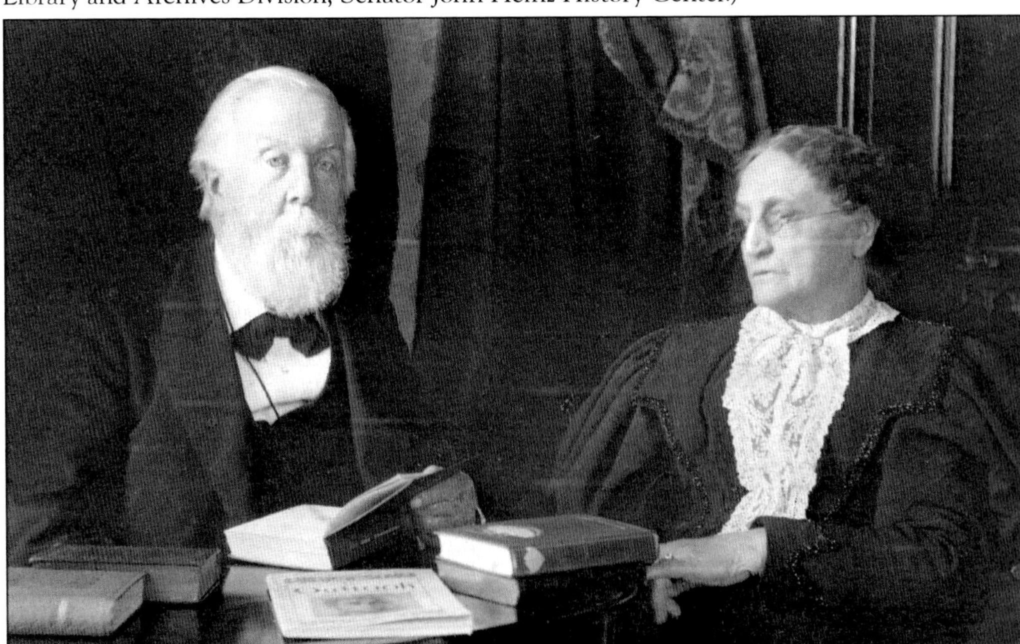

**ALEXANDER AND ELIZABETH STEWART BRADLEY, C. 1890.** Alexander Bradley was born on October 31, 1821, in Baltimore, Maryland, and arrived in Pittsburgh in 1927. In 1836, he started a foundry that manufactured stoves. He died in Pittsburgh on August 21, 1899, at the age of 87. (Courtesy of the Library and Archives Division, Senator John Heinz History Center.)

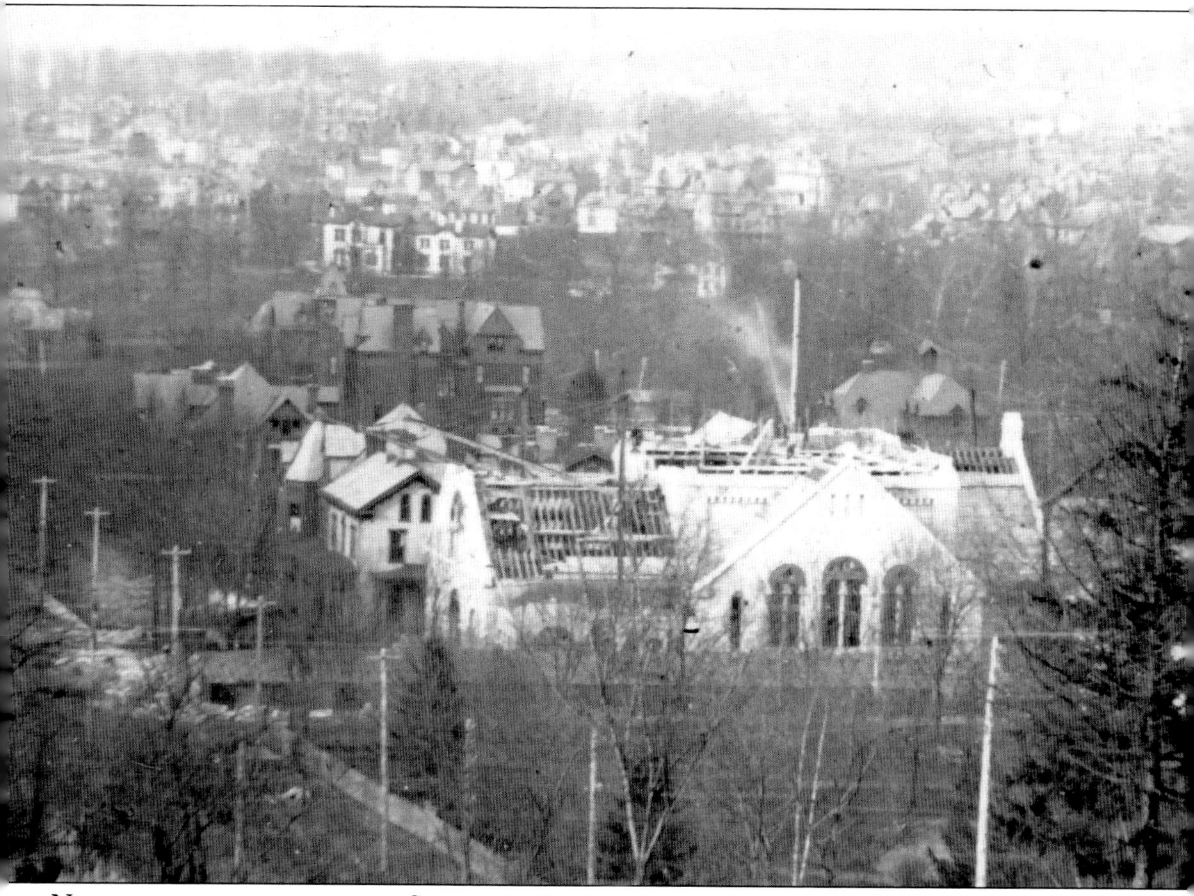

**NEIGHBORHOOD AROUND THE SHADYSIDE PRESBYTERIAN CHURCH, C. 1889.** Many of the early residents of Shadyside had homes close to the Shadyside Presbyterian Church. Amberson Avenue runs diagonally across the lower-left corner of the image with telephone poles tracing its path. In the foreground to the right of Amberson Avenue is the third building under construction for the Shadyside Presbyterian Church. At the left end of the church (toward Amberson Avenue) and just behind is the church's parsonage. Just behind and to the left of the parsonage is the Edwards house, which became the Lincoln home by 1897. Next the roof of the Snyder home (later the McClintock house) is visible and then the Spencer house and finally the Macbeth house. The very large structure to the right, looming behind the Spencer and Macbeth homes, is the Robert Pitcairn house. Friendship and East Liberty are visible in the distance. (Courtesy of the Shadyside Presbyterian Church Archives.)

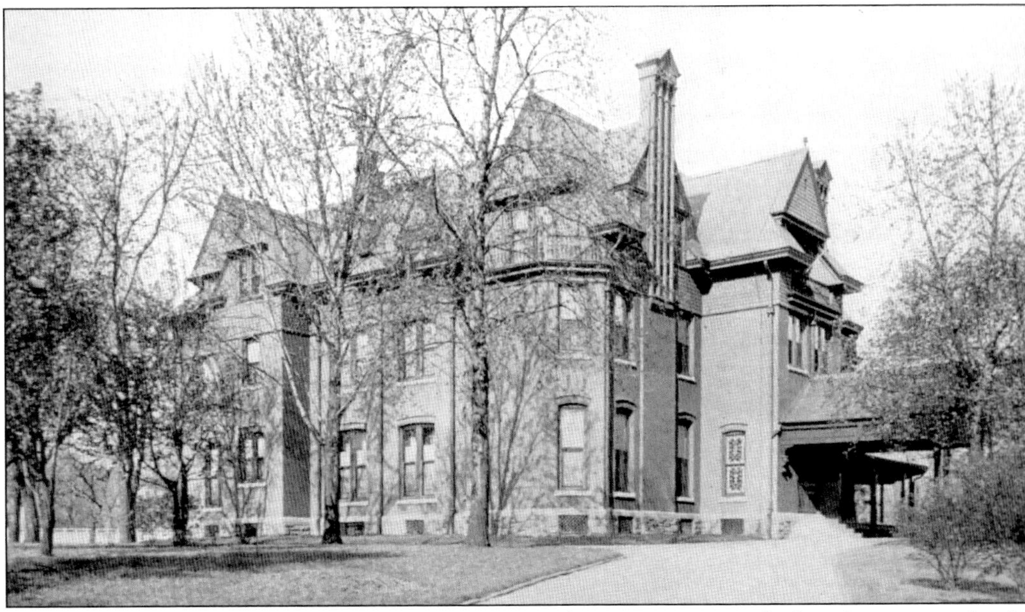

**RESIDENCE OF ROBERT PITCAIRN, C. 1905.** Robert Pitcairn made his fortune with the Pennsylvania Railroad. His childhood friend Andrew Carnegie got him a job as a ticket agent for the railroad. When Carnegie started his own business, Pitcairn was named to replace him as head of the Pittsburgh division of the railroad. In her memoirs, Ethel Spencer called the house "an elaborately ugly example of late Victorian architecture."

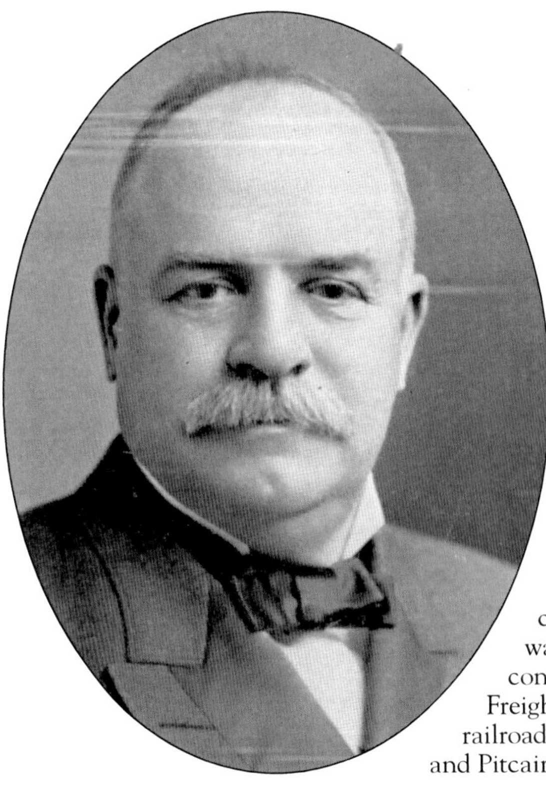

**ROBERT PITCAIRN, C. 1905.** Pitcairn began his career at the Pennsylvania Railroad with Carnegie, who remained a lifelong friend. In 1852, when the line was completed, Duncansville, or Hollidaysburg, was where the Pennsylvania Railroad connected with the Allegheny Portage Railroad. Freight and passengers were transferred between railroad cars and portage cars at this point. Carnegie and Pitcairn assisted in this transfer.

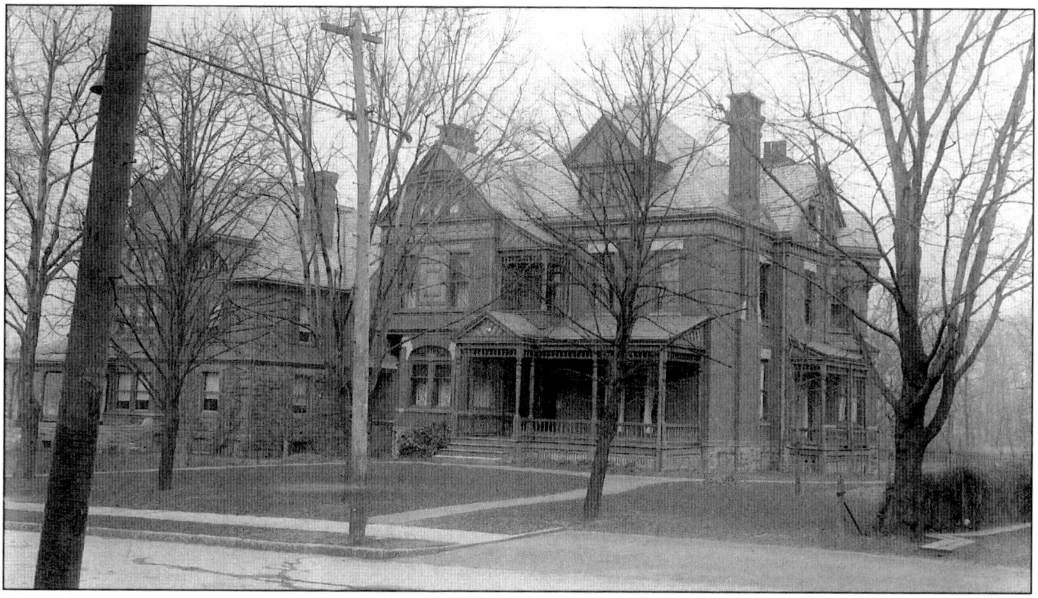

**THE SPENCER AND MACBETH HOUSES, C. 1900.** The Charles Hart Spencer family at 719 Amberson Avenue (right) and the George A. Macbeth family at 717 Amberson Avenue (left) were close neighbors. They lived only a short distance down Amberson Avenue from the Shadyside Presbyterian Church and from Spencer's father-in-law, Judge Marcus Acheson. Dahlia Street, now Pembroke Place, is not laid yet. (Courtesy of the Shadyside Presbyterian Church Archives.)

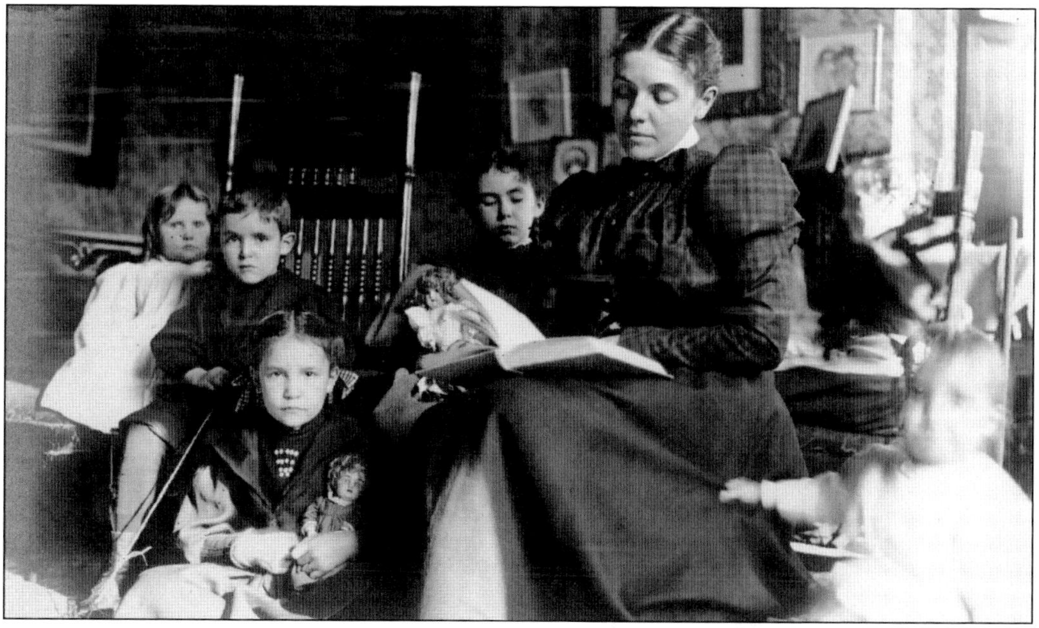

**MOTHER READING, C. 1898.** Mary Spencer is reading while surrounded by five of her seven children. Ethel Spencer is seated on the floor holding a doll. Mark Spencer is seated in a high-backed chair. Mary Wilson Spencer is sitting behind Mark. Kate Spencer is at her mother's right shoulder. Charles Spencer Jr. is the blur tugging on mommy's dress in the lower right corner. (Courtesy of the University of Pittsburgh Archives Service Center.)

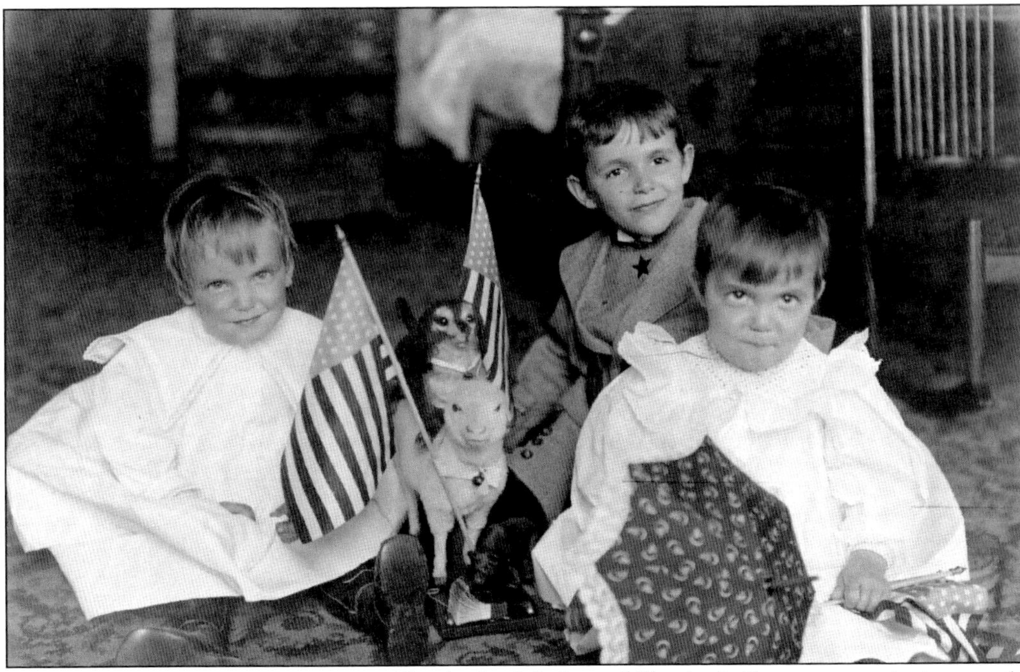

**CHILDREN PLAYING, APRIL 1898.** Charles Jr., Mark, and Elizabeth Spencer are playing on the bedroom floor with American flags and stuffed toys. (Courtesy of the University of Pittsburgh Archives Service Center.)

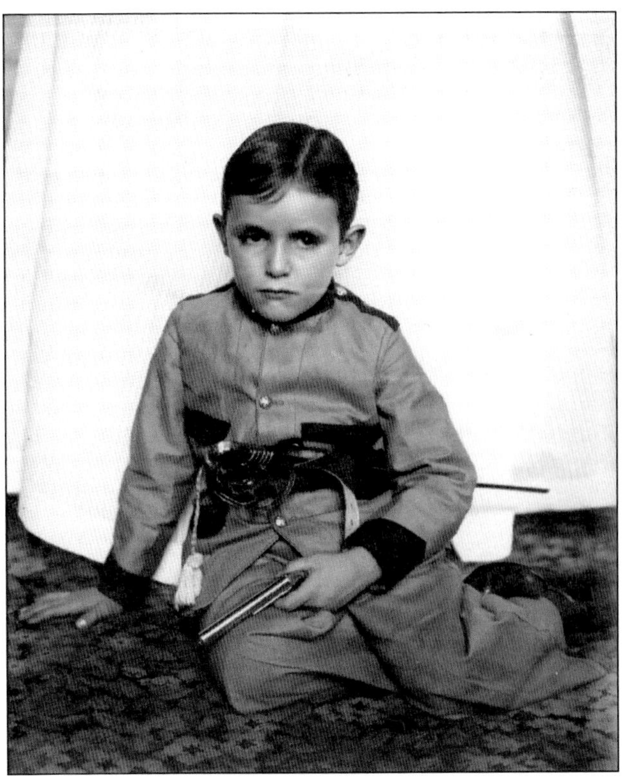

**SOLDIER MARK, APRIL 1899.** Mark is dressed like a soldier with a sword tucked in his belt and a toy gun in his hand. (Courtesy of the University of Pittsburgh Archives Service Center.)

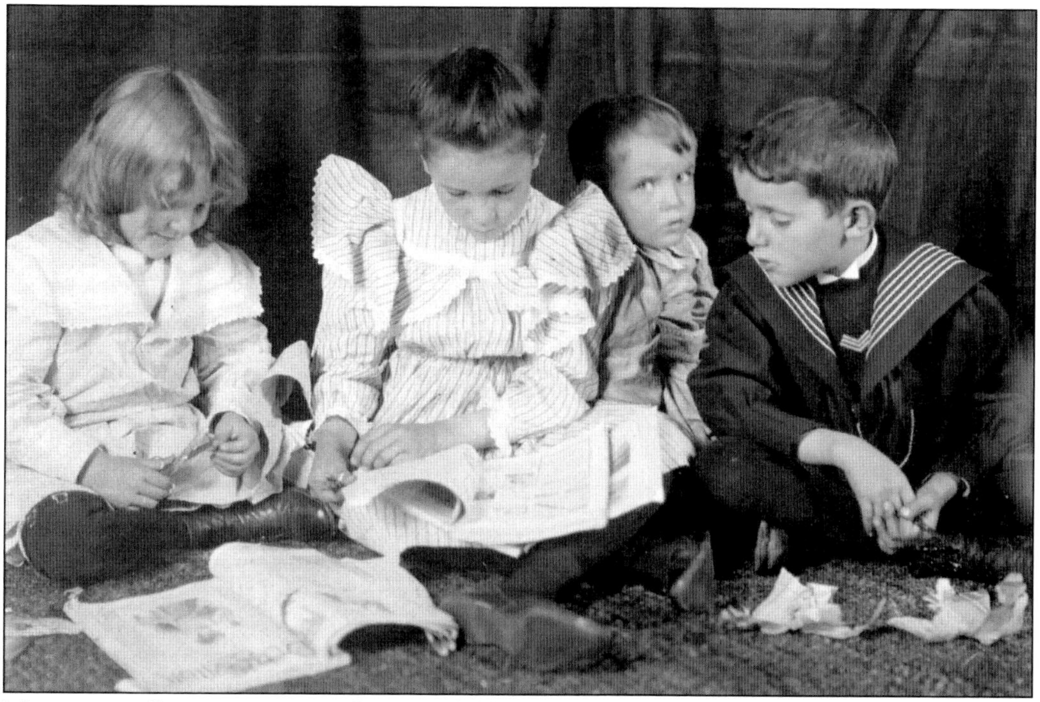

**Magazines, September 1899.** Spencer children Mary, Ethel, Charles Jr., and Mark are perusing and cutting up magazines. (Courtesy of the University of Pittsburgh Archives Service Center.)

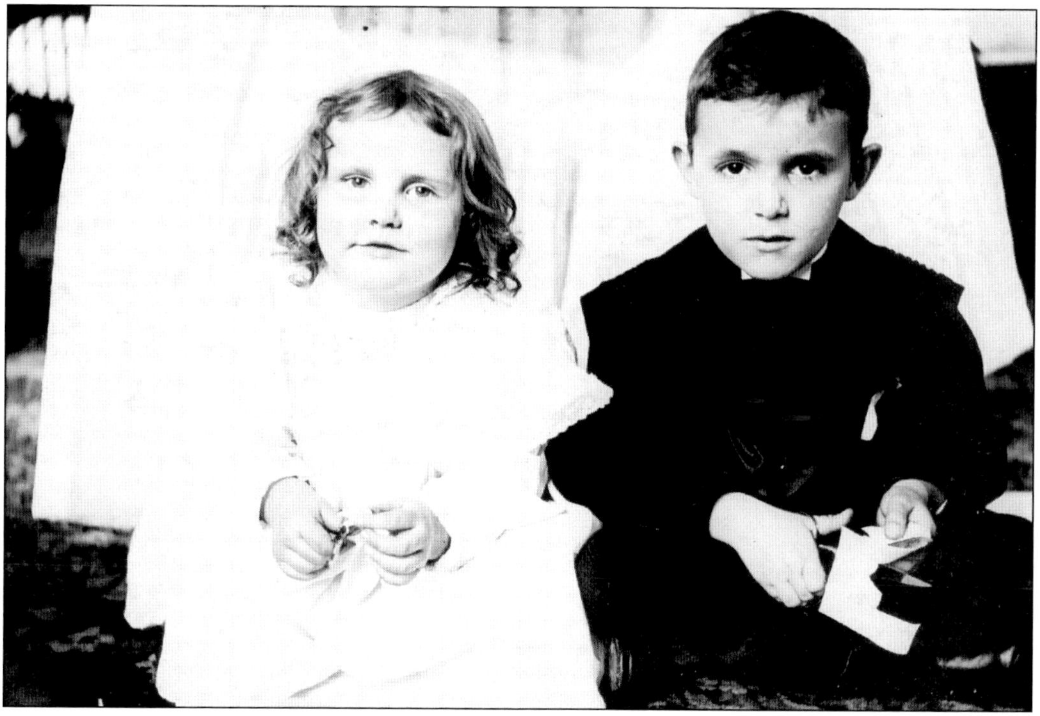

**Paper Dolls, March 1898.** Mary and Mark are cutting paper dolls. (Courtesy of the University of Pittsburgh Archives Service Center.)

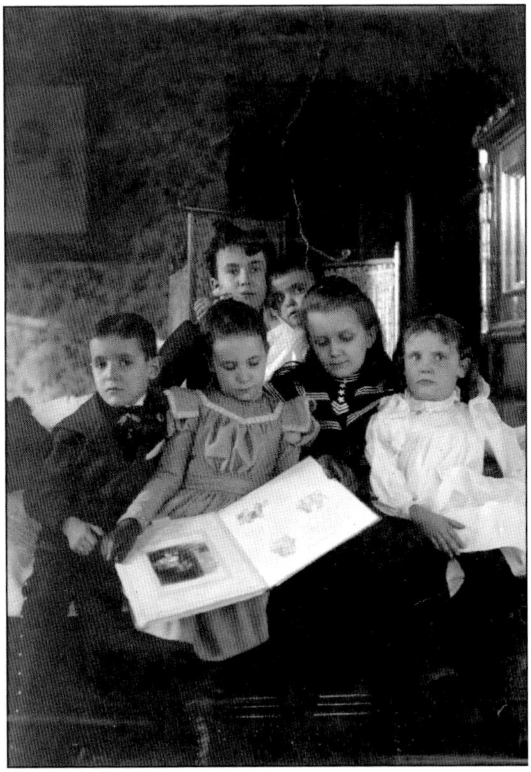

**CHILDREN READING, JANUARY 1899.** From left to right are (first row) Mark Spencer, Ethel Spencer, an unidentified girl, and Mary Spencer; (second row) Kate and Elizabeth Barrows. (Courtesy of the University of Pittsburgh Archives Service Center.)

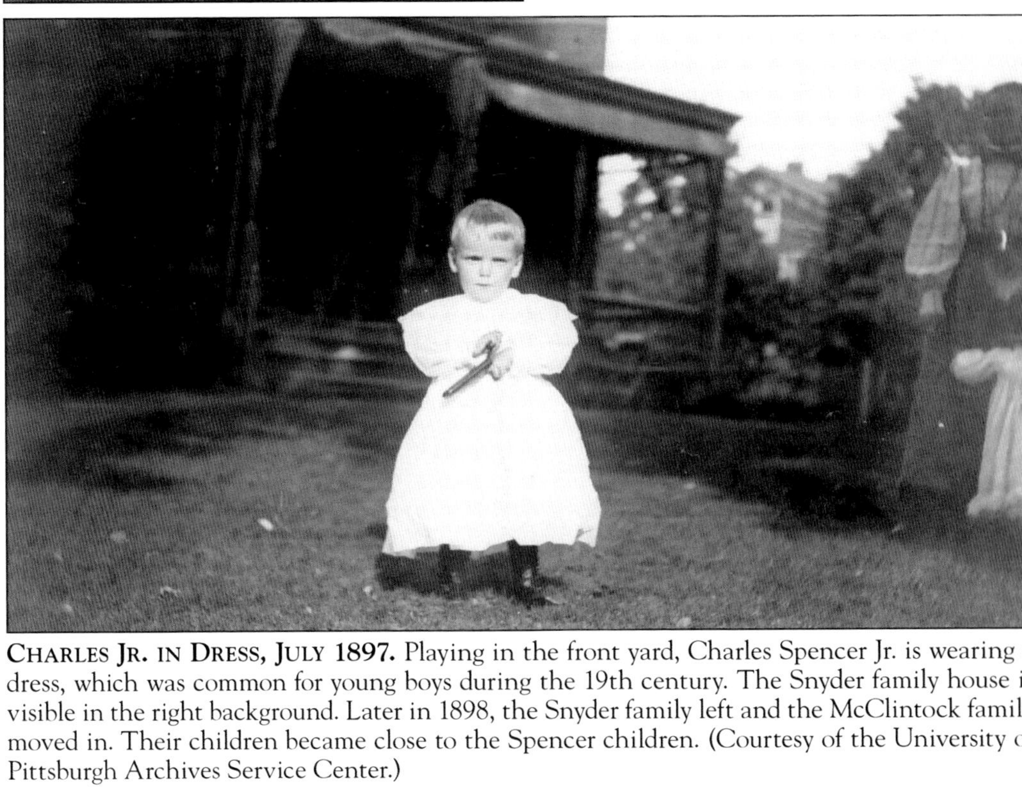

**CHARLES JR. IN DRESS, JULY 1897.** Playing in the front yard, Charles Spencer Jr. is wearing a dress, which was common for young boys during the 19th century. The Snyder family house is visible in the right background. Later in 1898, the Snyder family left and the McClintock family moved in. Their children became close to the Spencer children. (Courtesy of the University of Pittsburgh Archives Service Center.)

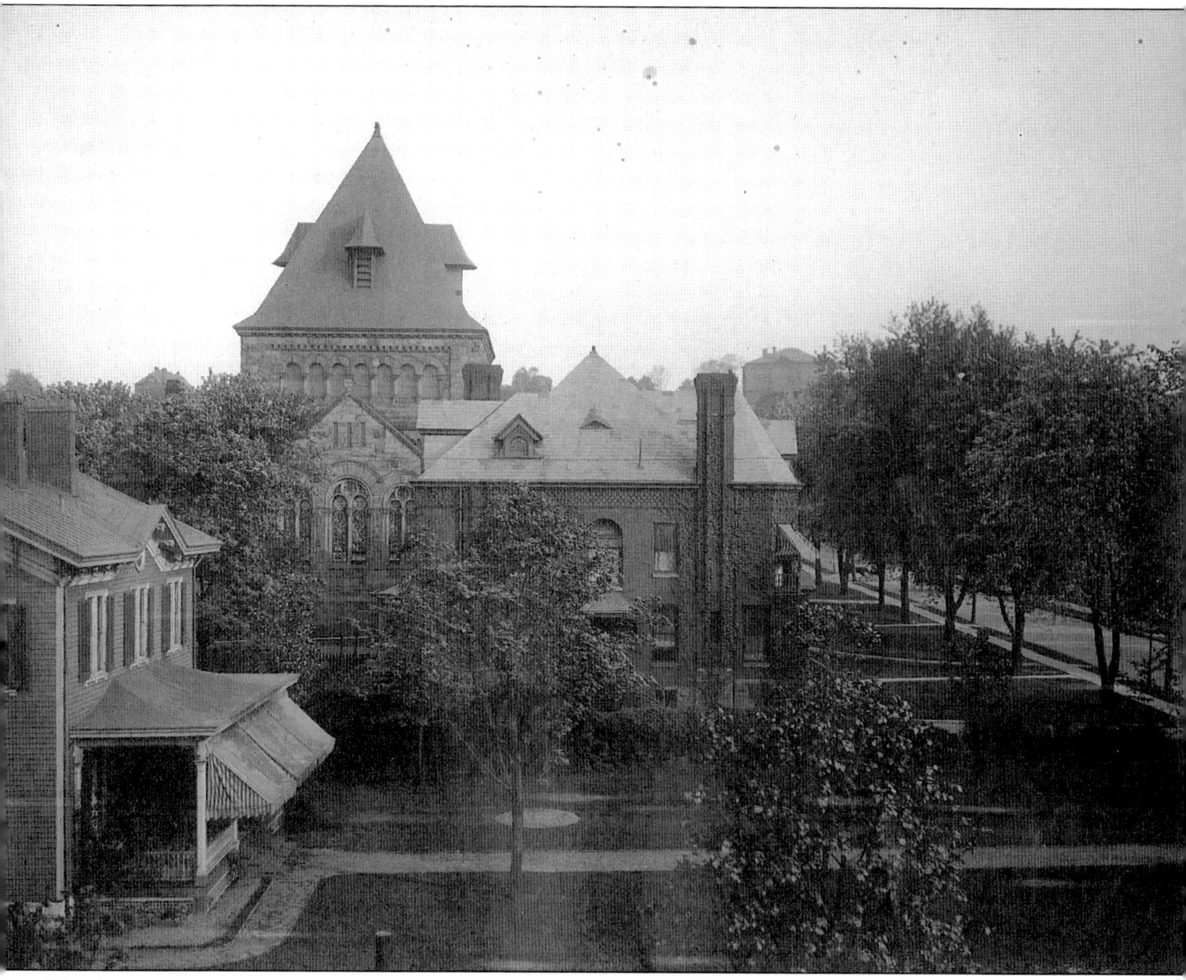

**UP AMBERSON AVENUE TOWARD FIFTH AVENUE, C. 1900.** This view from a Spencer house window shows the wood frame Frank T. McClintock house in the far left foreground (no longer standing). Next in the center of the image is the William E. Lincoln house (no longer standing). The Shadyside Presbyterian Church is clearly visible behind and to the left of the Lincoln house. Shadyside Presbyterian Church's parsonage (no longer standing) is hidden between the Lincoln house and the church. The Lawrence C. Phipps home (no longer standing) is visible on the distant hilltop above where Amberson Avenue ends at Fifth Avenue. (Courtesy of the Shadyside Presbyterian Church Archives.)

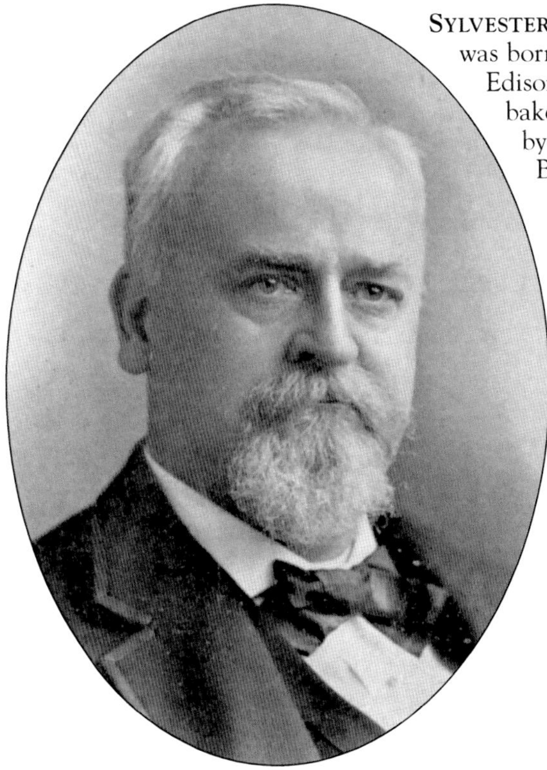

**SYLVESTER S. MARVIN, C. 1905.** Sylvester S. Marvin was born on November 18, 1841. He was called "the Edison of manufacturing" for his innovations in the bakery business—the largest in the United States by 1888—and the organization of the National Biscuit Company (Nabisco). Thereafter he founded the Pittsburgh Chocolate Company. He died on May 12, 1924, at his residence, Merimont, in Bryn Mawr at age 83.

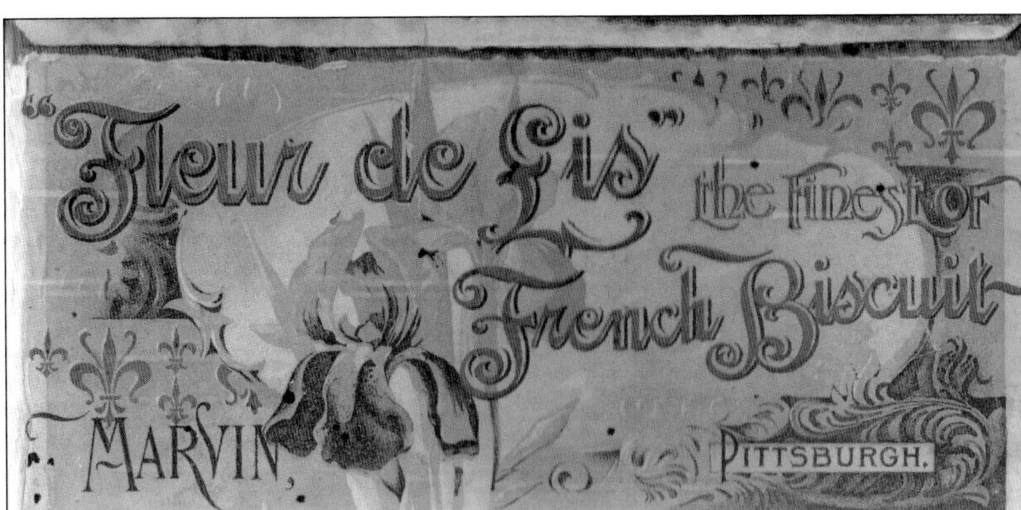


**MARVIN'S FRENCH BISCUIT, C. 1880.** The S. S. Marvin Company, manufacturers of crackers, cakes, and bread products, embraced every description of the baked products. With crackers, the business of the firm extended to every part of the United States. The company employed about 250 people in 1889.

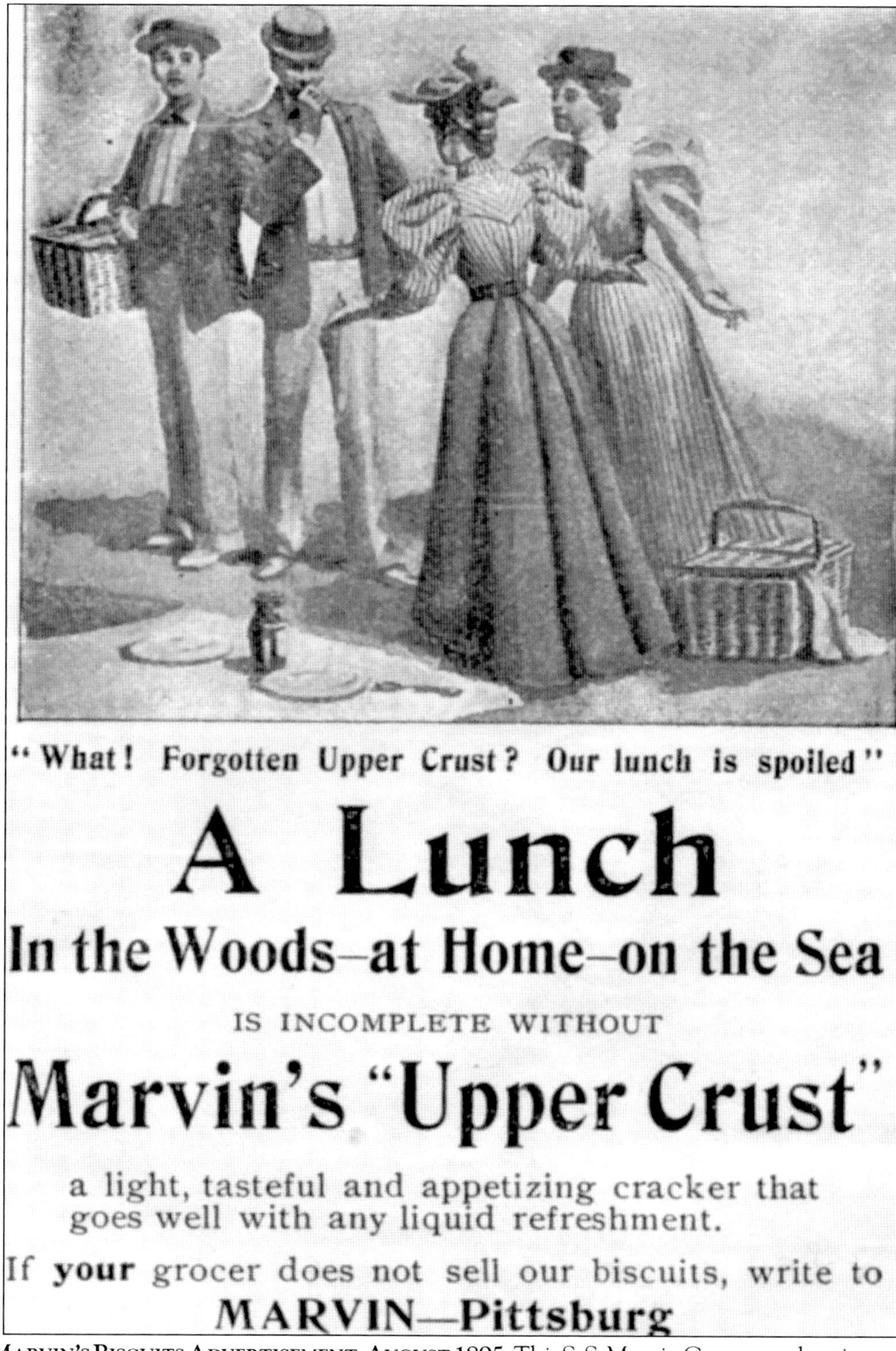


**MARVIN'S BISCUITS ADVERTISEMENT, AUGUST 1895.** This S. S. Marvin Company advertisement was published in the August 1895 issue of the *Ladies Home Journal.*

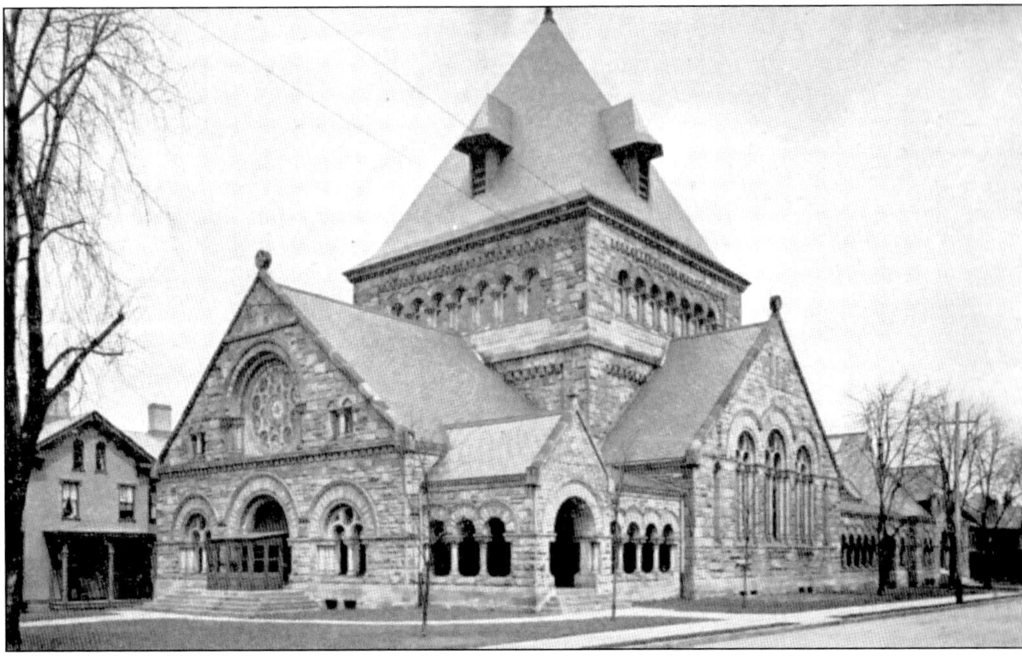

**SHADYSIDE PRESBYTERIAN CHURCH, C. 1905.** This stone structure was the third erected by the congregation and remains standing today. It was opened in 1890 and was designed by architects Rutan and Russel. Westminster Street runs to the right, and the parsonage is visible to the left.

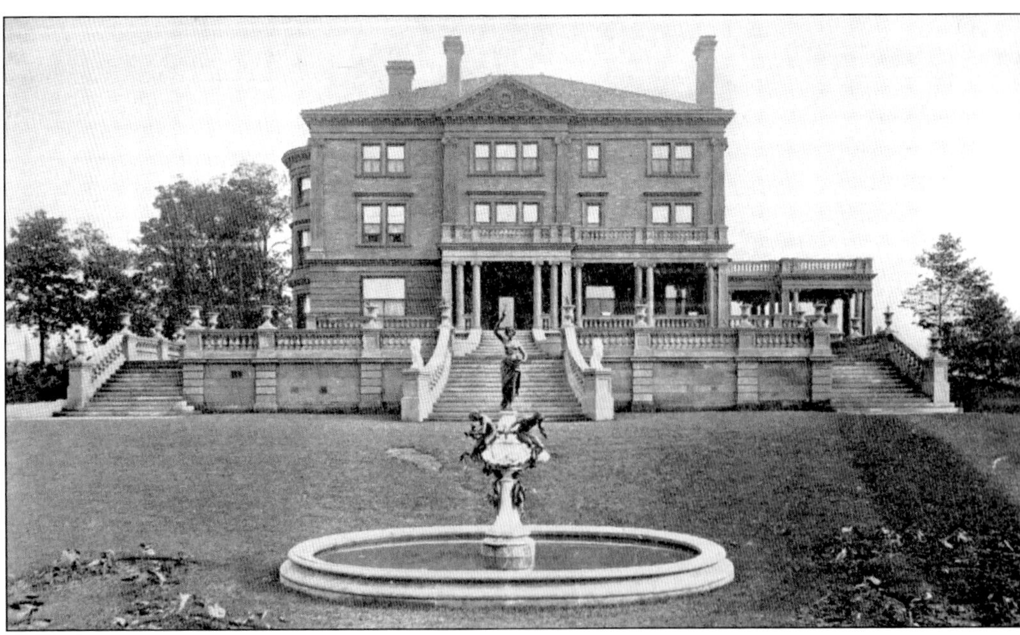

**GRANDVIEW, C. 1900.** Grandview was the residence of Lawrence Cowle Phipps. He joined Carnegie Steel as a clerk and eventually advanced to first vice president of the company. He retired from Carnegie Steel in 1901 and moved to Colorado, where he was active with investments. Phipps served two terms in the U.S. Senate from 1918 through 1929. He died on March 1, 1958.

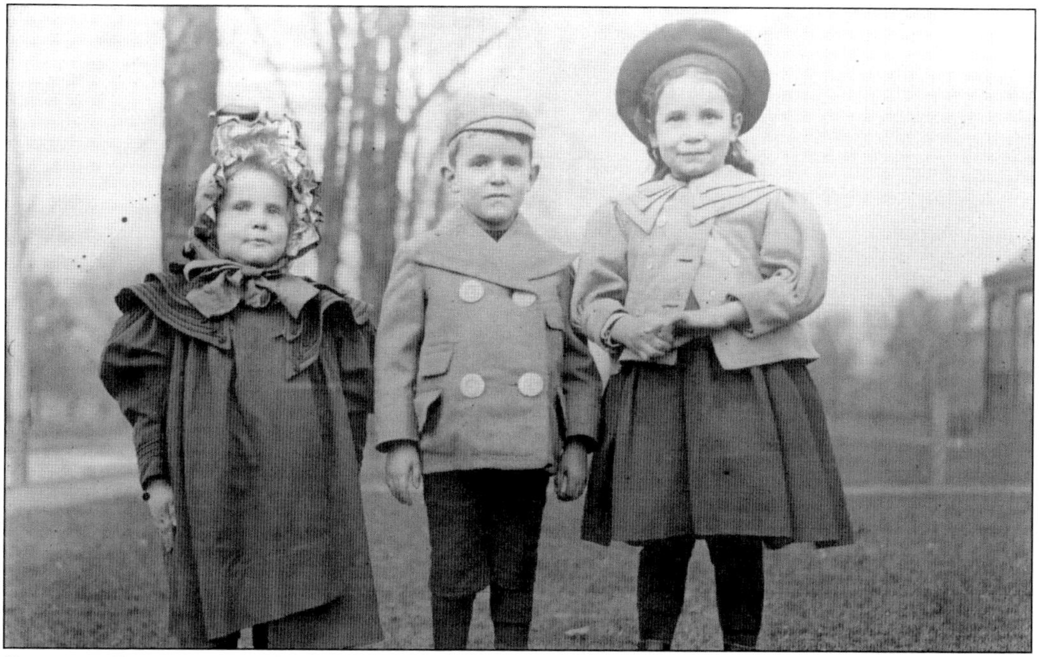

**SPENCER CHILDREN IN COATS, NOVEMBER 25, 1897.** From left to right are Mary, Mark, and Ethel Spencer standing on the family's front lawn looking down Amberson Avenue (far left) toward the Shady Side station. At the far right is just a bit of the Macbeth house porch. (Courtesy of the University of Pittsburgh Archives Service Center.)

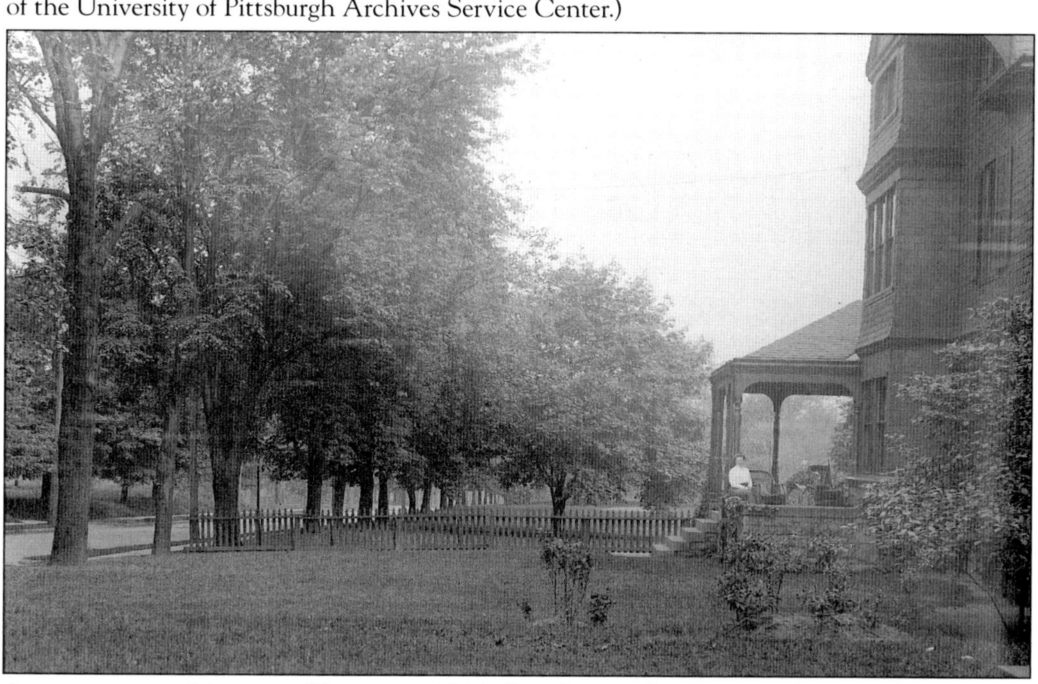

**AMBERSON AND MACBETH HOUSE, C. 1900.** Standing in the Spencer's front yard and looking down Amberson Avenue toward the Shady Side station, the planted trees along the road are striking. They were one of Shadyside's well-known attributes. The home at right is the Spencers' next-door neighbors, the Macbeths. (Courtesy of the Shadyside Presbyterian Church Archives.)

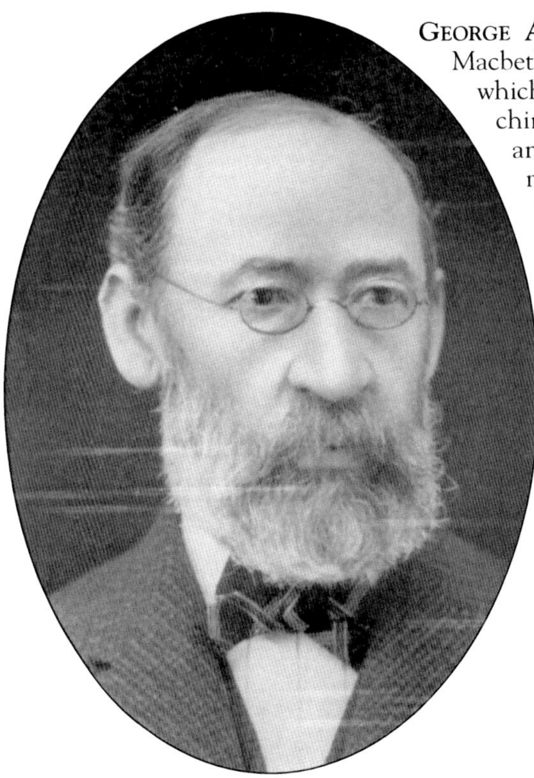

**GEORGE A. MACBETH, C. 1905.** In 1869, George A. Macbeth founded the George A. Macbeth Company, which claimed to be the largest producer of lamp chimneys for kerosene lamps in the United States and probably the world. In 1899, his company merged with the Thomas Evans Company and formed the Macbeth-Evans Glass Company. Macbeth was also a director of the Fort Pitt National Bank.

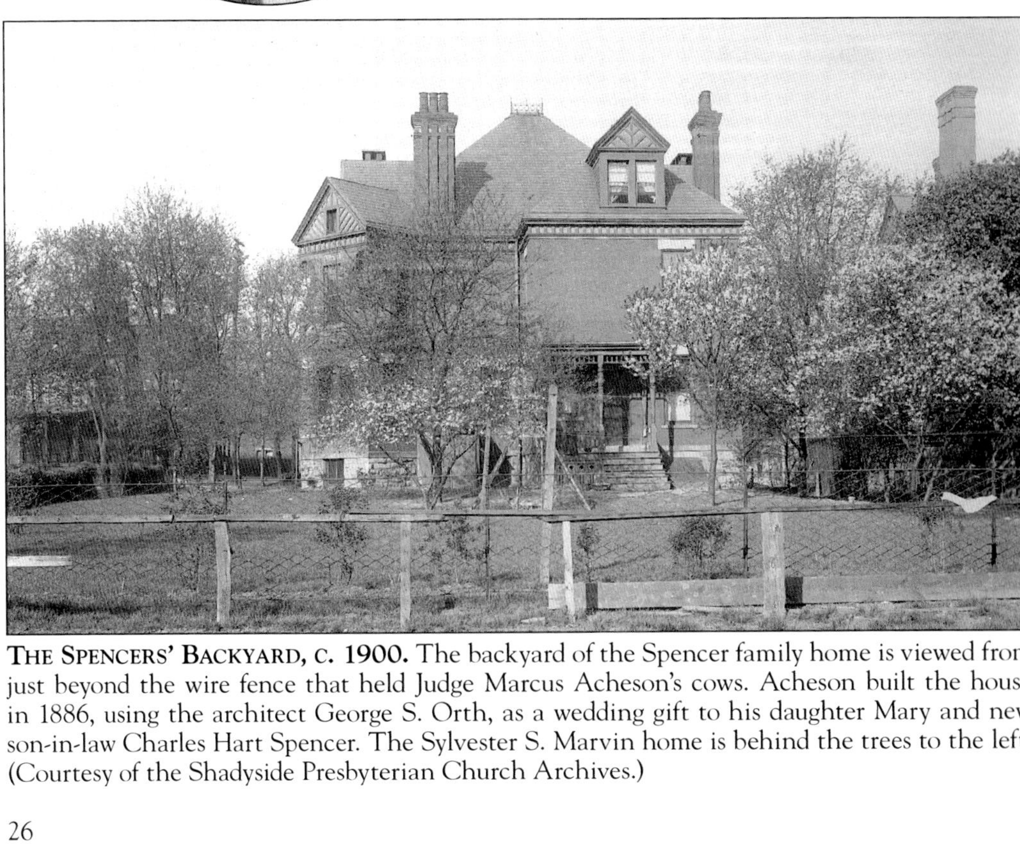

**THE SPENCERS' BACKYARD, C. 1900.** The backyard of the Spencer family home is viewed from just beyond the wire fence that held Judge Marcus Acheson's cows. Acheson built the house in 1886, using the architect George S. Orth, as a wedding gift to his daughter Mary and new son-in-law Charles Hart Spencer. The Sylvester S. Marvin home is behind the trees to the left. (Courtesy of the Shadyside Presbyterian Church Archives.)

**FLUFFY'S HAIRCUT, JUNE 1899.** Adeline Spencer is holding the family's dog Fluffy on the Spencers' back porch stairs while her father, Charles, cuts the dog's hair. Mark, Mary, and Elizabeth, under their father's right arm, and Ethel, with her back to the camera, gather around to help and watch. A chair and the Spencers' backyard swing set are visible on the lawn in the background. (Courtesy of the University of Pittsburgh Archives Service Center.)

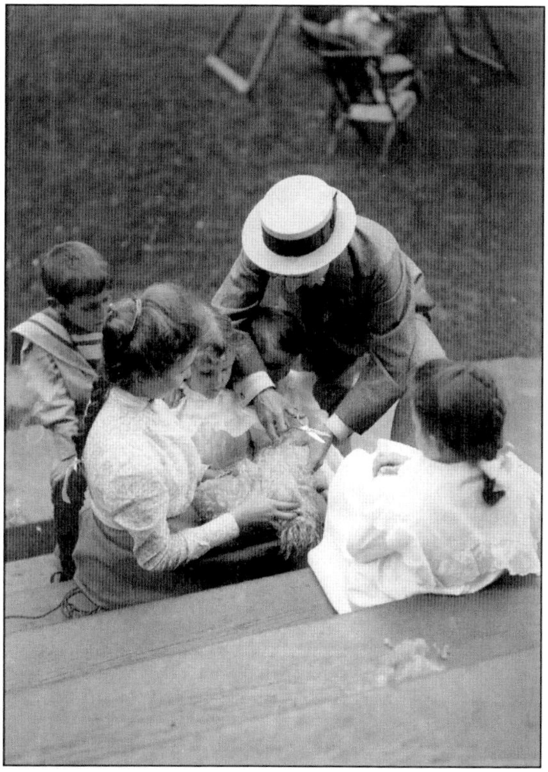

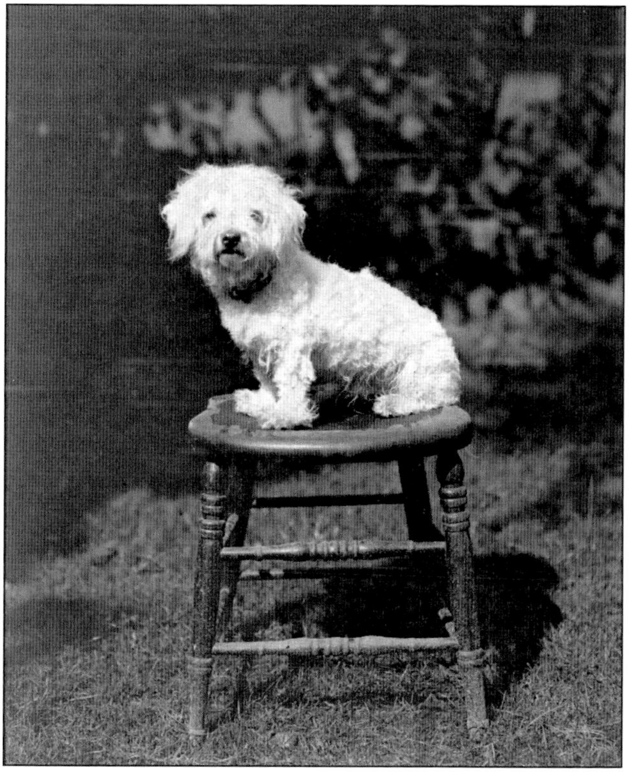

**FLUFFY, SEPTEMBER 1900.** The Spencer children grew up with a number of family pets, especially dogs. Their last dog was Lemmy, who lived to be 14 years old. When he died, their mother said that she had spent a large part of her life taking care of dogs and that she wanted no more. (Courtesy of the University of Pittsburgh Archives Service Center.)

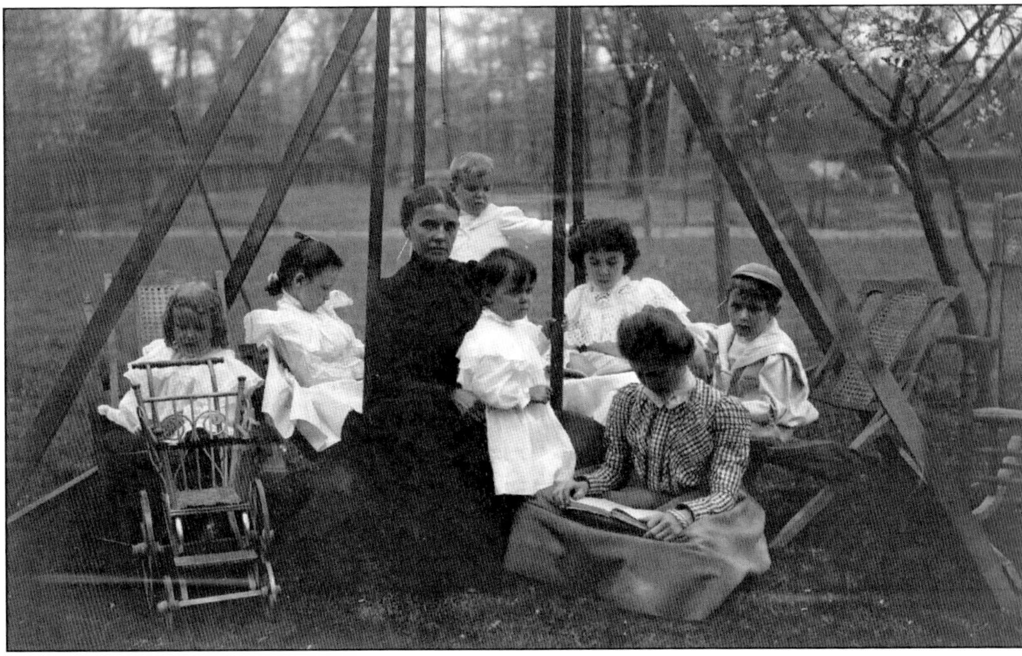

**MOTHER AND CHILDREN BY SWING, MAY 1899.** Mary Spencer is sitting in the backyard swing surrounded by all seven of her children. At far left, Mary Wilson is sitting behind her toy baby stroller. From left to right are Ethel, Mary, Charles Jr., Elizabeth, Kate, Adeline, and Mark. Two cows are standing in the distance to the right behind Mark. (Courtesy of the University of Pittsburgh Archives Service Center.)

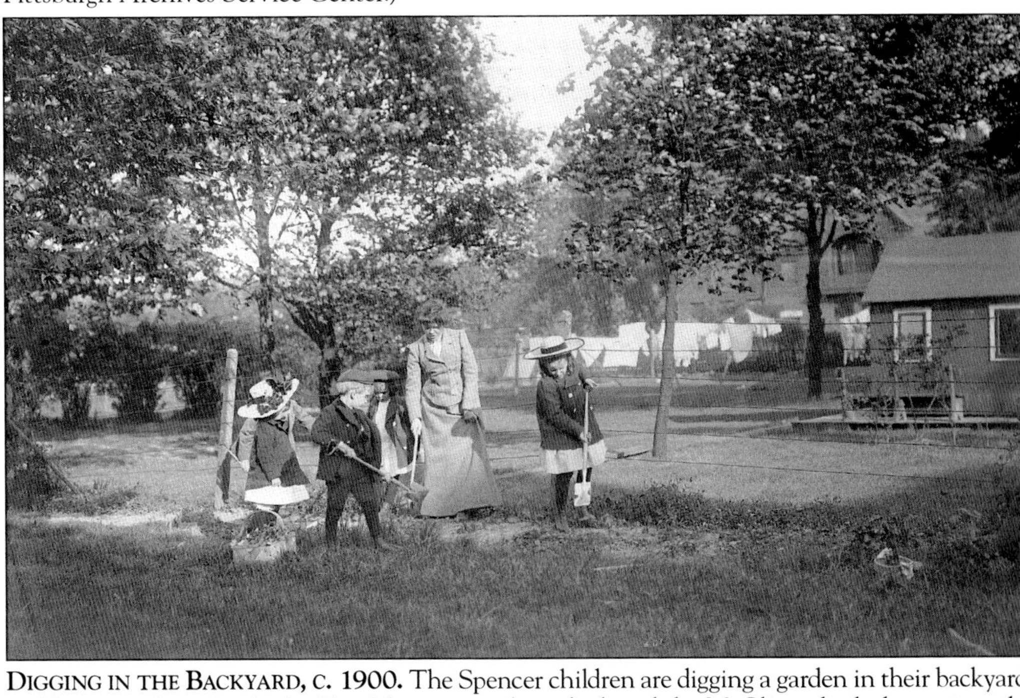

**DIGGING IN THE BACKYARD, C. 1900.** The Spencer children are digging a garden in their backyard. Dahlia Street (now Pembroke Place) has not yet been laid, and the McClintock playhouse is at the far right around 1900. (Courtesy of the Shadyside Presbyterian Church Archives.)

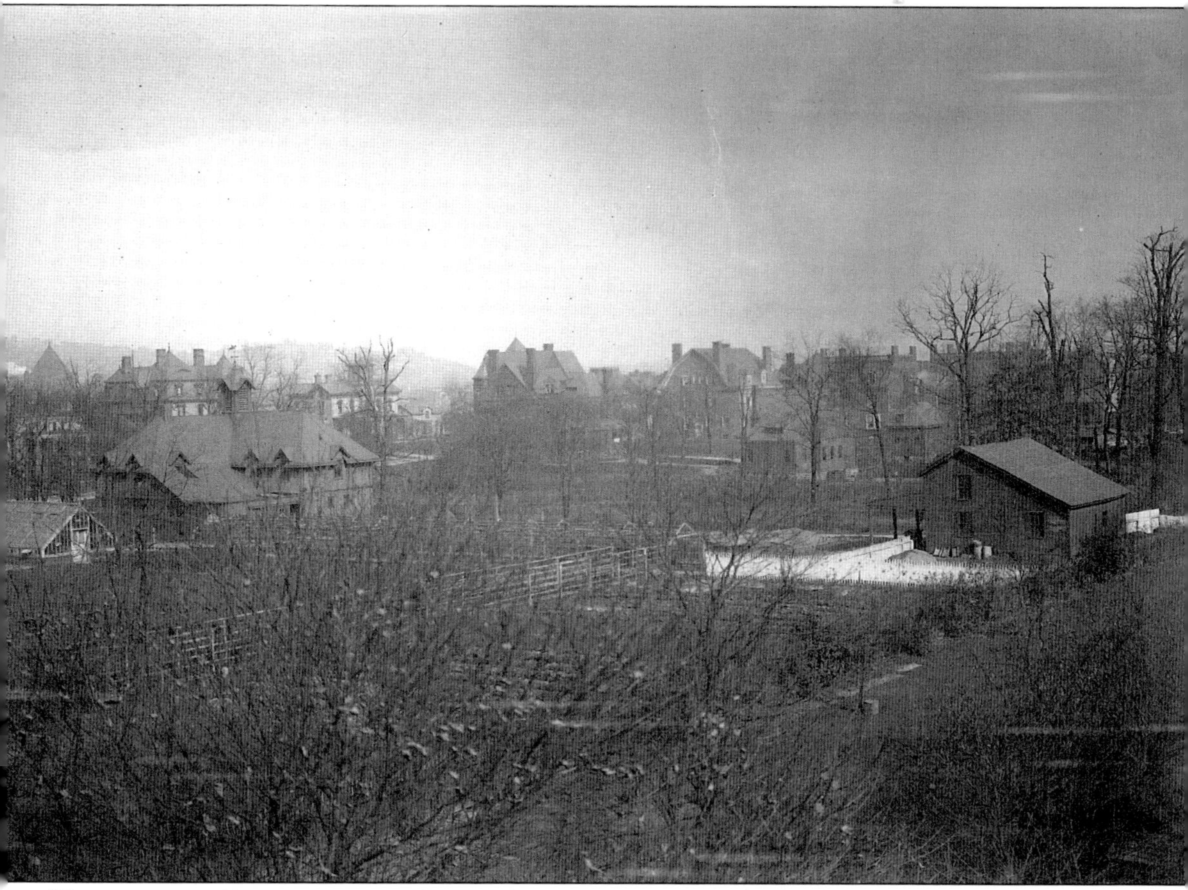

**VIEW TOWARD ELLSWORTH AND LILAC AVENUES, C. 1900.** Shadyside remained a suburb of country homes around 1900, as indicated by this view out of the Spencer house toward the intersection of Ellsworth Avenue and Lilac Avenue (now St. James Street). Robert Pitcairn's greenhouse (far left) and stables (to the right of the greenhouse) are clearly visible. The structure in the center distance is the back and west side of the James McCrea house (no longer standing). The structure to the right of the McCrea house is the Percifor Frazer Smith house. Ellsworth Avenue runs diagonally from about the center of the left edge of the image up along the other side of the McCrea and Smith houses. Lilac Avenue connects with Ellsworth Avenue on the other side of the Smith property (see page 113). The pyramid in the distance at far left behind the Pitcairn greenhouse and carriage house is the Christ Methodist Church at the intersection of Aiken and Centre Avenues (see pages 87 and 116). (Courtesy of the Shadyside Presbyterian Church Archives.)

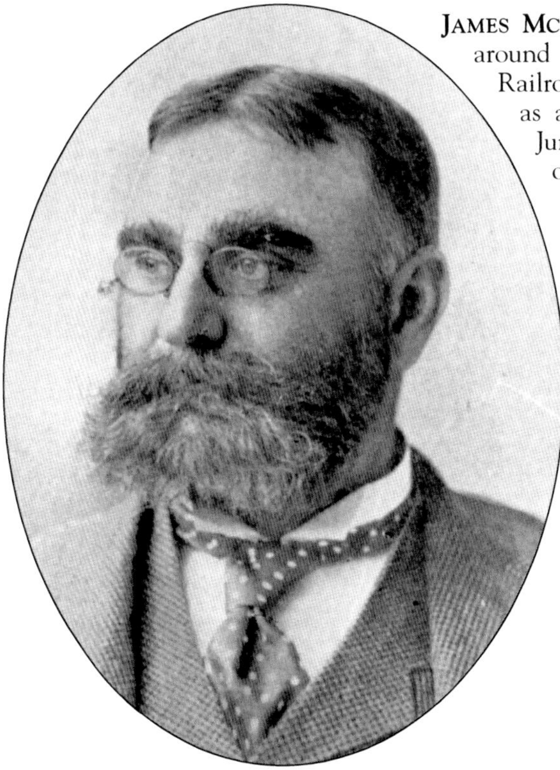

**JAMES MCCREA, C. 1905.** James McCrea was born around 1847. He worked for the Pennsylvania Railroad for 48 years beginning in June 1865 as a rodman and an assistant engineer. On June 8, 1899, McCrea was elected a director of the railroad, and on January 2, 1907, he became president. He was president until he resigned on January 1, 1913. He died on March 28, 1913, at his home, Greygange, near Ardmore.

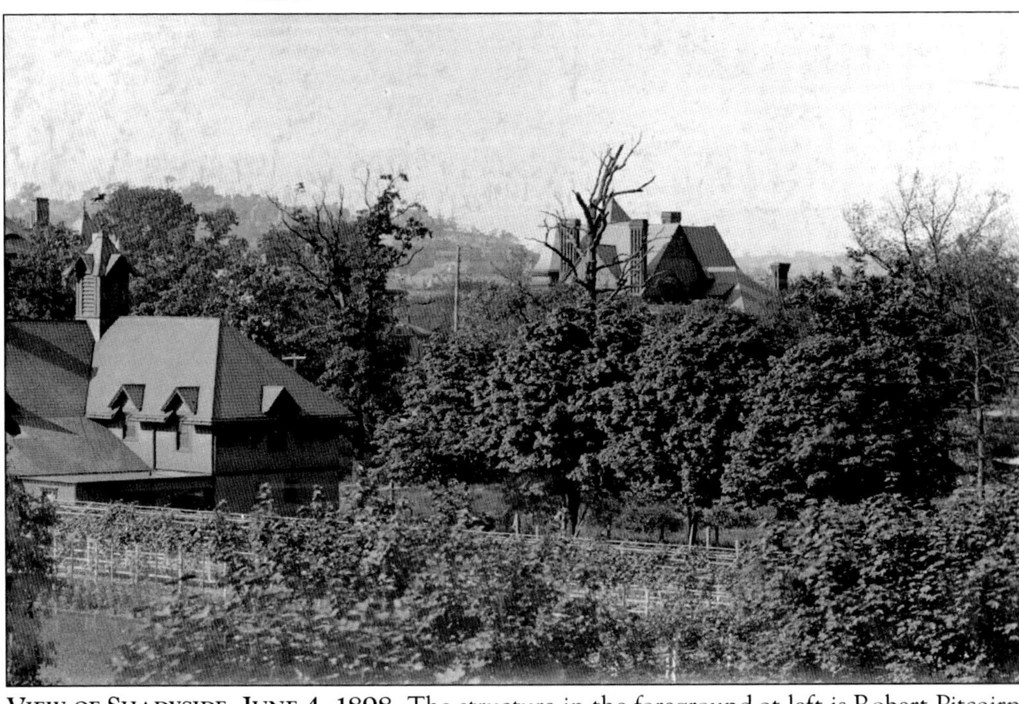

**VIEW OF SHADYSIDE, JUNE 4, 1898.** The structure in the foreground at left is Robert Pitcairn's carriage house, and the structure in the center distance is the back and west side of the McCrea house. (Courtesy of the University of Pittsburgh Archives Service Center.)

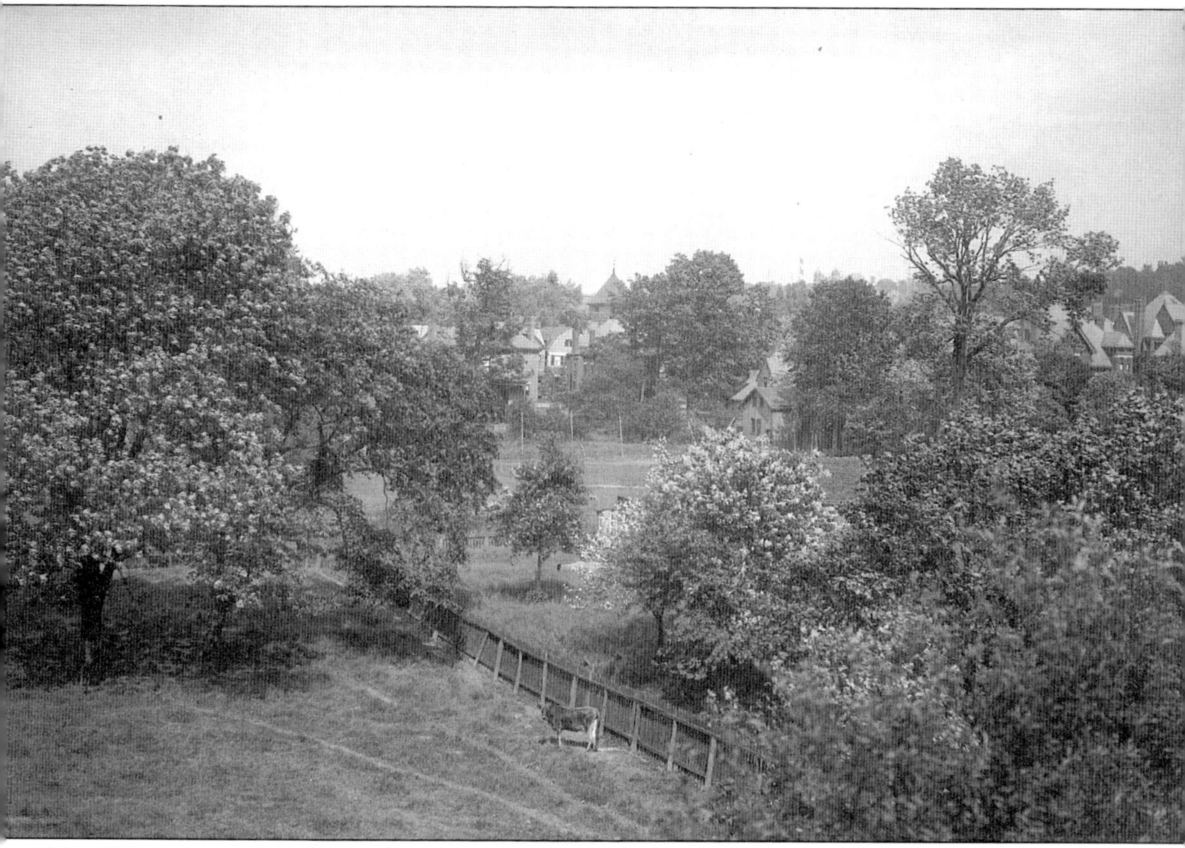

**THE WOODS TOWARD LILAC AVENUE, C. 1900.** This view from the third-floor rear window of the Spencer house looks over the area the Spencers called "the woods" toward Lilac Avenue (now St. James Street). Dahlia Street (now Pembroke Place) does not yet exist. One of Judge Marcus Acheson's cows is visible at bottom center. At center where the sky meets the buildings and trees is the tower of the First Methodist Church at South Aiken Avenue and Howe Street. (Courtesy of the Shadyside Presbyterian Church Archives.)

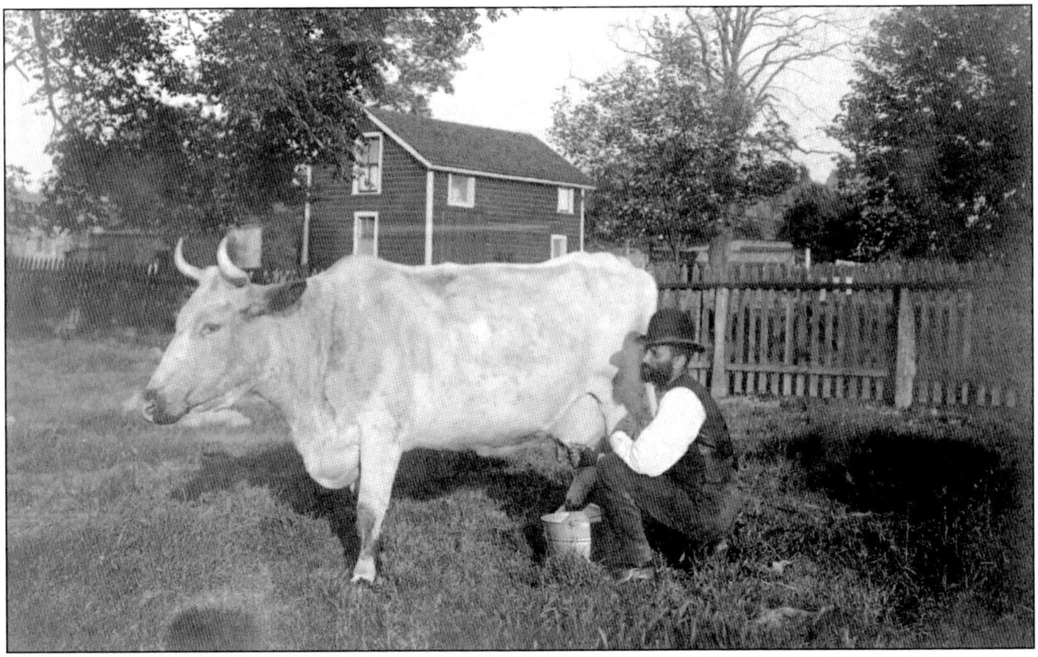

**MILKING THE COW, JUNE 4, 1898.** Cows were still common in Shadyside during the late 19th century. John Organ is shown here milking a cow. A structure belonging to Sylvester S. Marvin that was perhaps used by the McClintock family is visible behind the cow. (Courtesy of the University of Pittsburgh Archives Service Center.)

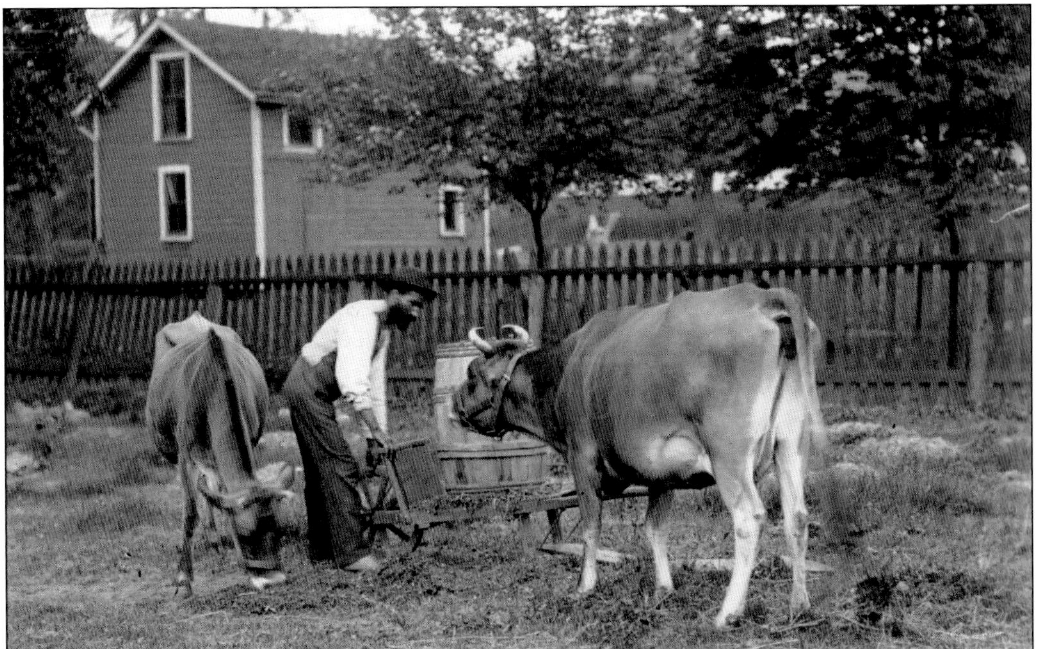

**TENDING THE COWS, JULY 1900.** Organ is tending the cows behind the Spencer home. Dahlia Street (now Pembroke Place) has not been laid yet. (Courtesy of the University of Pittsburgh Archives Service Center.)

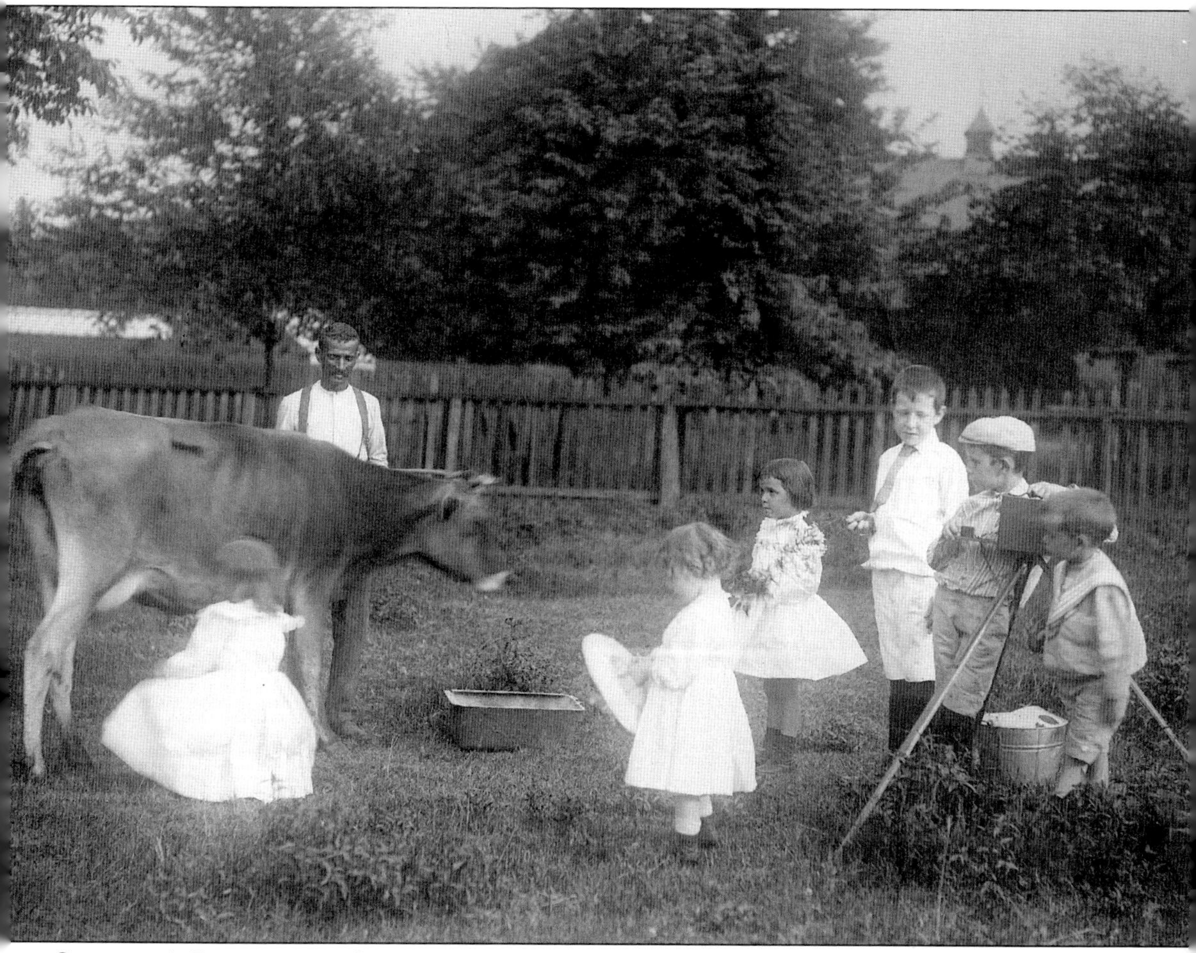

**CHILDREN'S PHOTOGRAPH SHOOT, C. 1900.** Some of the Spencer children and a few friends are posing for a photograph while milking the cow in the Spencer backyard. Perhaps Mary Spencer is at the cow, the next little girl to the right is unidentified, and Elizabeth Spencer is holding the flowers. To the right of Elizabeth are neighbor George Macbeth, Mark (at the camera), and Charles Jr. Organ, who worked for Judge Marcus Acheson (the Spencer children's grandfather) as a coachman, supervises from behind the cow. Robert Picairn's greenhouse (left) and stables (right) are visible. (Courtesy of the Shadyside Presbyterian Church Archives.)

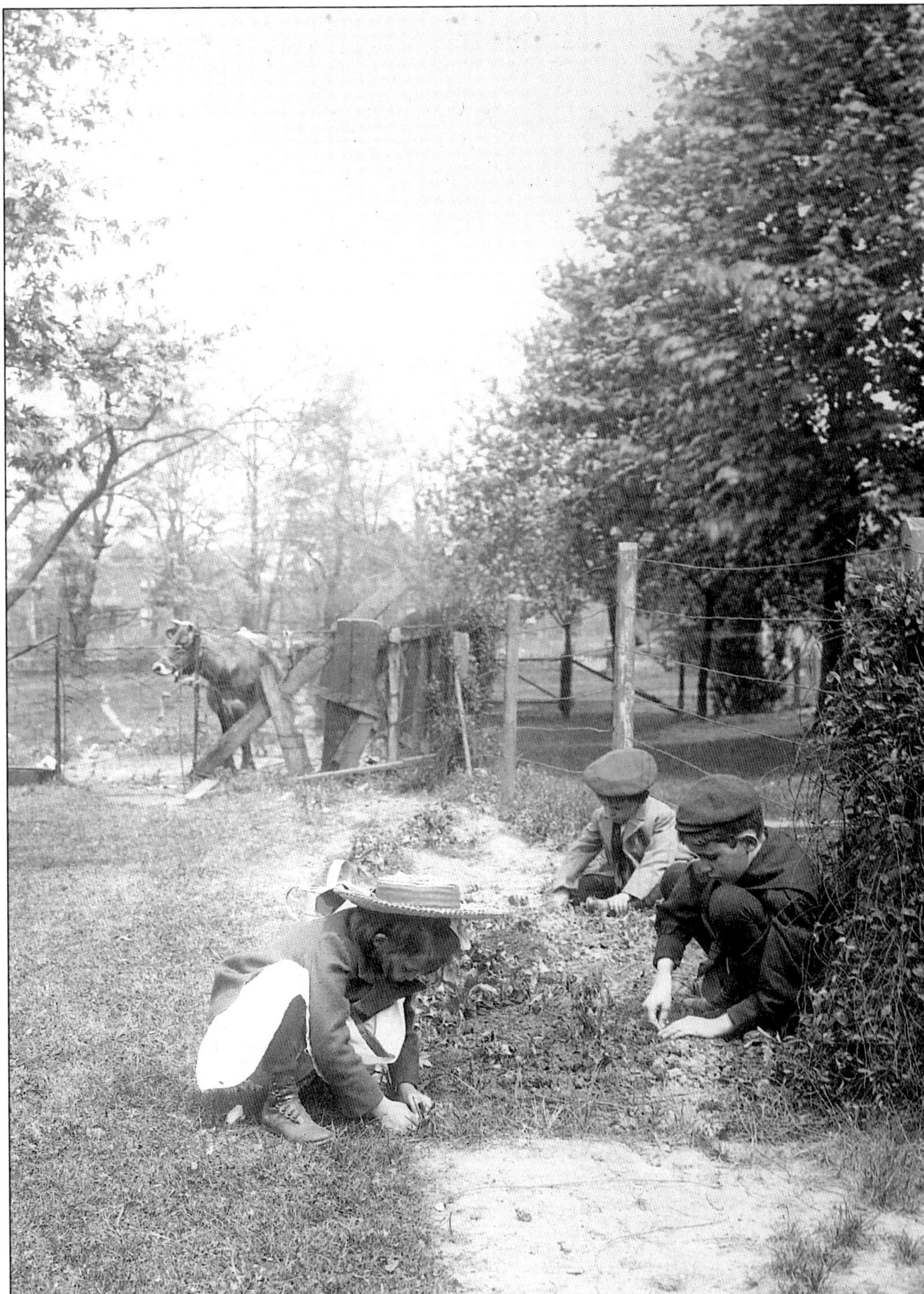

**SPENCER CHILDREN GARDENING, C. 1900.** The Spencer children were often in their backyard gardening. Judge Marcus Acheson's cow appears to watch with some interest. (Courtesy of the Shadyside Presbyterian Church Archives.)

**READING IN THE SWING, JUNE 1899.** The Spencer children are gathered around their mother, who is reading to them in and around their backyard swing. From left to right are Elizabeth, Mark, and Charles Jr., and Ethel is in the seat at right. The McClintock house is visible through the trees behind them. (Courtesy of the University of Pittsburgh Archives Service Center.)

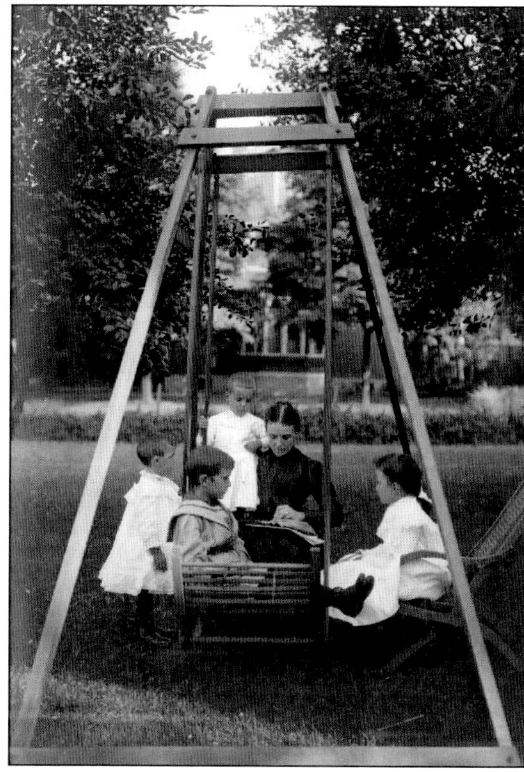

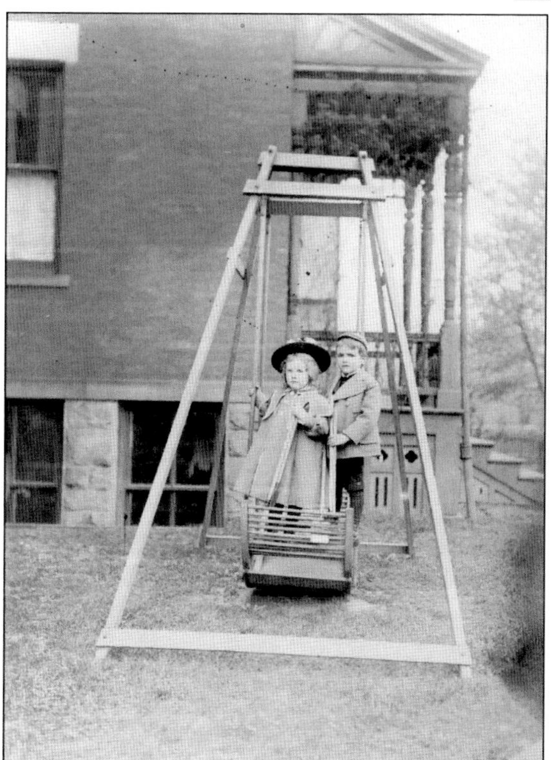

**ON THE SWING, APRIL 24, 1898.** Mary Wilson and Mark are playing on their swing in their backyard. At right, the back porch stairs are clearly visible. (Courtesy of the University of Pittsburgh Archives Service Center.)

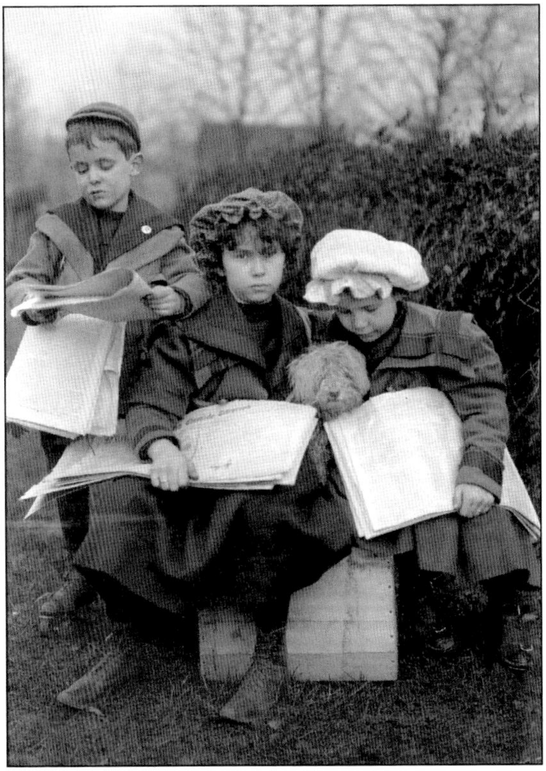

**PITTSBURGH CHRONICLE TELEGRAPH, MARCH 1899.** Mark, Kate, and Ethel Spencer (from left to right) are in their yard with their dog, looking at copies of the *Pittsburgh Chronicle Telegraph*. (Courtesy of the University of Pittsburgh Archives Service Center.)

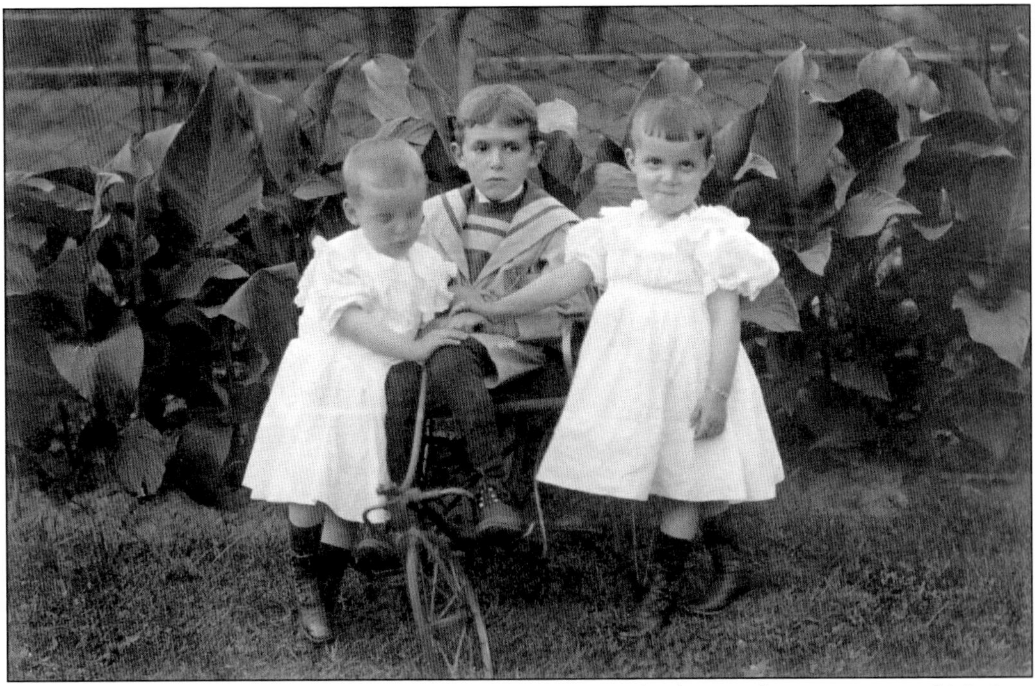

**TRICYCLE, JUNE 1899.** Charles Jr. and Elizabeth Spencer, the fraternal twins, surround Mark as he sits on a tricycle in front of the *Cannas* in the Spencers' backyard. (Courtesy of the University of Pittsburgh Archives Service Center.)

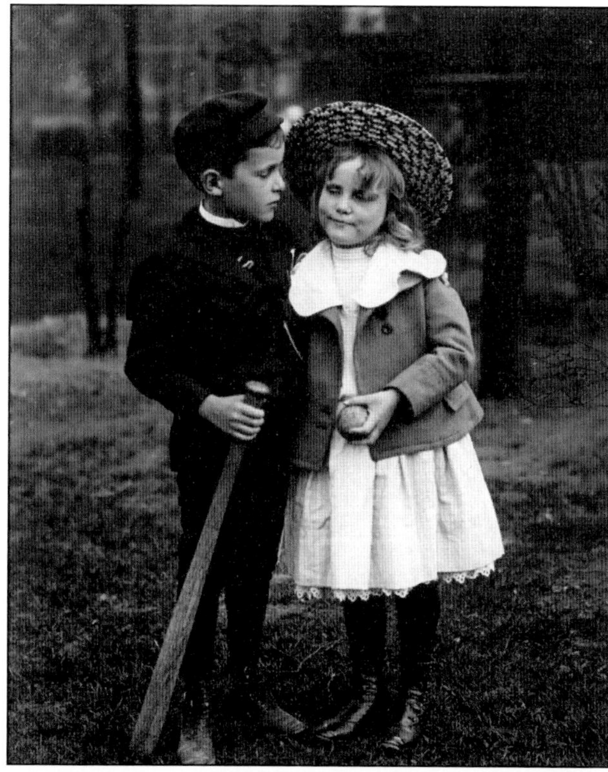

**BASEBALL, MAY 1900.** Mark holds a baseball bat while his sister Mary Wilson holds a baseball. (Courtesy of the University of Pittsburgh Archives Service Center.)

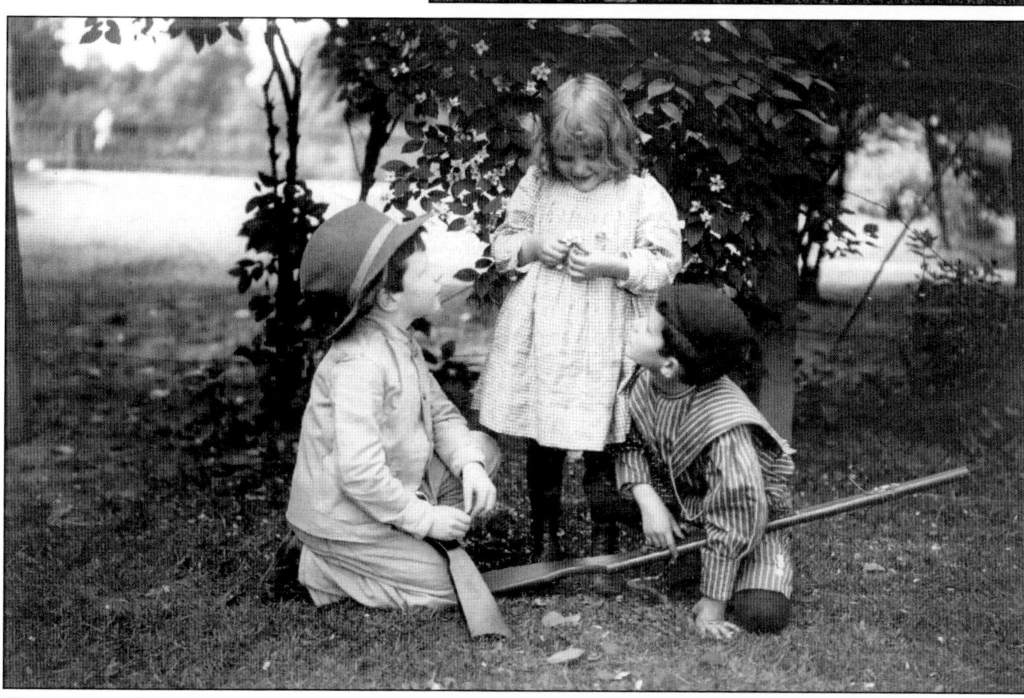

**GUNS AND FLOWERS, JUNE 1899.** George Macbeth (left) and Mark (right) are armed with toy rifles while Mary Wilson holds flowers she picked from the bush behind them. (Courtesy of the University of Pittsburgh Archives Service Center.)

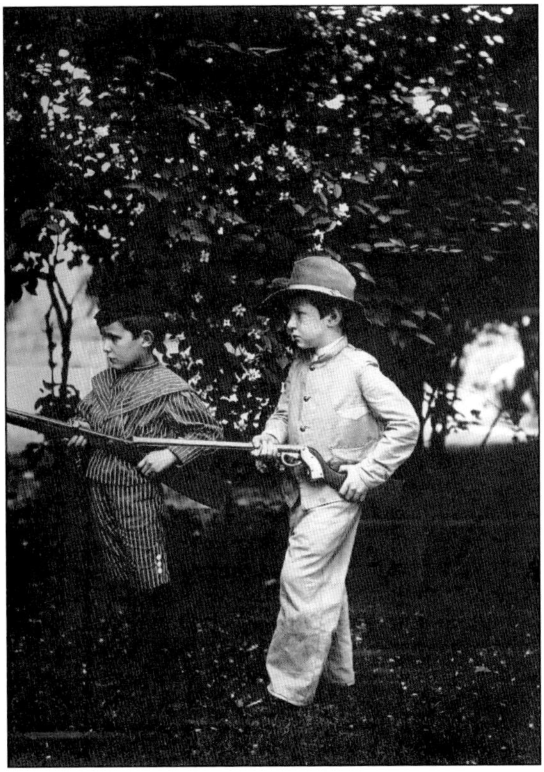

**OUTDOOR PLAY, JUNE 1899.** Mark Spencer (left) and George Macbeth (right) are playing with toy guns. (Courtesy of the University of Pittsburgh Archives Service Center.)

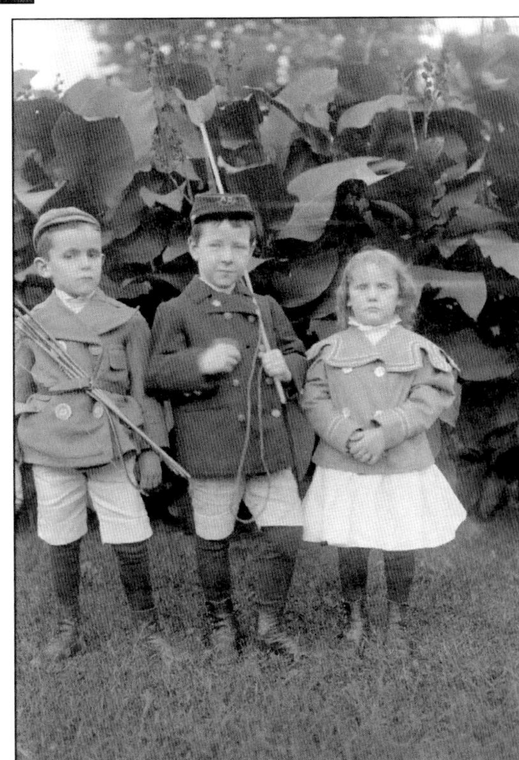

**BOW HUNTING, SEPTEMBER 1898.** Mark (left), George Macbeth (center), and Mary Wilson Spencer are preparing to play with bows and arrows. Mark has three arrows and a bow tucked into his belt. (Courtesy of the University of Pittsburgh Archives Service Center.)

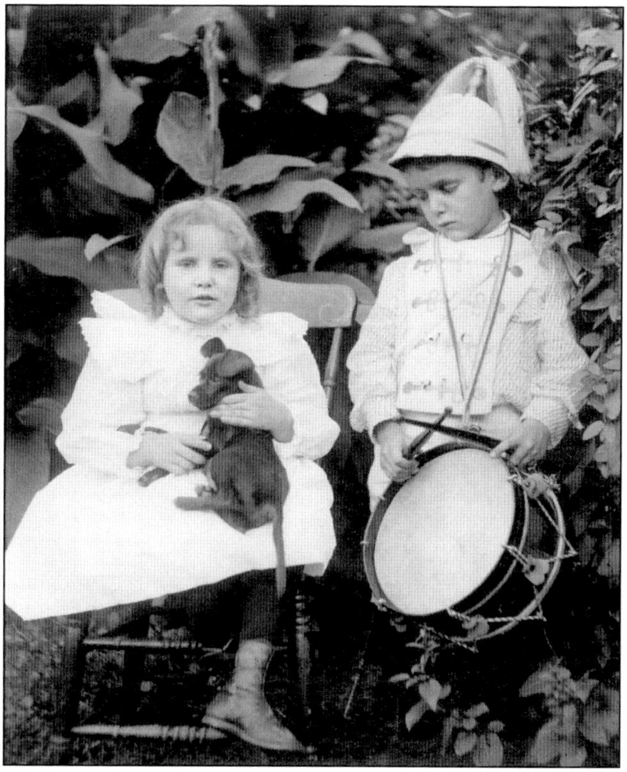

**MARY WILSON AND MARK PLAYING, AUGUST 1898.** Mary Wilson is holding a puppy while Mark pretends to be a drumming soldier. (Courtesy of the University of Pittsburgh Archives Service Center.)

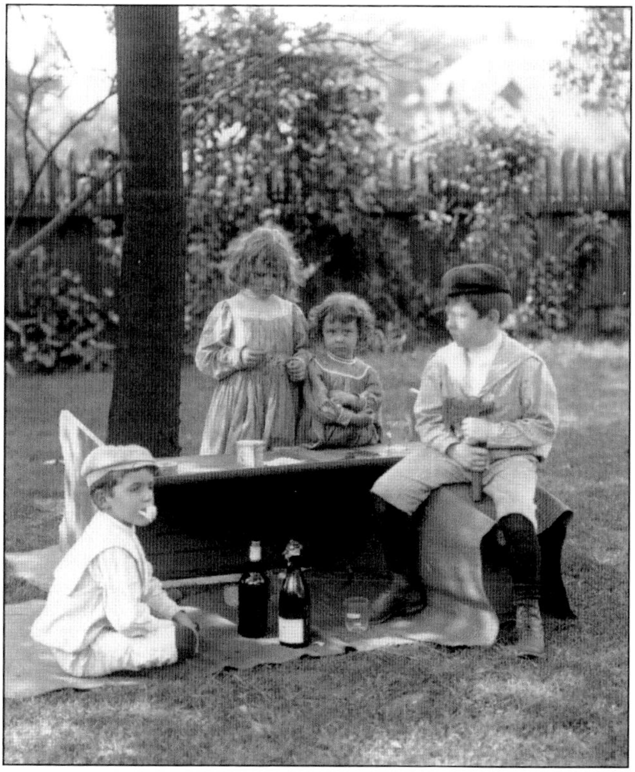

**PLAYING BAR, JUNE 1900.** Mark, Mary Wilson, an unidentified girl, and George Macbeth are playing bar. (Courtesy of the University of Pittsburgh Archives Service Center.)

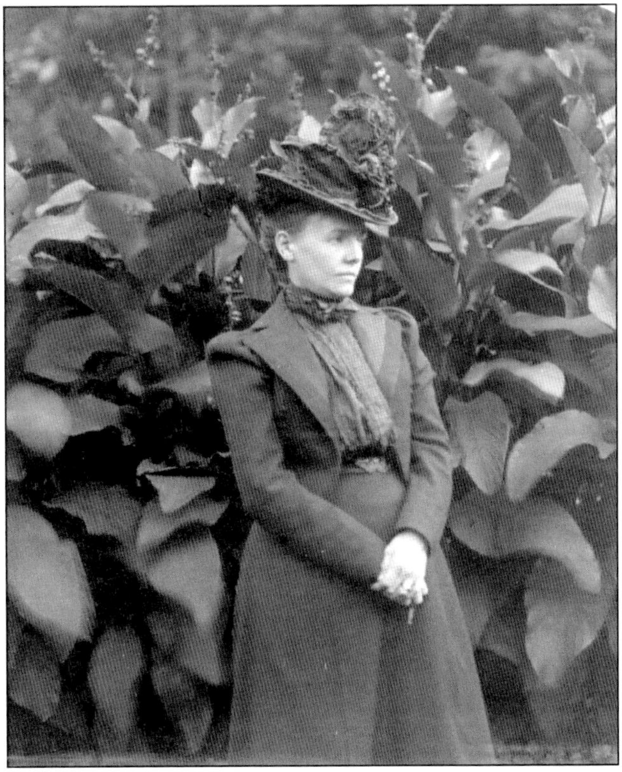

**MARY SPENCER IN BACKYARD, SEPTEMBER 1899.** Mary Spencer is standing in her backyard dressed in formal attire. (Courtesy of the University of Pittsburgh Archives Service Center.)

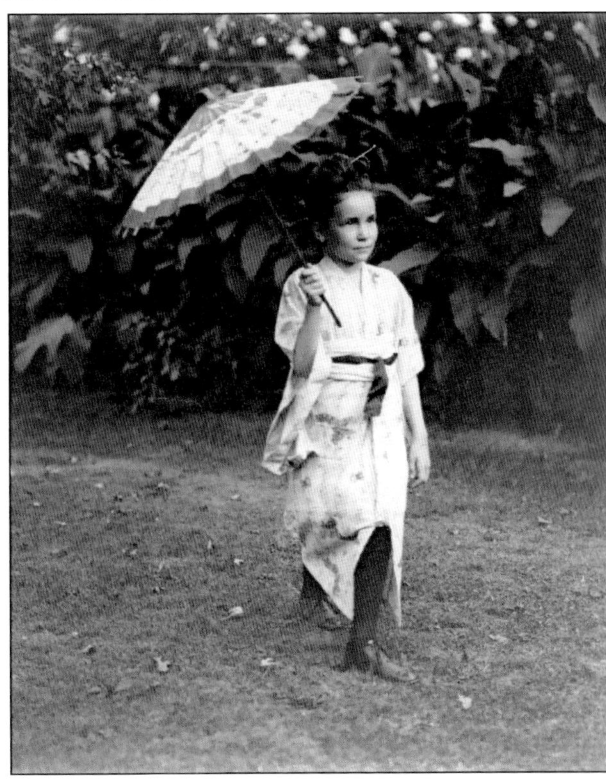

**COSTUMED, SEPTEMBER 1900.** Ethel Spencer is dressed in an Asian costume. (Courtesy of the University of Pittsburgh Archives Service Center.)

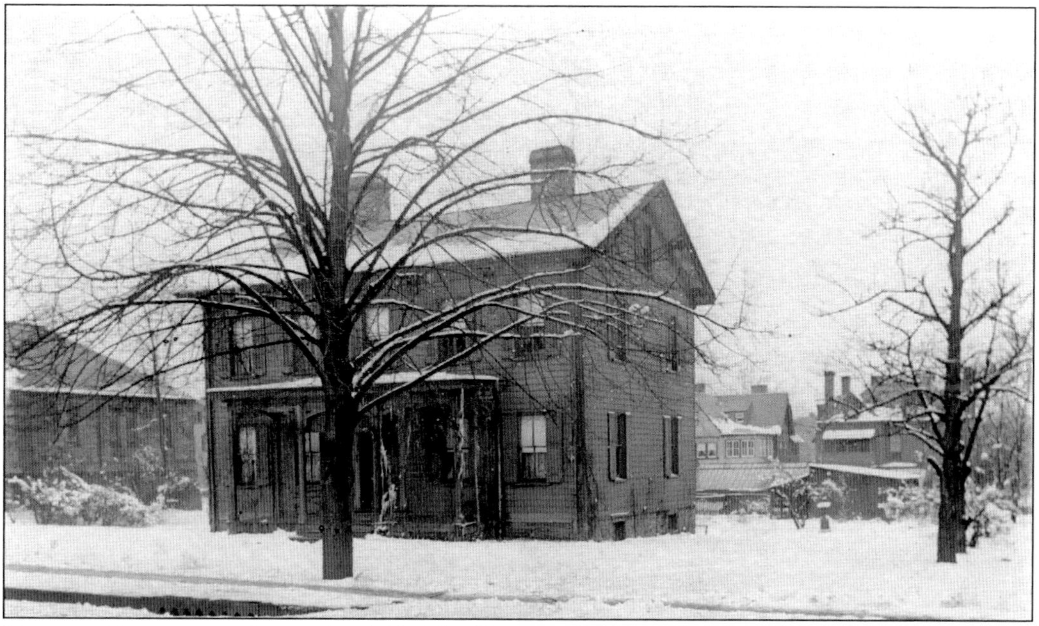

**DAWSON RESIDENCE, APRIL 6, 1902.** The Dawson residence stood at 5131 Westminster Street next to the Shadyside Presbyterian Church. The east edge of the church is seen on the far left, and the backs of homes on Dahlia Street (now Pembroke Place) are in the distance at right. (Courtesy of the Library and Archives Division, Senator John Heinz History Center.)

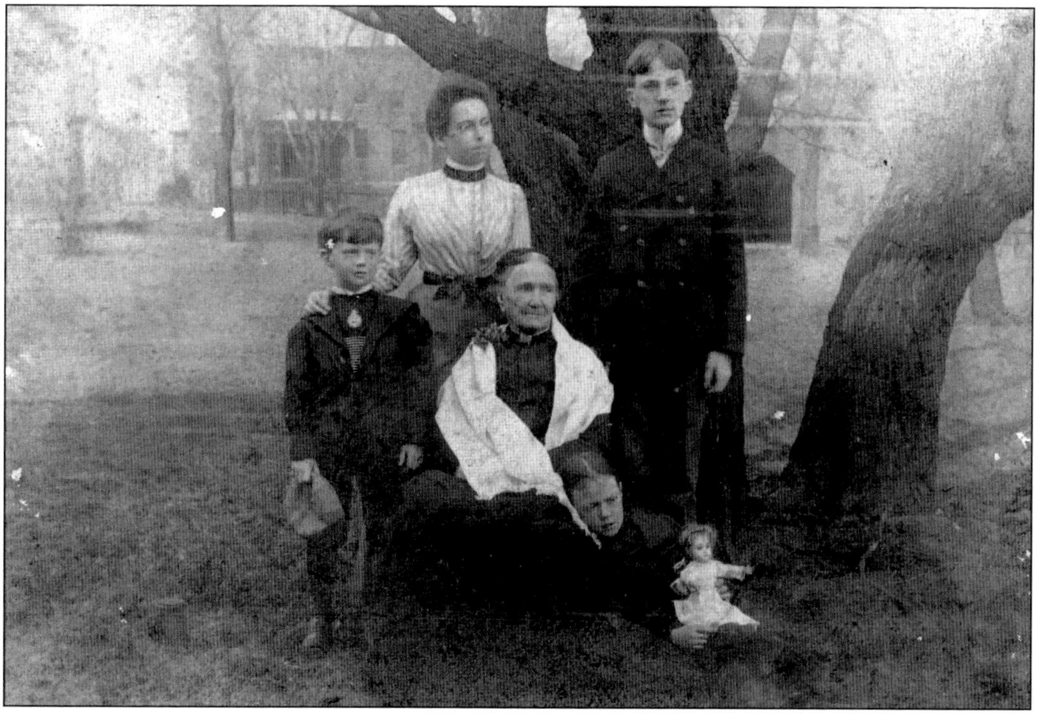

**DAWSON FAMILY, APRIL 6, 1902.** Susanna Scott Dawson poses with her daughter Anne Dawson Montgomery and three grandchildren on her 92nd birthday. (Courtesy of the Library and Archives Division, Senator John Heinz History Center.)

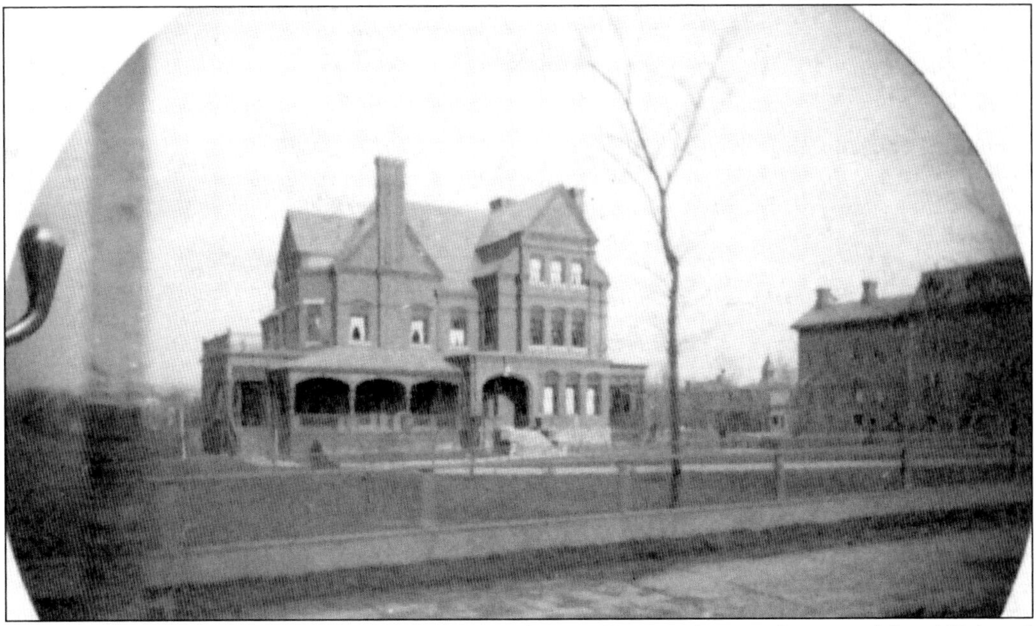

**THOMAS D. MESSLER RESIDENCE, C. 1889.** Thomas D. Messler was born in May 1834 and entered the service of the New York and Erie Railroad in 1858. He was considered one of the most well-known railroad men at the time. His home in Shadyside was located on Fifth Avenue and Amberson Street. He died on August 11, 1893. (Courtesy of the University of Pittsburgh Archives Service Center.)

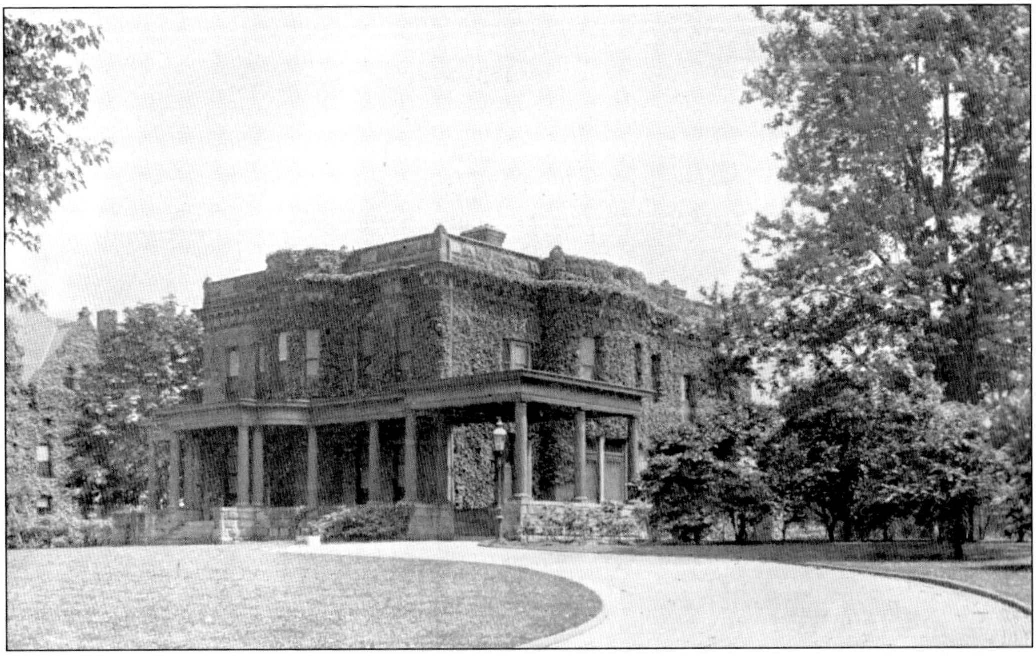

**RESIDENCE OF REUBEN MILLER, C. 1905.** Reuben Miller was born in 1839 and worked as a steelmaker, the same line of work as his father. His home, Ivy House, was located at 4900 Fifth Avenue near Bidwell Street (now Devonshire Avenue). Miller was also a director of the Fidelity Trust Company and a member of the Americus Club.

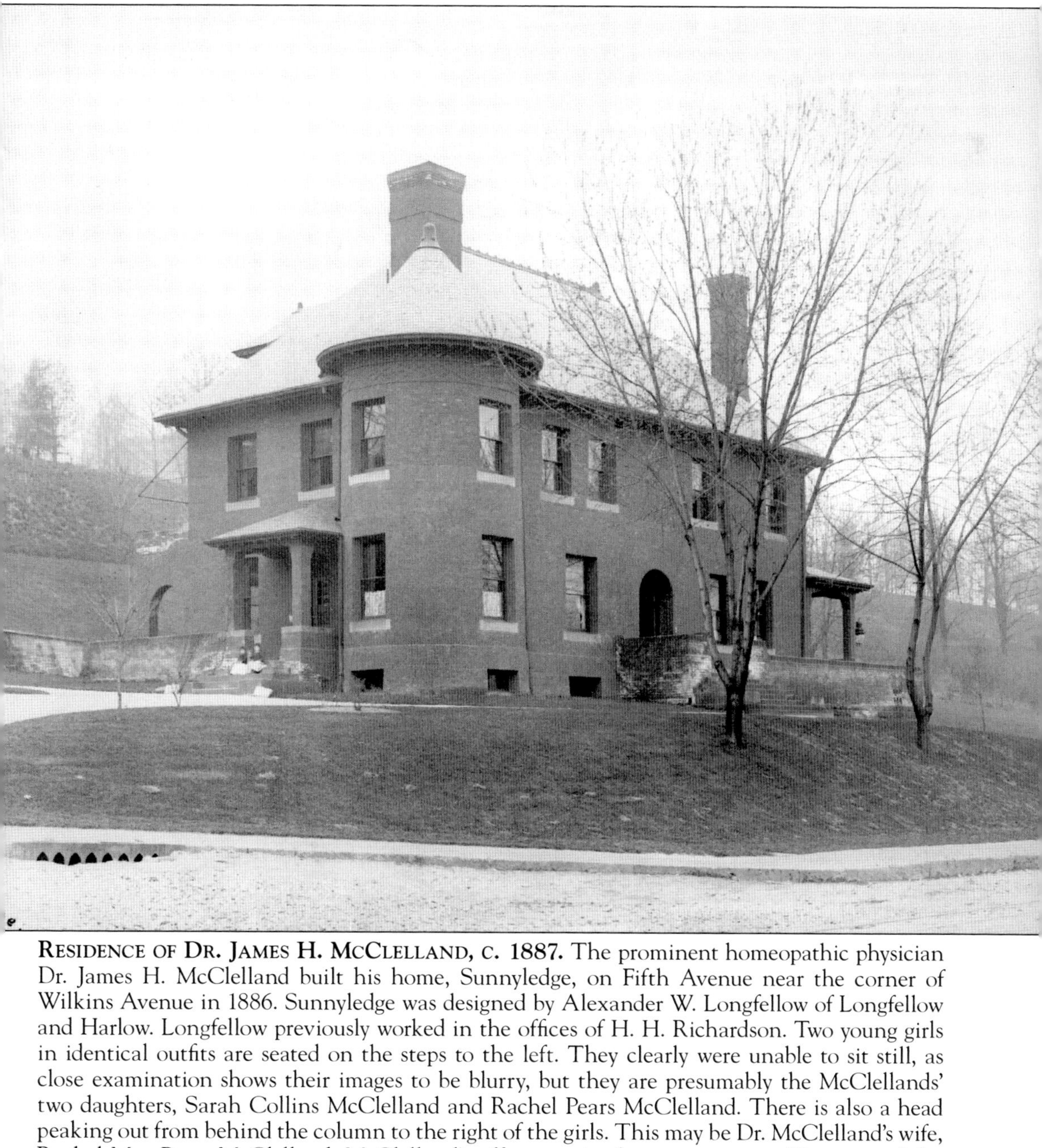

**RESIDENCE OF DR. JAMES H. MCCLELLAND, C. 1887.** The prominent homeopathic physician Dr. James H. McClelland built his home, Sunnyledge, on Fifth Avenue near the corner of Wilkins Avenue in 1886. Sunnyledge was designed by Alexander W. Longfellow of Longfellow and Harlow. Longfellow previously worked in the offices of H. H. Richardson. Two young girls in identical outfits are seated on the steps to the left. They clearly were unable to sit still, as close examination shows their images to be blurry, but they are presumably the McClellands' two daughters, Sarah Collins McClelland and Rachel Pears McClelland. There is also a head peaking out from behind the column to the right of the girls. This may be Dr. McClelland's wife, Rachel May Pears McClelland. McClelland's office was in the corner tower. (Courtesy of the Library and Archives Division, Senator John Heinz History Center.)

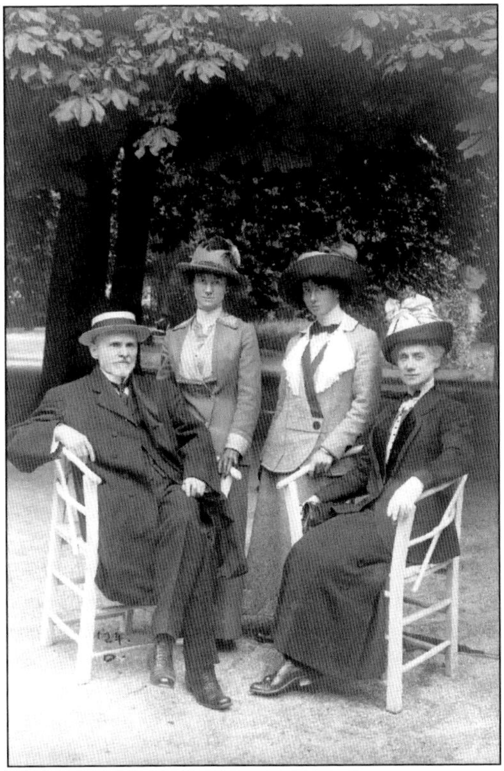

**Dr. James H. McClelland's Family, c. 1907.** The McClelland family included, from left to right, father McClelland, mother Rachel May Pears, and their two daughters, Rachel Pears and Sarah Collins. (Courtesy of the Library and Archives Division, Senator John Heinz History Center.)

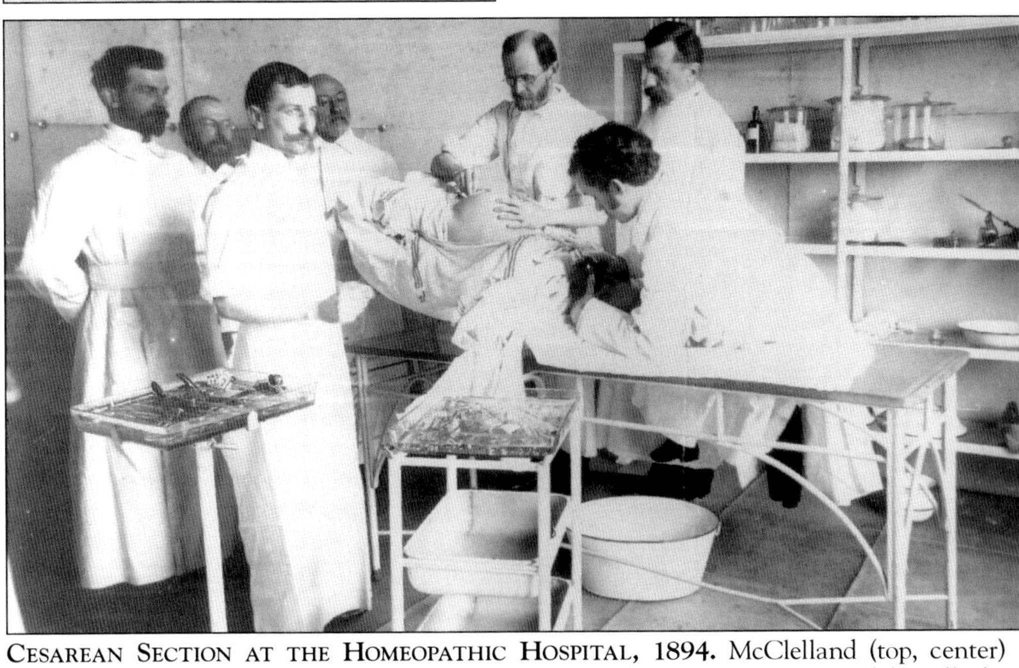

**Cesarean Section at the Homeopathic Hospital, 1894.** McClelland (top, center) is shown performing what is thought to have been the first cesarean section west of the Allegheny Mountains. The operation took place in a new operating room with glass floors, walls, and ceiling at the Homeopathic Hospital in downtown Pittsburgh. (Courtesy of the Library and Archives Division, Senator John Heinz History Center.)

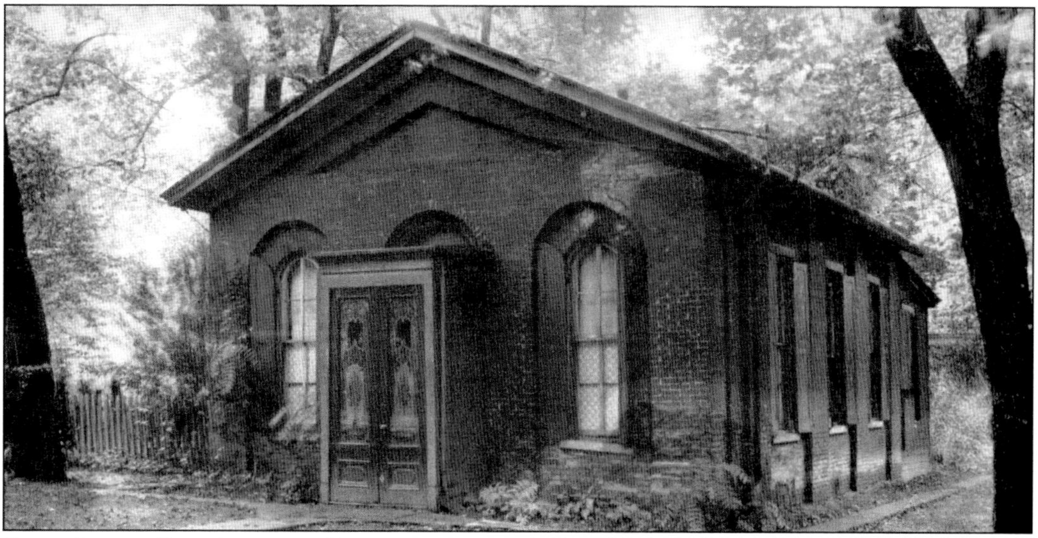

**FIRST SHADY SIDE ACADEMY BUILDING, C. 1885.** The Shady Side Academy college preparatory school for boys, then known as the Shady Side Classical Academy, held its first classes in September 1883 and began meeting in this one-room brick building at 926 Aiken Avenue that same year. In September 1885, the Shady Side Academy moved to a new building at Morewood and Ellsworth Avenues (see page 80).

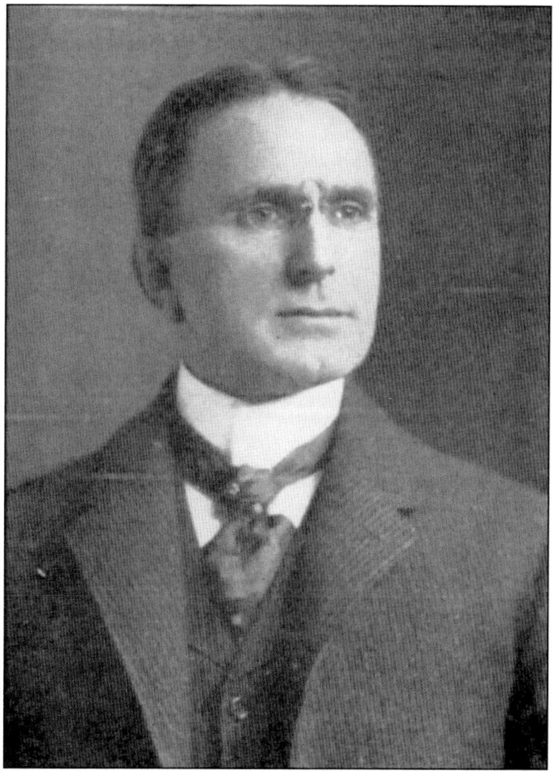

**WILLIAM RALSTON CRABBE, PH.D., C. 1895.** Dr. William Ralston Crabbe, the founder and principal of the Shady Side Academy, was born on May 4, 1854, in Ashland, Ohio. He graduated from Wooster University (now the College of Wooster) in 1877 and then from Pittsburgh's Western Theological Seminary in 1881. He lived with his wife and two daughters at 5053 Castleman Street. Crabbe died on October 15, 1915.

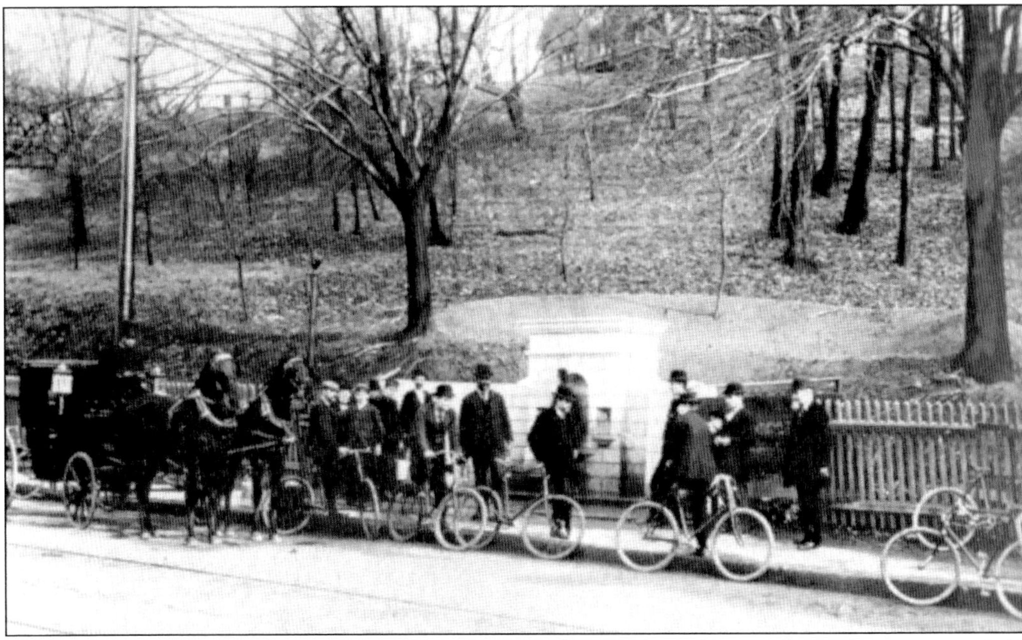

**HOWE SPRINGS, C. 1880.** Howe Springs provided these bicyclists with fresh water on Fifth Avenue. The springs were on the Thomas Marshall Howe estate known as Graystone. The Howe home is visible through the trees at the top of the hill where there was a fine view of Shadyside and much of the East End.

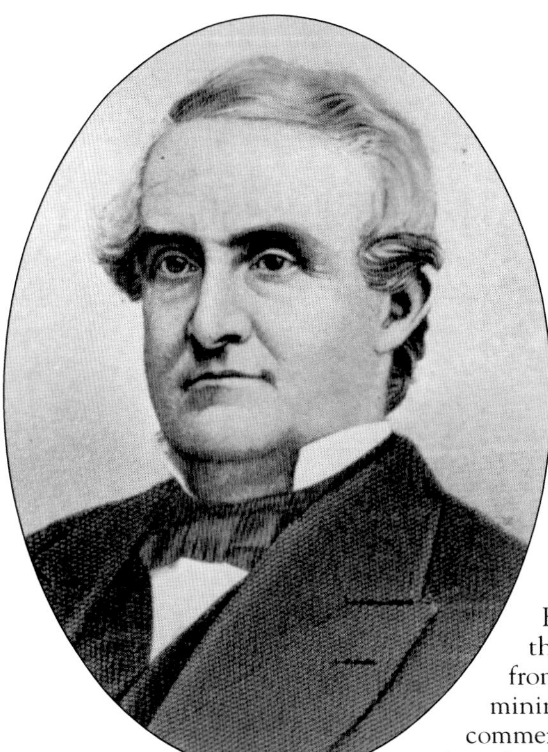

**THOMAS MARSHALL HOWE, C. 1870.** Howe served as a cashier and president of the Exchange National Bank of Pittsburgh from 1839 to 1859. He also engaged in copper mining, copper and steel manufacturing, commercial pursuits, and banking. Howe was twice elected to the U.S. Senate. He died in 1877.

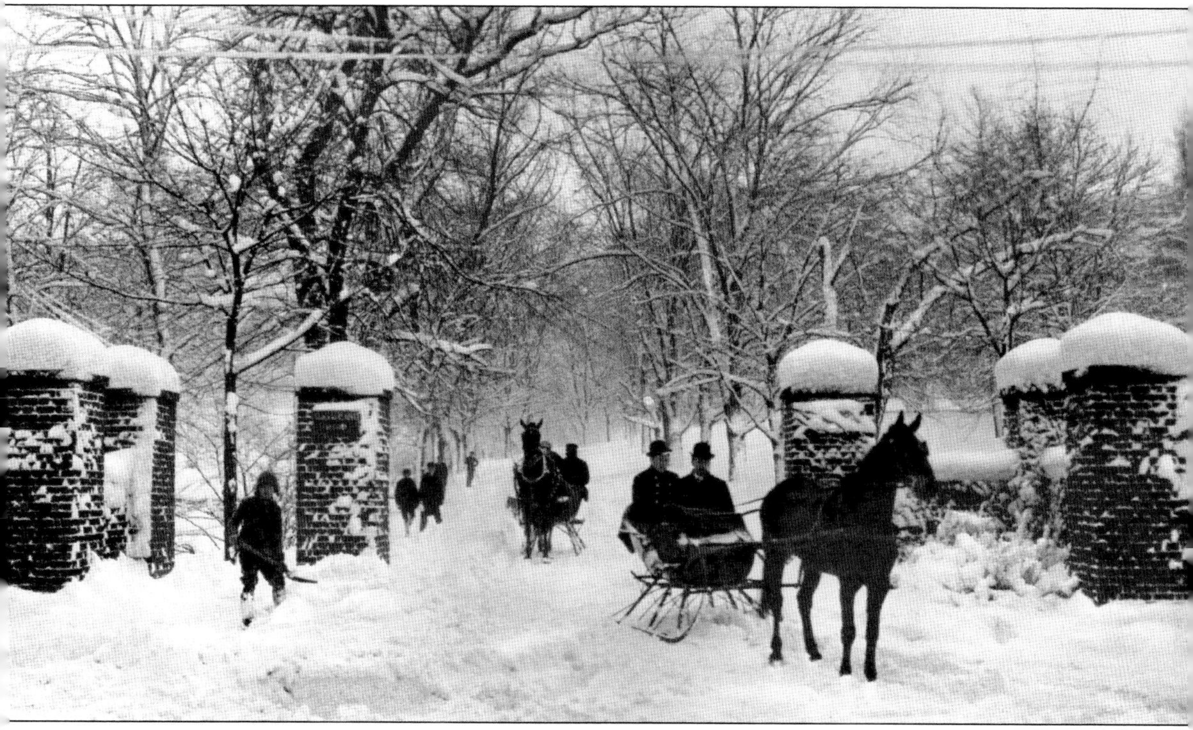

**WOODLAND ROAD AND FIFTH AVENUE, C. 1890.** Horse-drawn sleighs are traveling down Woodland Road through the gate that opens onto Fifth Avenue. Woodland Road is a private drive that leads to Chatham University, known as the Pennsylvania Female College in 1869 and then the Pennsylvania College for Women beginning in 1890, and several private residences.

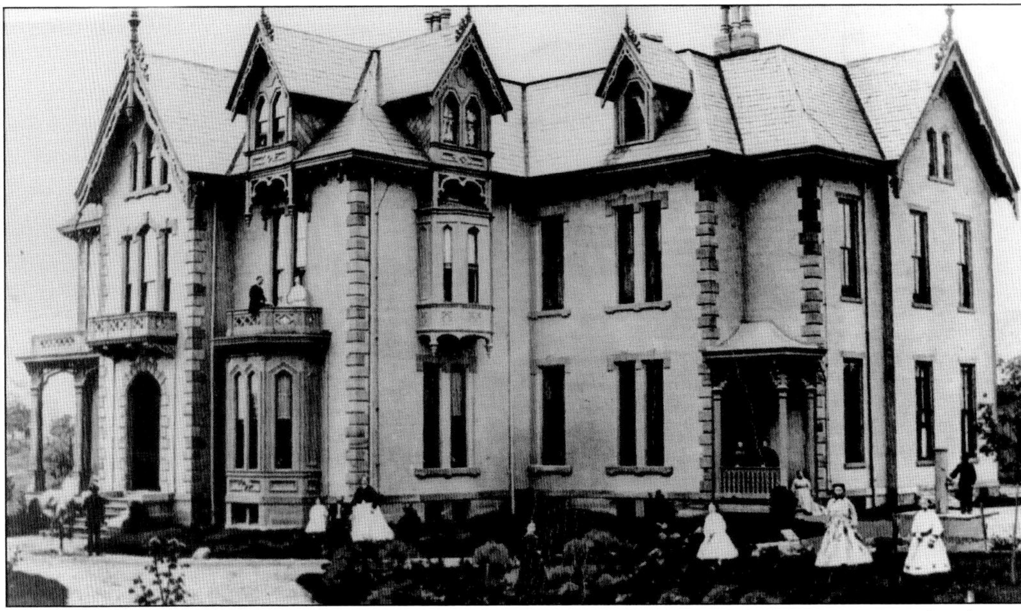

**GEORGE A. BERRY MANSION, C. 1865.** The residence of George A. Berry was the largest private residence in Allegheny County at the time. When the Pennsylvania Female College was chartered on December 11, 1869, it was decided to purchase the Berry estate to house the college. Rev. William Trimble Beatty, pastor of the Shadyside Presbyterian Church, led the creation of the college. (Courtesy of the Chatham College Archives.)

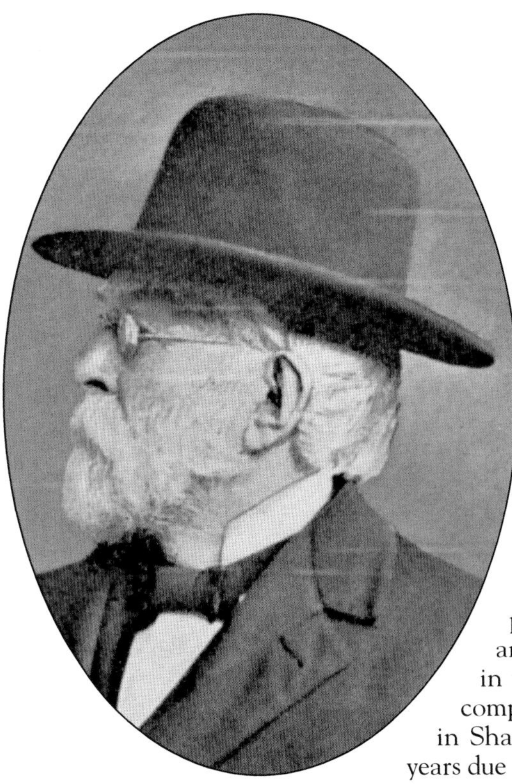

**GEORGE A. BERRY C. 1890.** Berry was the president of Citizens' National Bank (1865–1901) and a grandson of George Anshutz, the pioneer in the manufacture of iron in Pittsburgh. Anshutz completed a small furnace, the first one in the region, in Shadyside in 1792, which was in use for only two years due to a lack of local ore.

**BERRY HALL I TOWER, C. 1890.** Modifications were made to the Berry mansion to transform it into Berry Hall. Early in the Pennsylvania Female College history, everything took place in Berry Hall, including classes, dining, student boarding, faculty offices, and administration. The building was demolished in 1952. (Courtesy of the Chatham College Archives.)

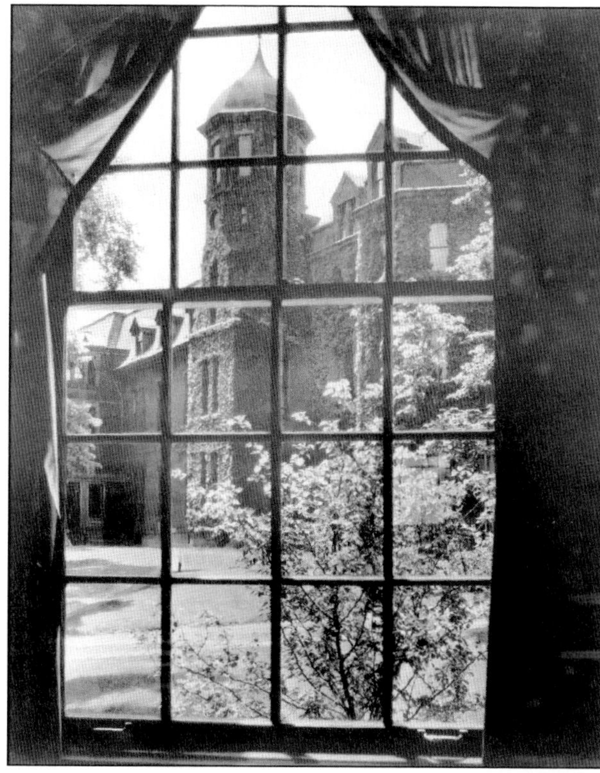

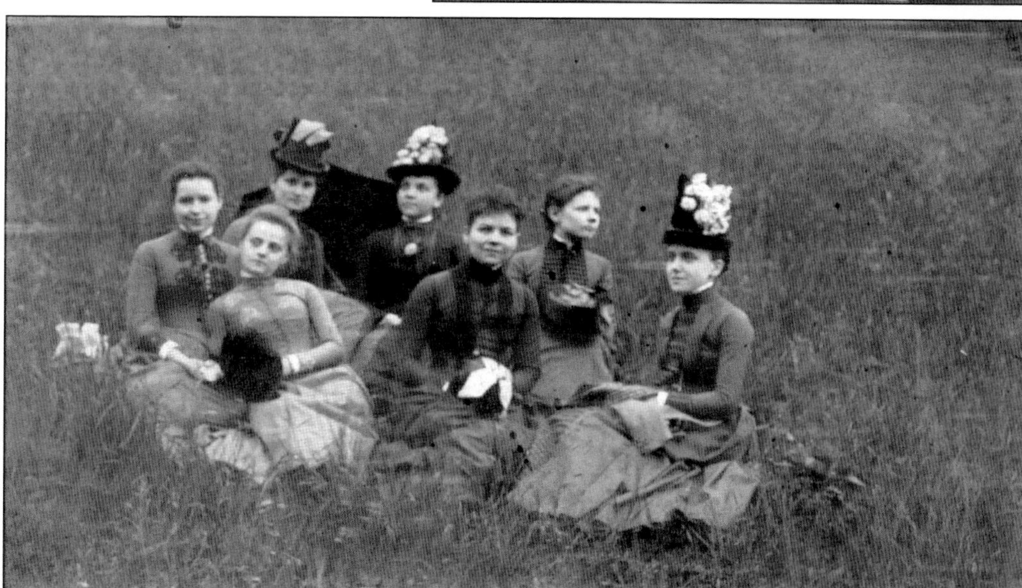

**PENNSYLVANIA FEMALE COLLEGE CLASS OF 1888.** The number of graduating seniors from the Pennsylvania Female College (renamed Pennsylvania College for Women in 1890 and then Chatham College in 1955) was still small in 1888. Sitting on the lawn, from left to right, are (first row) Elizabeth Simpson, Dorcas Beer, and Martha Lockhart; (second row) Alice Stockton, Elizabeth Kirk, Hetty Boyle, and Elizabeth Boale. (Courtesy of the Chatham College Archives.)

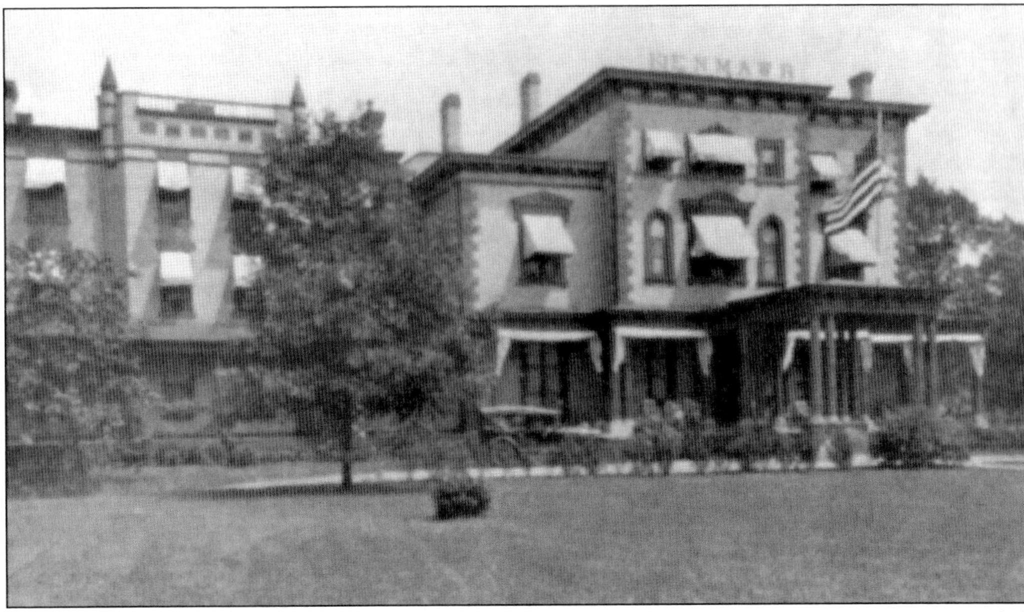

**The Kenmawr, c. 1890.** The Kenmawr hotel at Shady Avenue and Walnut Street was a stylish place to live for many years. Many prominent Pittsburghers made it their home.

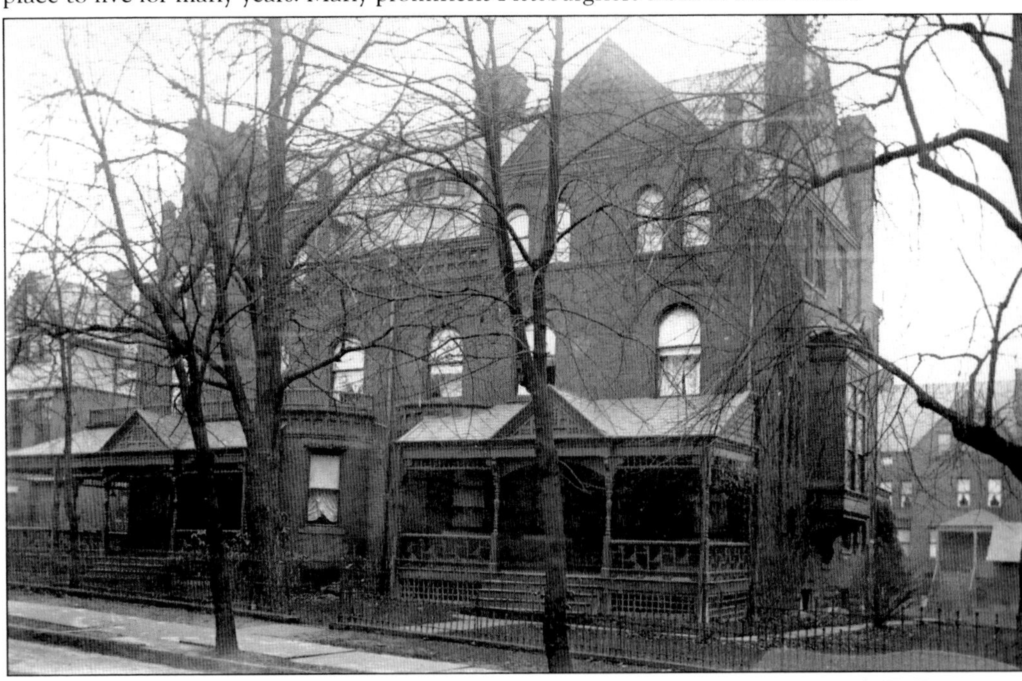

**Double House on Denniston, c. 1890.** On December 7, 1888, Maj. Joseph F. Denniston, the county and city treasurer, was issued a building permit to build a double house at 428 and 432 Denniston Avenue that was estimated to cost $12,000. Denniston was a member of the Grand Army of the Republic Post 117, the Veteran Legion, and the Loyal Legion. Denniston, his wife, Nannie C. Boulton, and three children, Bertha, Rachel, and Joseph, lived at 428 Denniston Avenue. Denniston died on November 24, 1897, due to wounds received during the Civil War. (Courtesy of Nancy McNary Smith.)

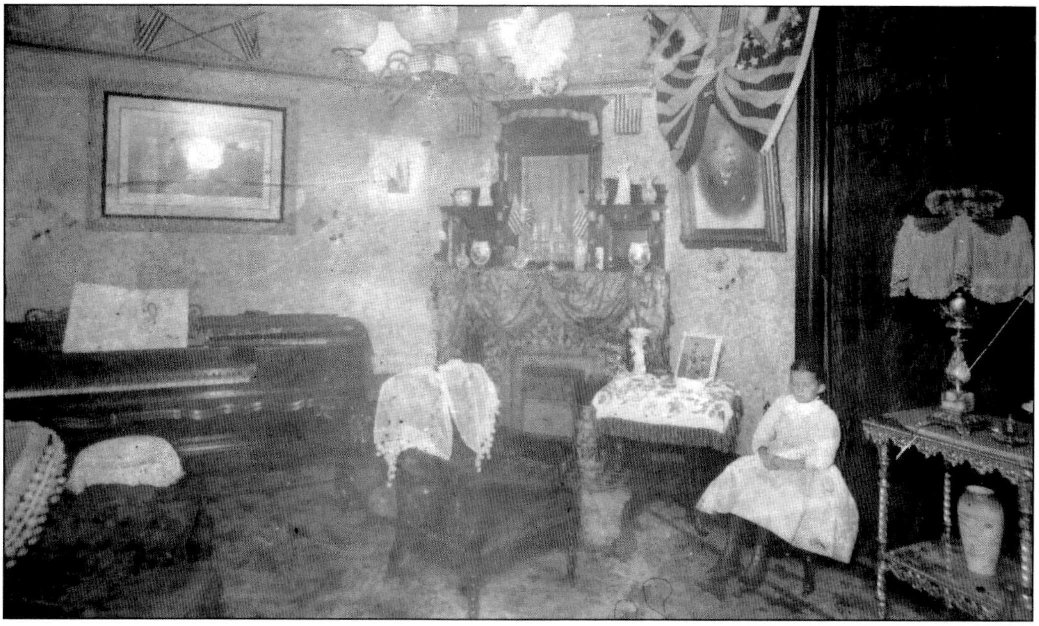

**MAJ. JOSEPH F. DENNISTON'S PARLOR, C. 1890.** Denniston's first-floor parlor is decorated in flags, suggesting a celebration or remembrance. Perhaps the celebration was for the major's Civil War service, or perhaps they are in somber remembrance of the late major at his early death in 1897 due to wounds from the war. The unidentified girl may be one of the major's two daughters. (Courtesy of Nancy McNary Smith.)

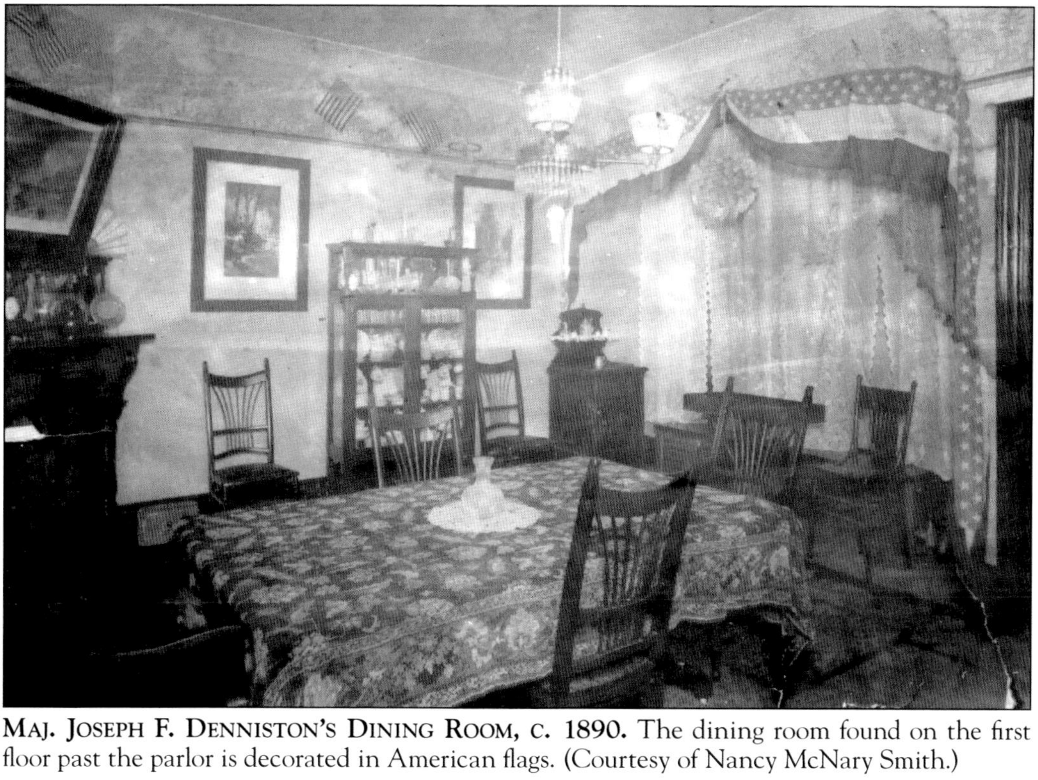

**MAJ. JOSEPH F. DENNISTON'S DINING ROOM, C. 1890.** The dining room found on the first floor past the parlor is decorated in American flags. (Courtesy of Nancy McNary Smith.)

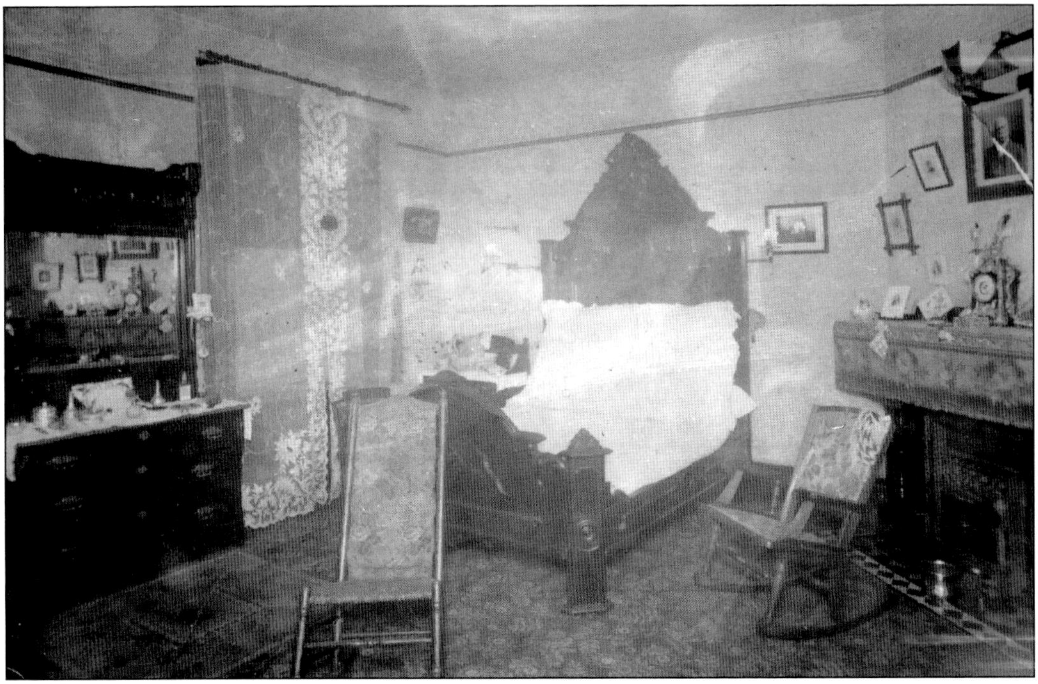

**MAJ. JOSEPH F. DENNISTON'S MASTER BEDROOM, C. 1890.** The master bedroom on the second floor contains an impressive carved-wood bed. On each side of the headboard is an adjustable lighting fixture. (Courtesy of Nancy McNary Smith.)

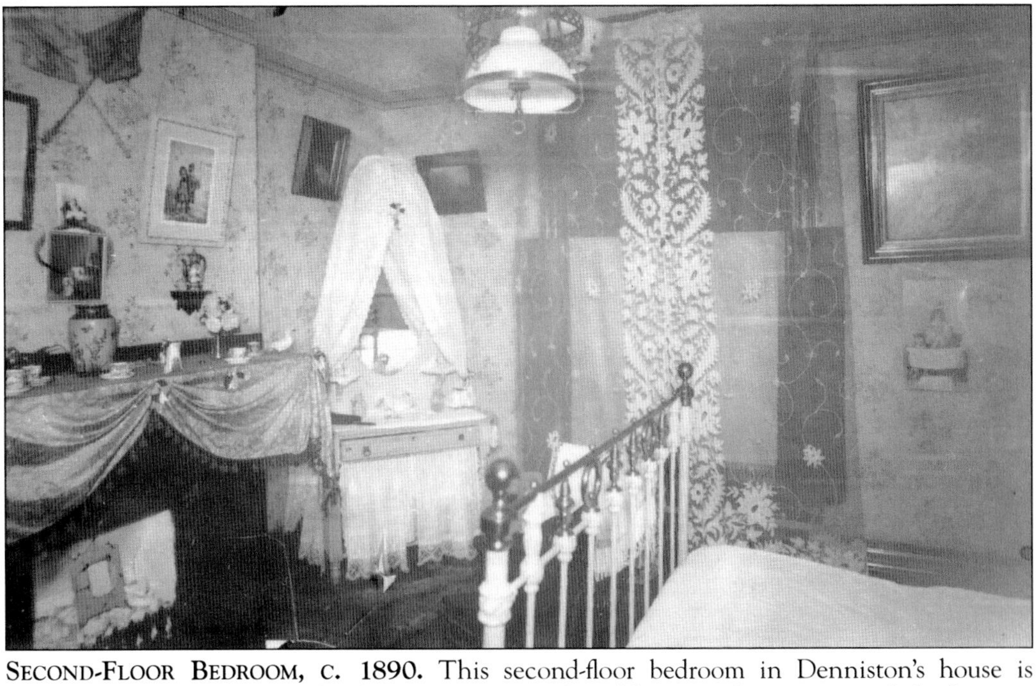

**SECOND-FLOOR BEDROOM, C. 1890.** This second-floor bedroom in Denniston's house is apparently for a woman or girl. There is a vanity and washbasin in the corner just left of center. This could have been a bedroom for one of his daughters, Bertha or Rachel, or it may have been his wife's bedroom. (Courtesy of Nancy McNary Smith.)

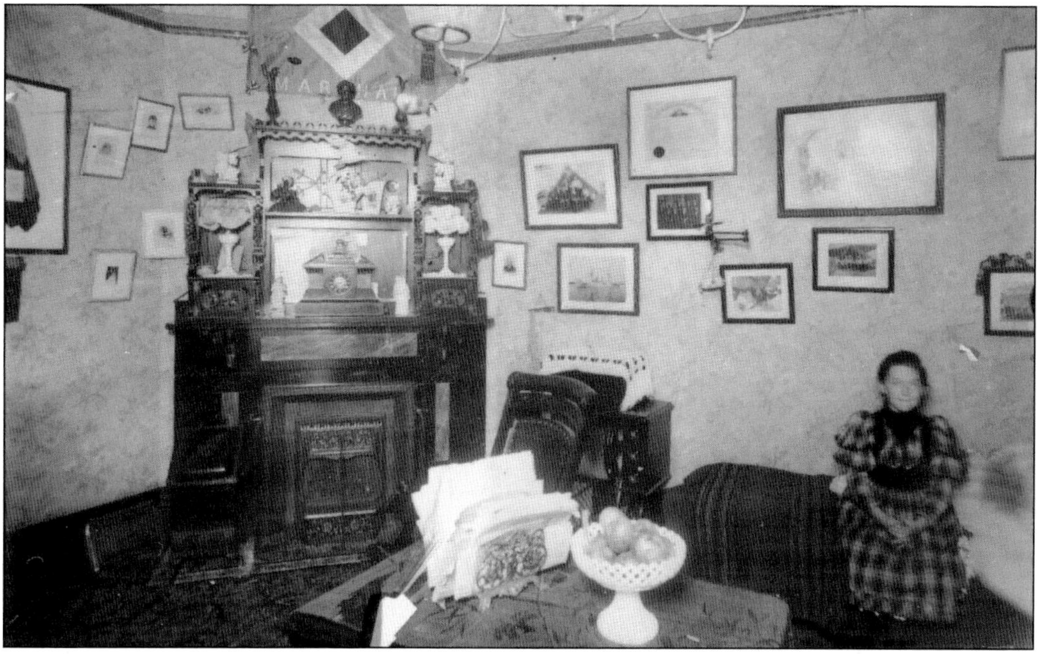

**SECOND-FLOOR OFFICE, C. 1890.** This room in Denniston's house appears to be a man's den, office, or study. Above the fireplace hangs a flag declaring chief marshal, and on close inspection, the images on the wall on the right are war related. The unidentified girl in this photograph may be one of his two daughters. (Courtesy of Nancy McNary Smith.)

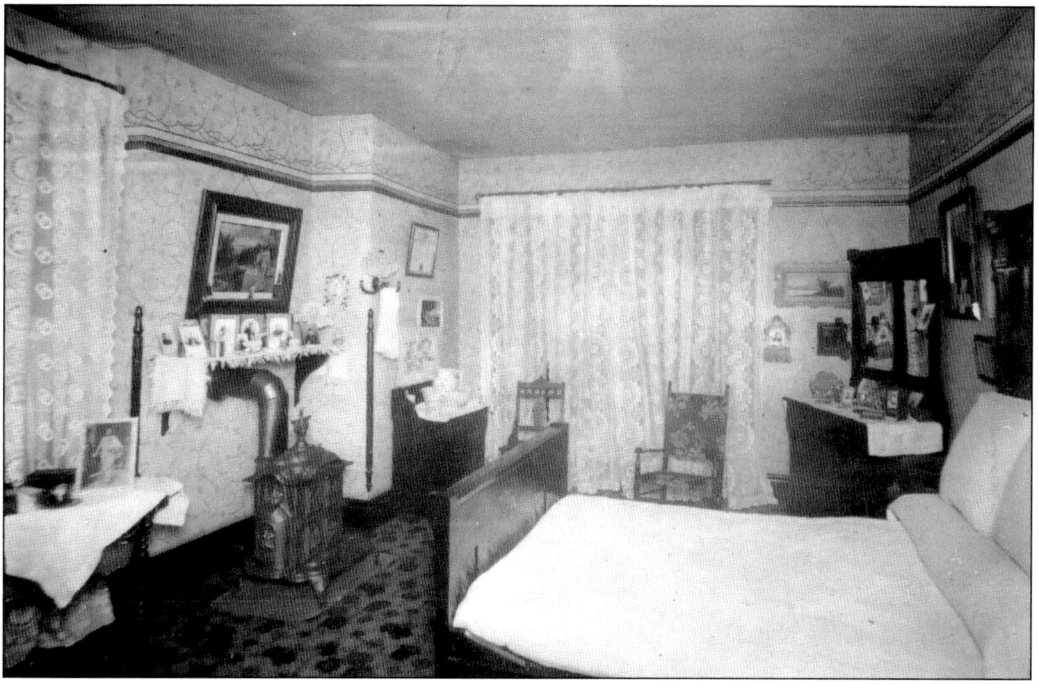

**THIRD-FLOOR BEDROOM, C. 1890.** This third-floor bedroom was probably occupied by household staff or renters. The 1895 *Pittsburg and Allegheny Blue Book* lists a Richard Alexander Beatty and M. Rena Beatty as living with the Denniston family. (Courtesy of Nancy McNary Smith.)

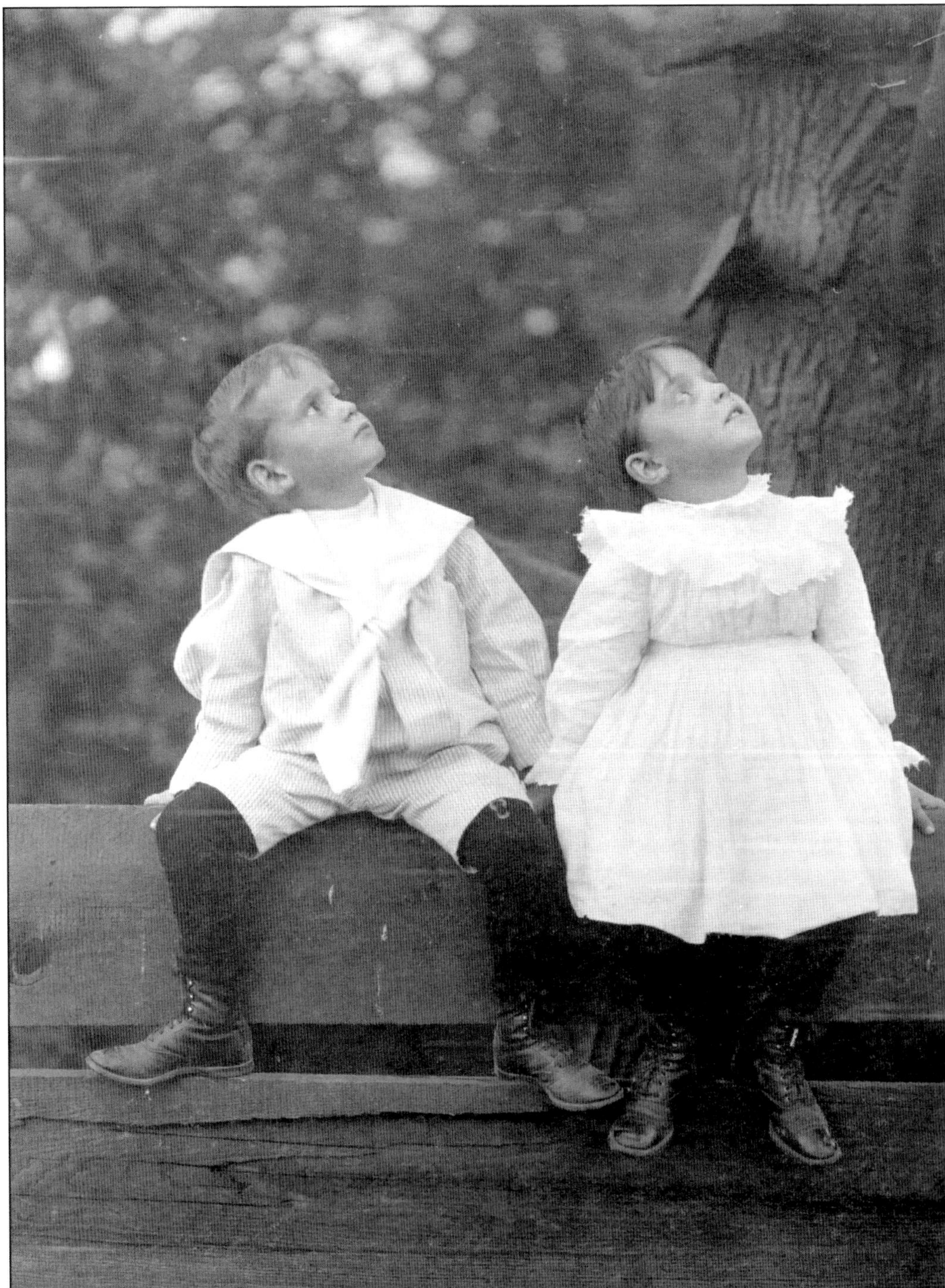

**TWINS LOOKING UP, 1900.** Charles Jr. and Elizabeth Spencer are sitting atop a wood fence and looking skyward. (Courtesy of the University of Pittsburgh Archives Service Center.)

# *Two*

# RAPID GROWTH AND INDUSTRIALIZATION 1901–1919

In 1910, Shadyside was built up and had a population of 13,263, but the neighborhood still retained much of its suburban character. New technologies such as electricity, telephone, and the automobile started having an impact. These expensive new services and items were snapped up by Shadyside residents, and by 1907, a strip along the edge of Shadyside was known as Automobile Row. The construction of new roads, sewers, and other infrastructure were common sights in Shadyside during these years.

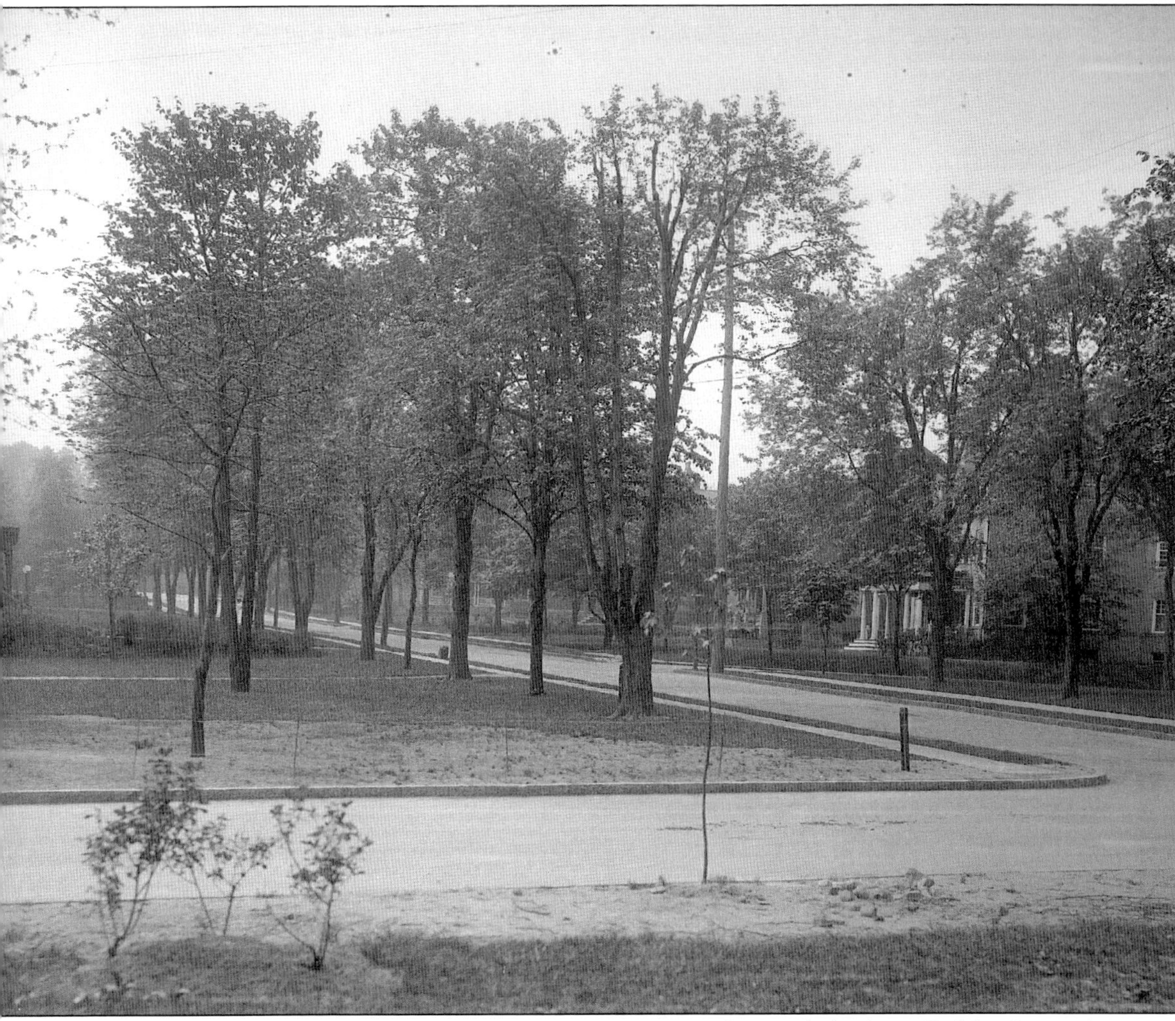

**DAHLIA STREET AND AMBERSON AVENUE, C. 1902.** The newly laid out Dahlia Street (now Pembroke Place) is clearly visible from the Spencers' side yard. The yellow brick house at right sits on Amberson Avenue at the corner of Castleman Street. The connection of the two roads is visible just to the right of the tree in the center foreground next to Amberson Avenue and just behind the telephone pole. Located at 826 Amberson Avenue, this was the home of Wenman Abner Lewis. It still stands today but without the front porch. The Lewis family lived at 5336 Westminster Street until April 1, 1898, when they moved into their Amberson Avenue house. (Courtesy of the Shadyside Presbyterian Church Archives.)

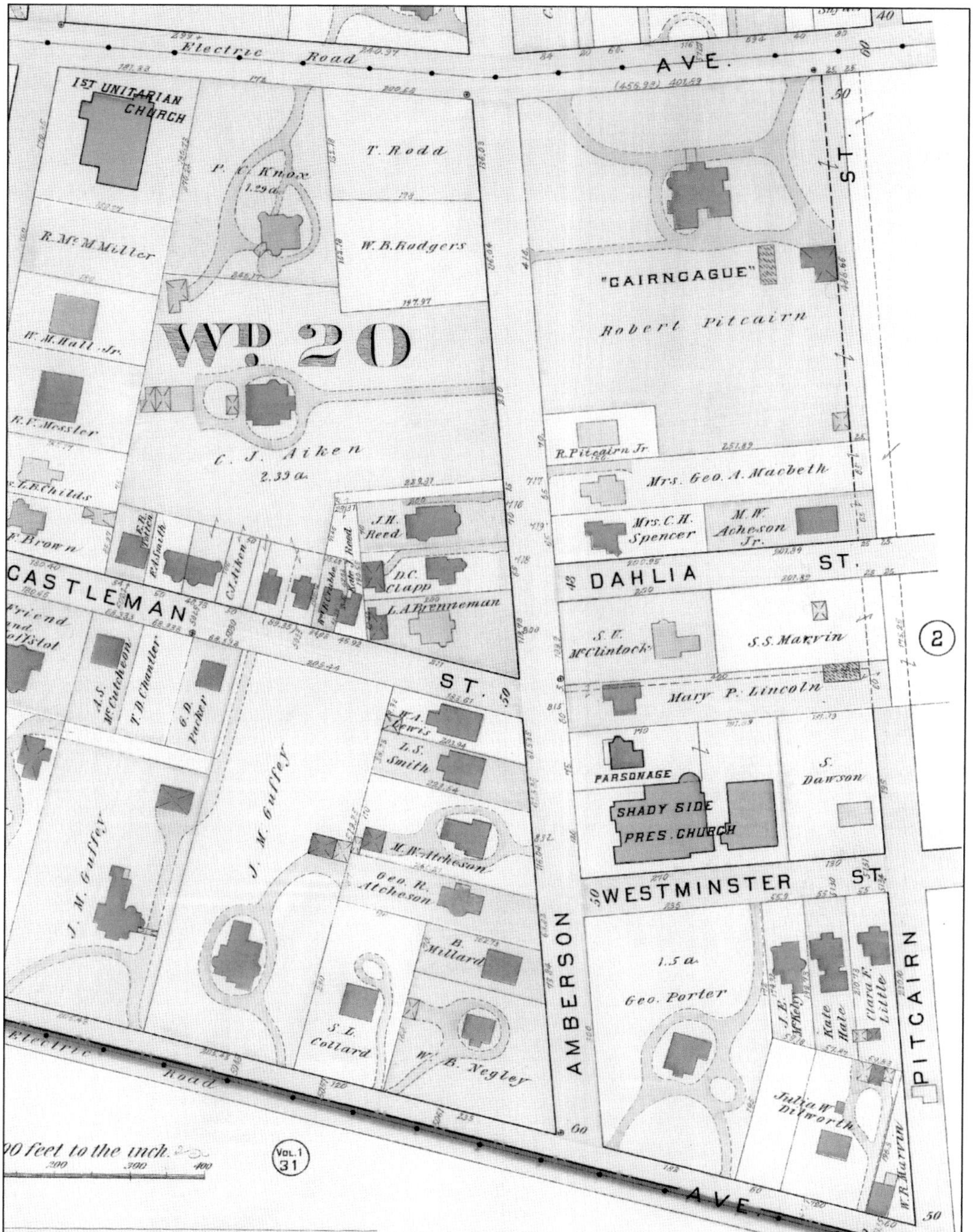


**SHADYSIDE AREA MAP, 1904.** By 1904, most of the main roads had been laid in Shadyside. This map details the neighborhood around the Shadyside Presbyterian Church and the Aiken estate, which was the residence of the owners of the farm that made up much of Shadyside. During the first decade of the 20th century, the large estates, like those of the Aikens and the Pitcairns, gave way to more densely packed subdivisions. (Courtesy of the University of Pittsburgh's Digital Research Library.)

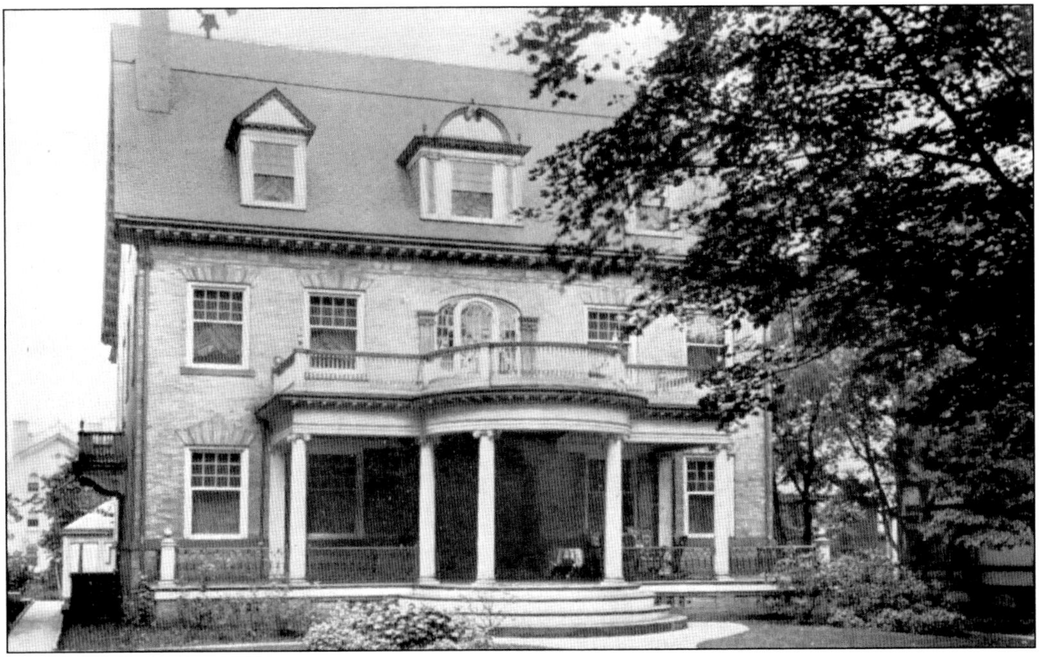

**RESIDENCE OF WENMAN ABNER LEWIS, C. 1905.** The Lewis family lived at 826 Amberson Avenue beginning on April 1, 1898. Wenman Abner Lewis graduated from Allegheny College, and his wife graduated from the Pittsburgh Female College. Lewis was a principal in the Lewis-Findley Coal Company where his son Bernard was made partner. In 1911, the company was reorganized into the West Virginia Pittsburgh Coal Company with Lewis acting as president.

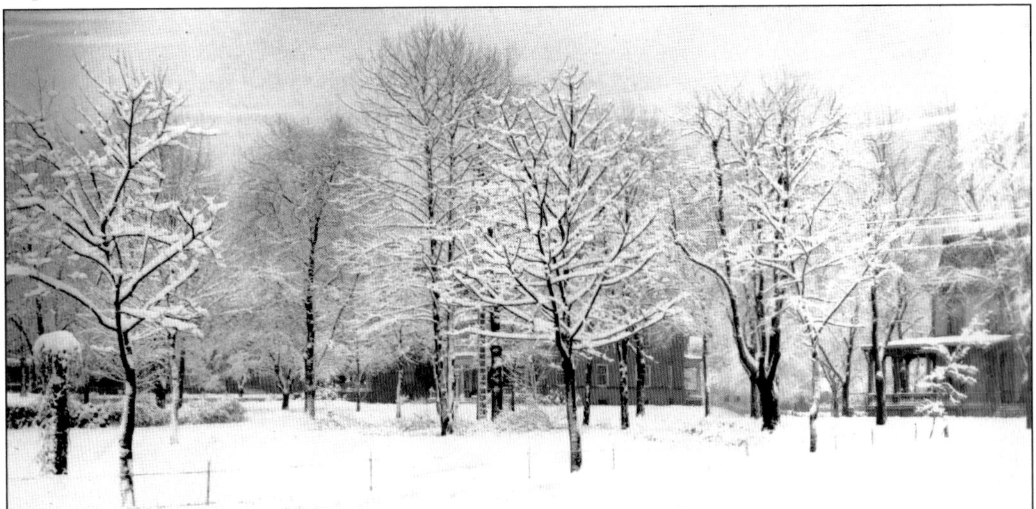

**WINTER, MARCH 1906.** Snow softens the view across Dahlia Street (now Pembroke Place) toward Amberson Avenue from the Spencer family backyard. The Lewis home is visible through the trees at center. On the other side of Castleman Street to the right is the wood home (no longer standing) that belonged to Sylvester S. Marvin until he sold it to Brenneman in 1901. (Courtesy of the University of Pittsburgh Archives Service Center.)

**CHARLES SPENCER JR. RIDING A BICYCLE, APRIL 1903.** Charles Spencer Jr. is sitting on a bicycle and steadying himself by resting his right foot on a recently laid flagstone curb. He is probably next to his house on Dahlia Street (now Pembroke Place) in a view looking toward Lilac Avenue (now St. James Street). (Courtesy of the University of Pittsburgh Archives Service Center.)

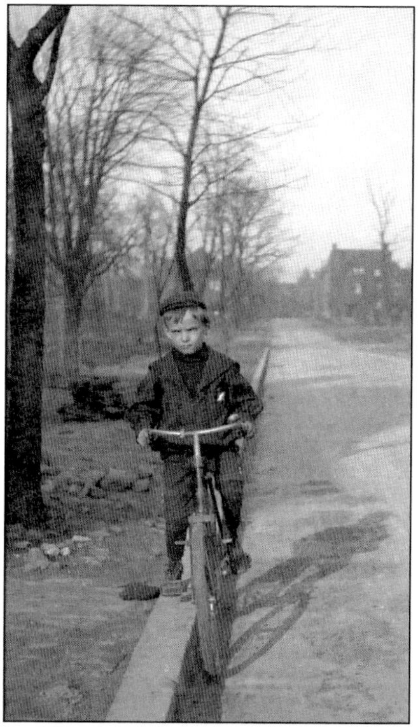

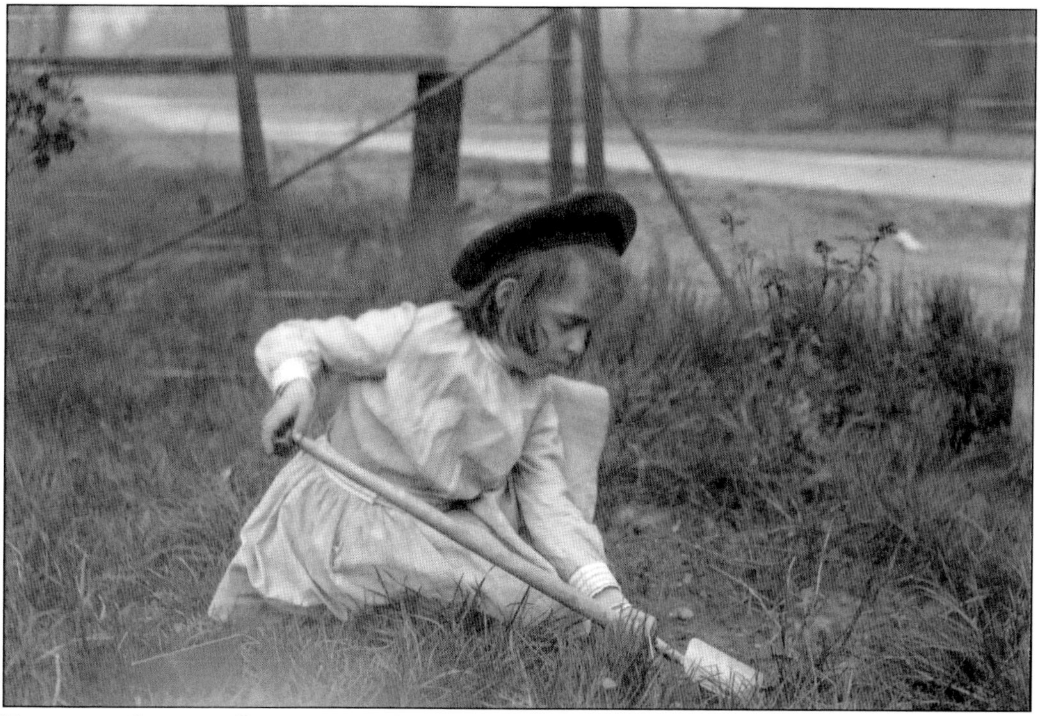

**ELIZABETH SPENCER GARDENING, APRIL 1903.** Elizabeth Spencer is gardening in her backyard along the new Dahlia Street with a structure still apparently owned by Sylvester S. Marvin at right on the other side of the street. (Courtesy of the University of Pittsburgh Archives Service Center.)

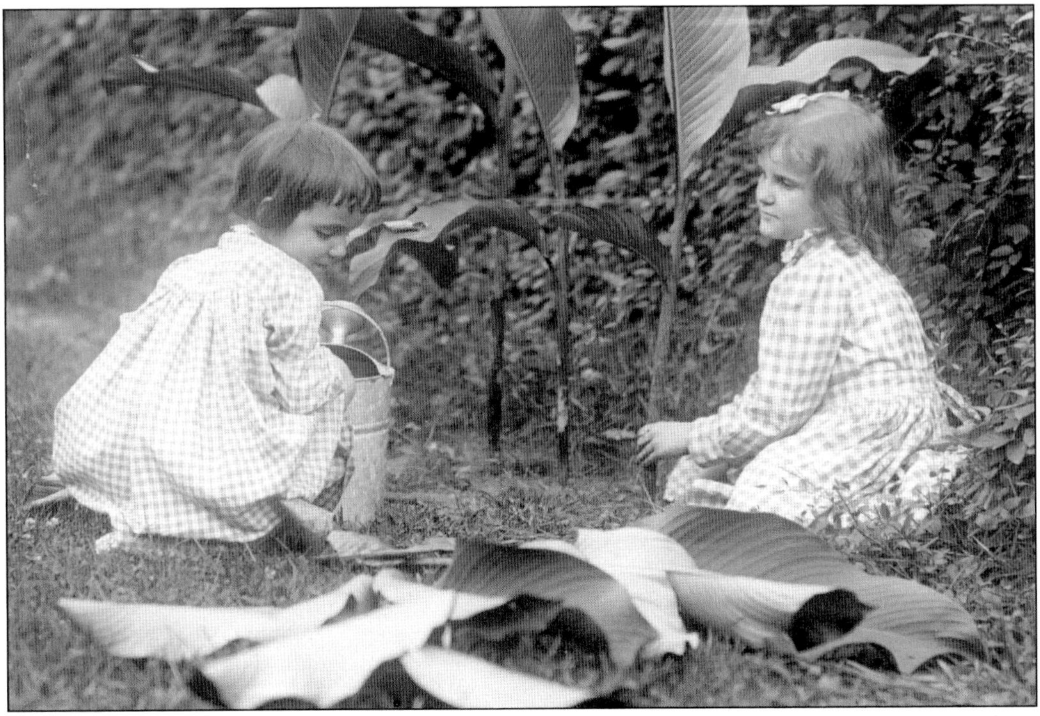

**YOUNG GARDENERS, JULY 1901.** Elizabeth Spencer is watering the *Canna* plants as Mary Wilson Spencer sits and watches. (Courtesy of the University of Pittsburgh Archives Service Center.)

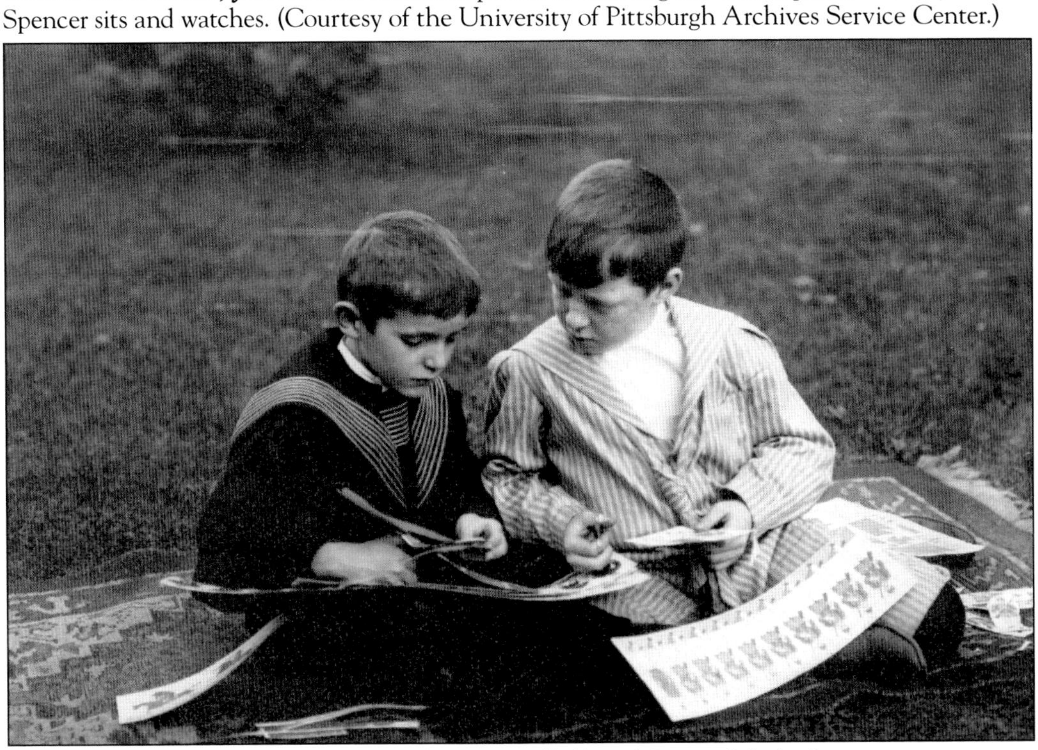

**PAPER SOLDIERS, OCTOBER 1901.** Mark Spencer (left) and George Macbeth are sitting on a rug cutting paper soldiers. (Courtesy of the University of Pittsburgh Archives Service Center.)

**TETHERBALL, SEPTEMBER 1901.** Mark (left) and George Macbeth play tetherball with rackets. (Courtesy of the University of Pittsburgh Archives Service Center.)

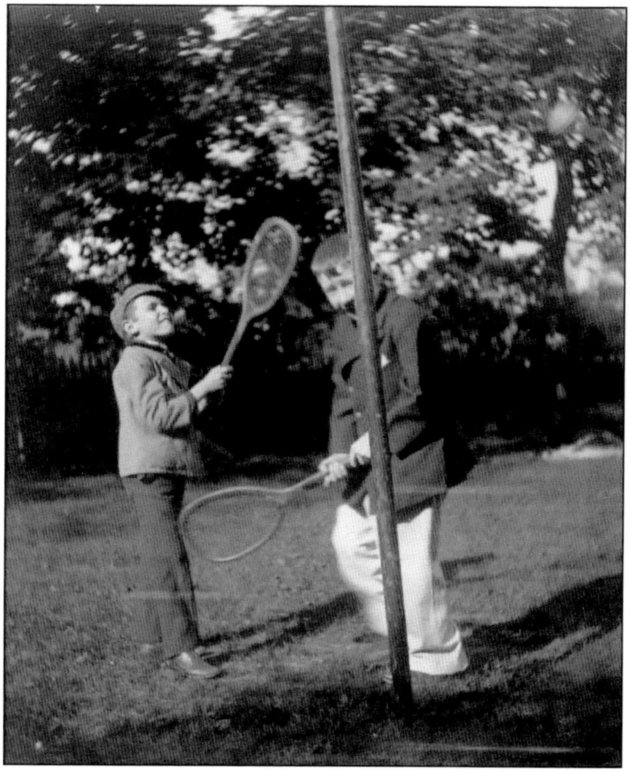

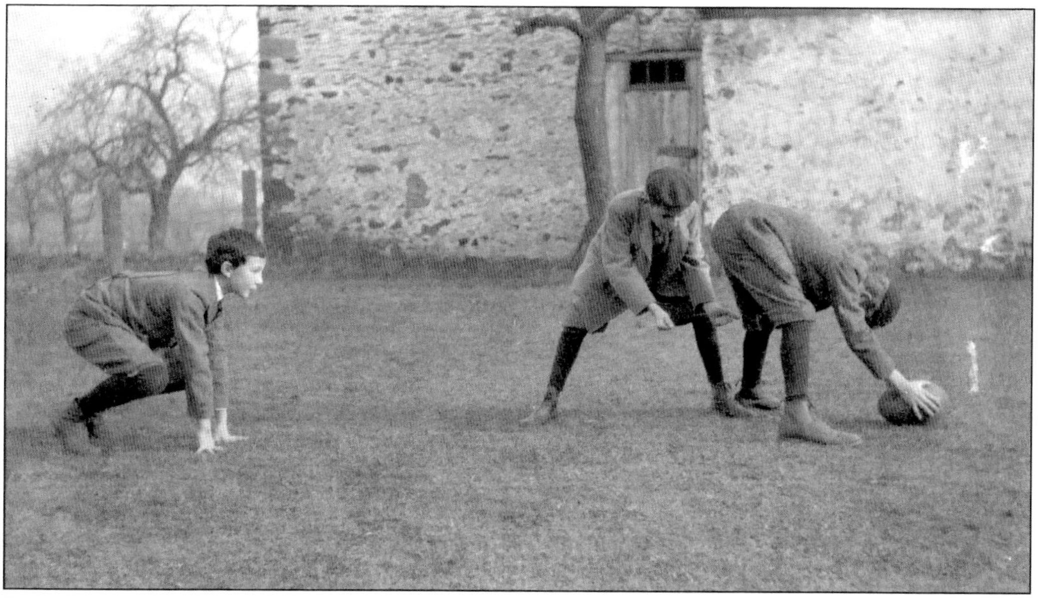

**FOOTBALL, NOVEMBER 1904.** Mark plays football with two other boys on Thanksgiving day. (Courtesy of the University of Pittsburgh Archives Service Center.)

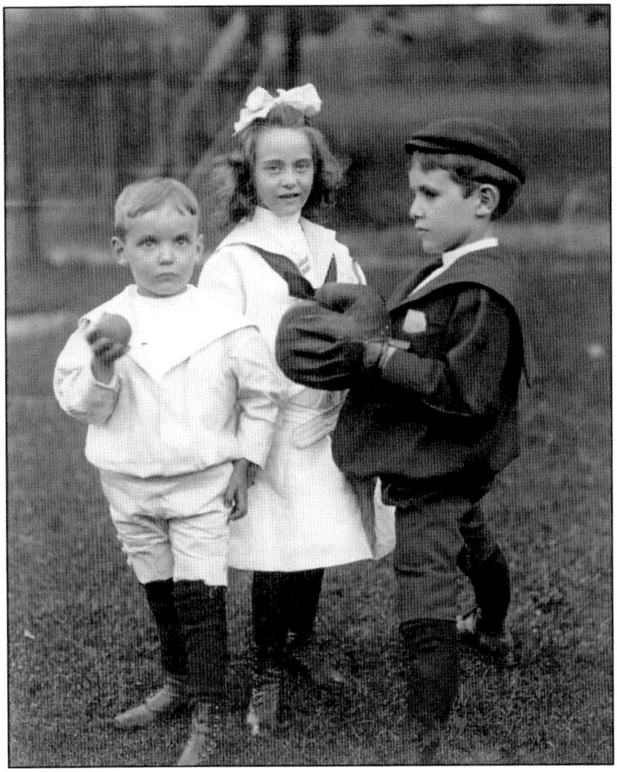

**BASEBALL, MAY 1901.** Charles Spencer Jr. holds a baseball with an unidentified girl, and Mark Spencer is wearing a baseball glove. (Courtesy of the University of Pittsburgh Archives Service Center.)

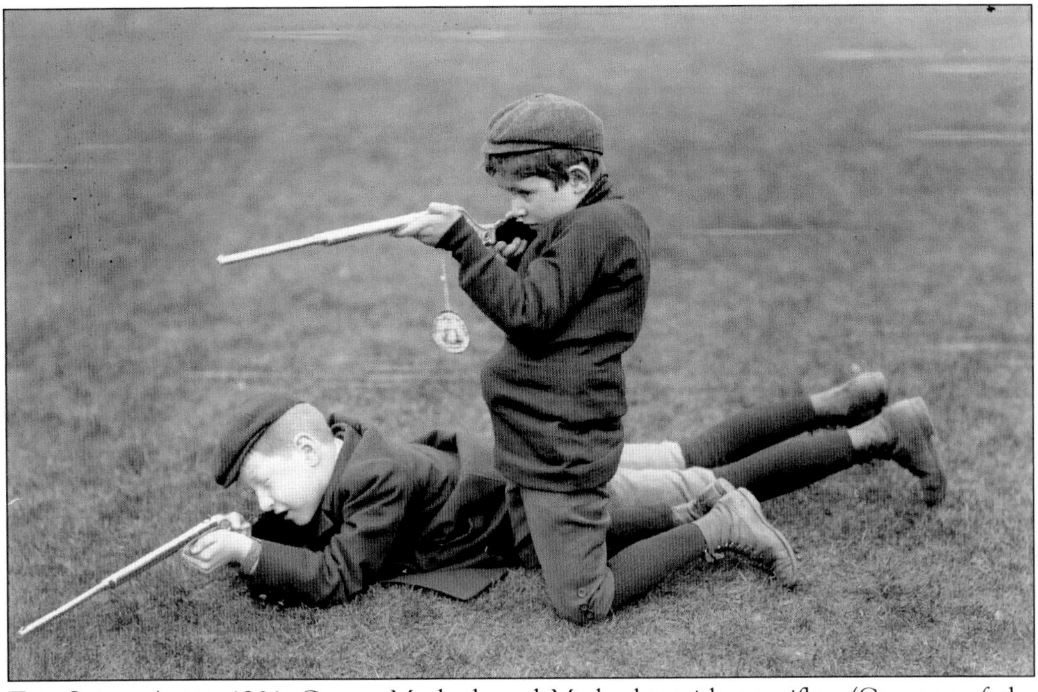

**TOY GUNS, APRIL 1901.** George Macbeth and Mark play with toy rifles. (Courtesy of the University of Pittsburgh Archives Service Center.)

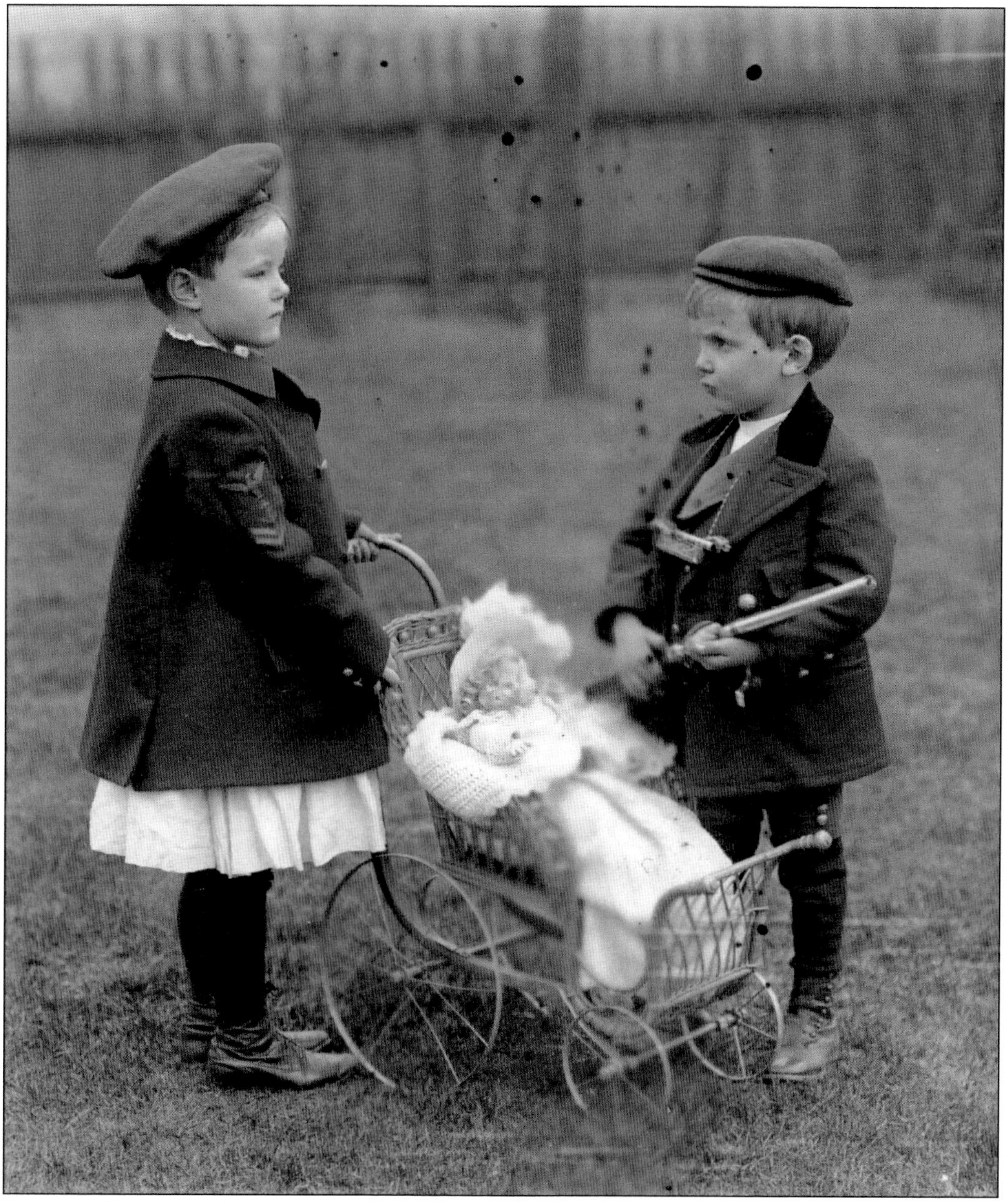

**PLAYING OUTSIDE, APRIL 1901.** An unidentified girl pushes a toy baby carriage with a doll in it while Charles Spencer Jr. stands guard with a toy rifle. (Courtesy of the University of Pittsburgh Archives Service Center.)

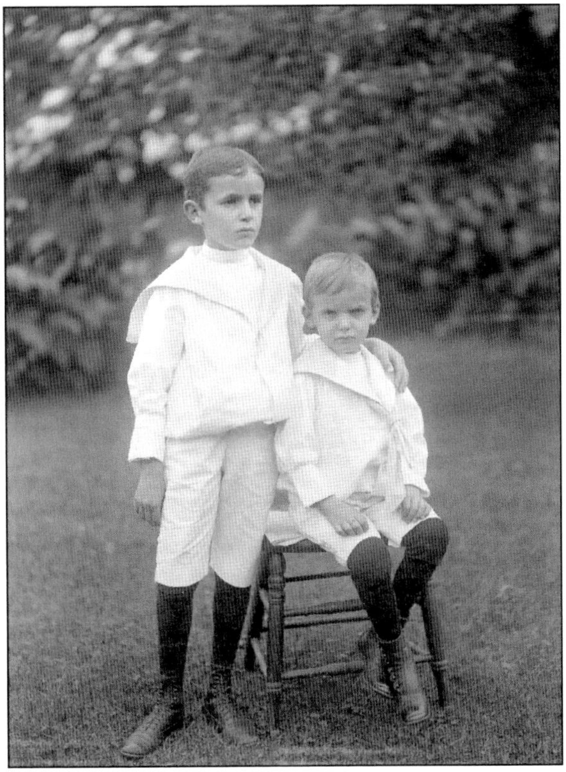

**WEARING WHITE, SEPTEMBER 1901.** Mark and Charles Spencer Jr. wear white sailor's outfits. (Courtesy of the University of Pittsburgh Archives Service Center.)

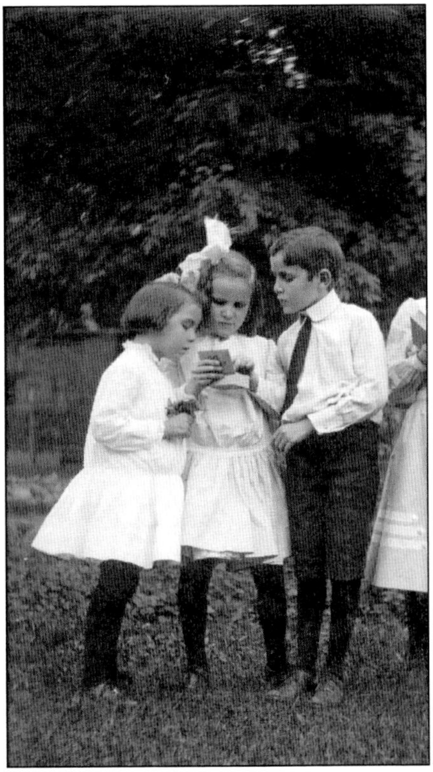

**BOX, AUGUST 1902.** Spencer children Elizabeth, Mary Wilson, and Mark examine the contents of the small box that Mary Wilson is holding. (Courtesy of the University of Pittsburgh Archives Service Center.)

**PATRIOTIC BICYCLE, JUNE 1901.** Mark and an unidentified girl display their patriotism. (Courtesy of the University of Pittsburgh Archives Service Center.)

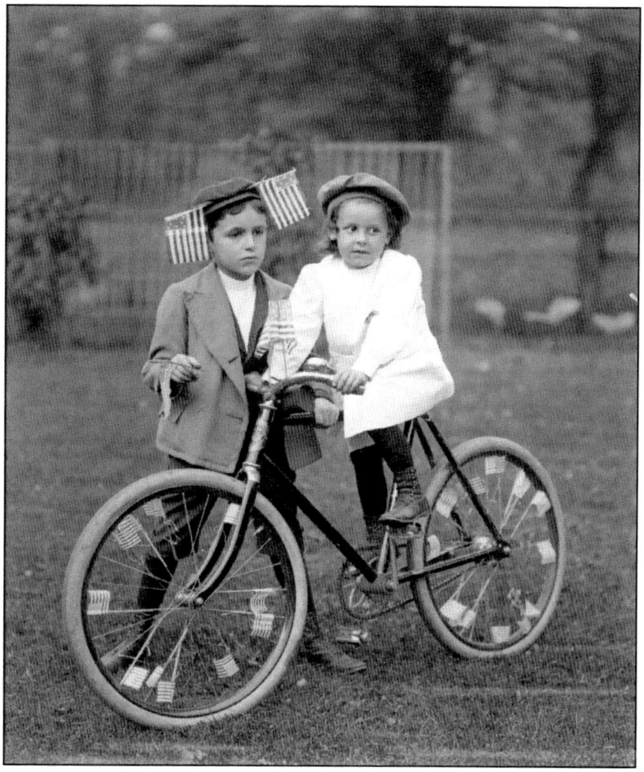

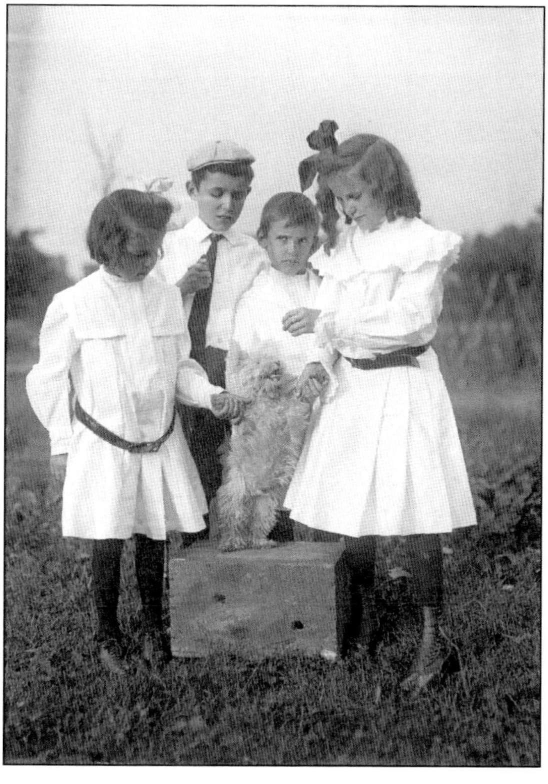

**PLAYING WITH DOG, JUNE 1904.** Elizabeth, Mark, Charles Jr., and Mary Wilson play with one of their pet dogs. (Courtesy of the University of Pittsburgh Archives Service Center.)

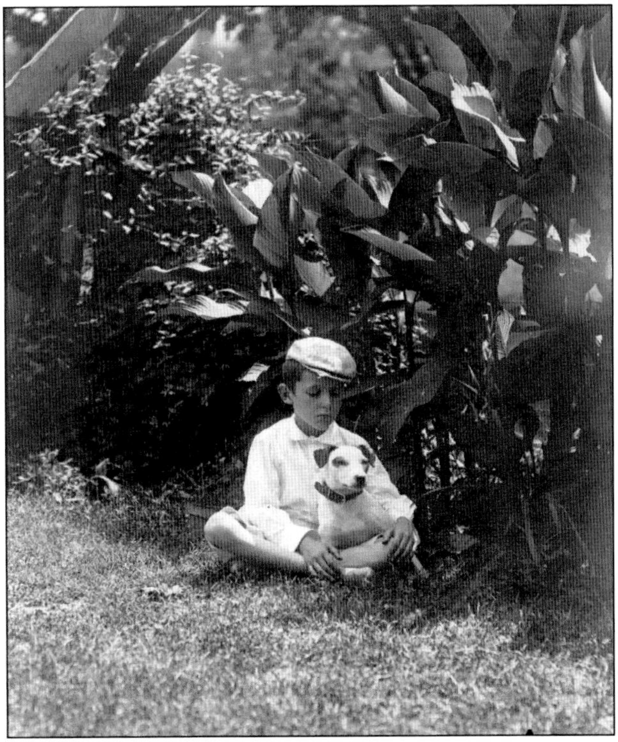

**Mark Spencer and Dog, June 1901.** Mark Spencer sits on the grass with a pet dog. (Courtesy of the University of Pittsburgh Archives Service Center.)

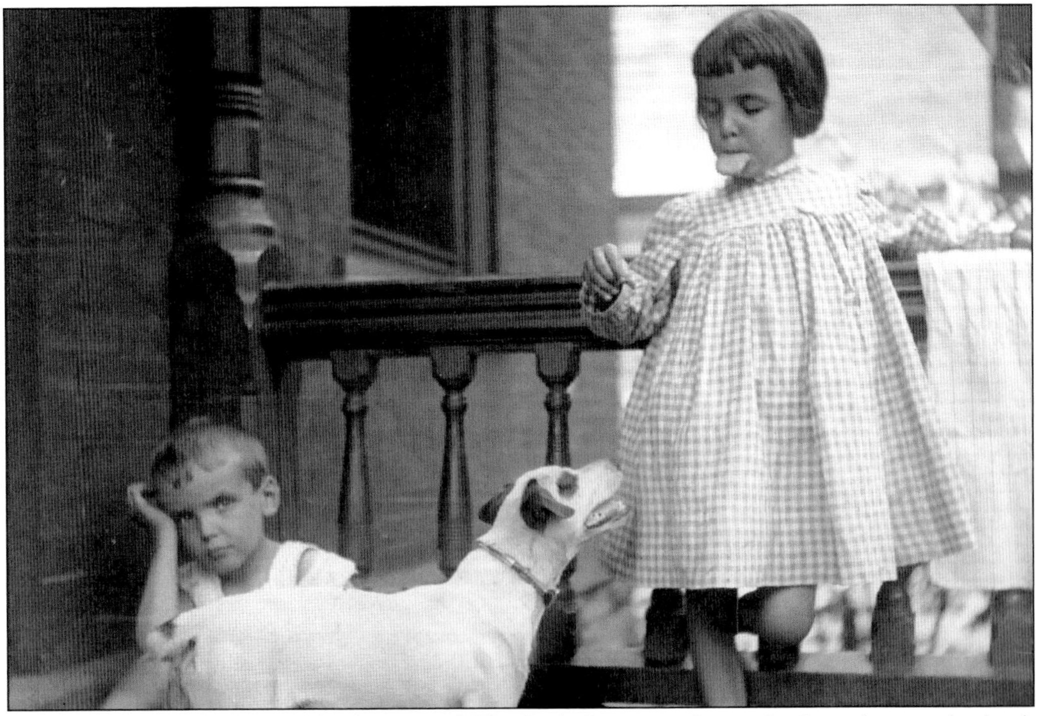

**Dog Tricks, July 1901.** Charles Jr. and Elizabeth Spencer play with their dog on the back porch. The fraternal twins are six years old here. (Courtesy of the University of Pittsburgh Archives Service Center.)

**KATE SPENCER, AUGUST 1903.** Kate Spencer is reading on her front porch. The DeWitt C. Clapp house is visible behind her across the street at 718 Amberson Avenue. Clapp was in the iron and steel business. (Courtesy of the University of Pittsburgh Archives Service Center.)

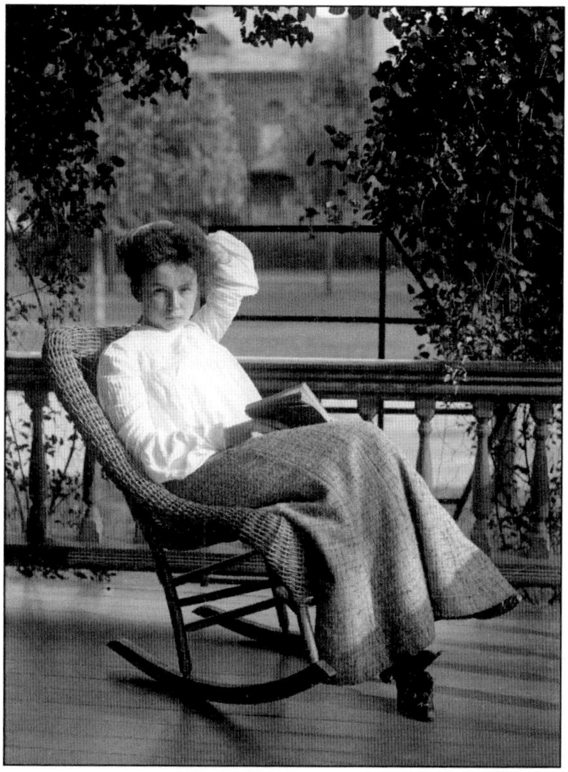

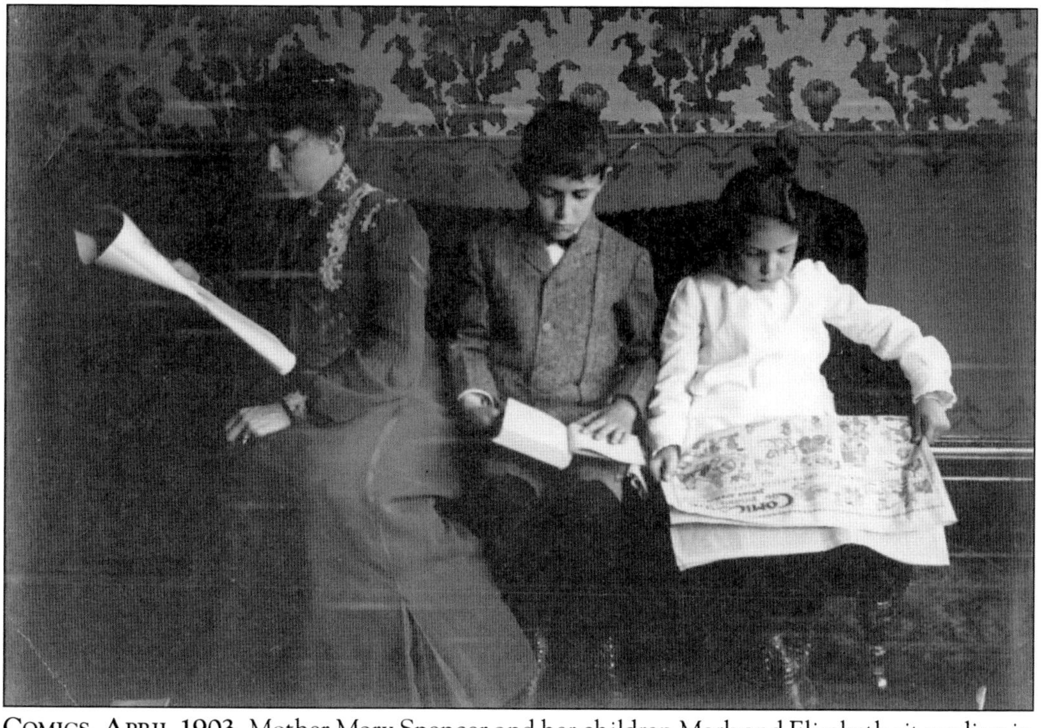

**COMICS, APRIL 1903.** Mother Mary Spencer and her children Mark and Elizabeth sit reading in their home. (Courtesy of the University of Pittsburgh Archives Service Center.)

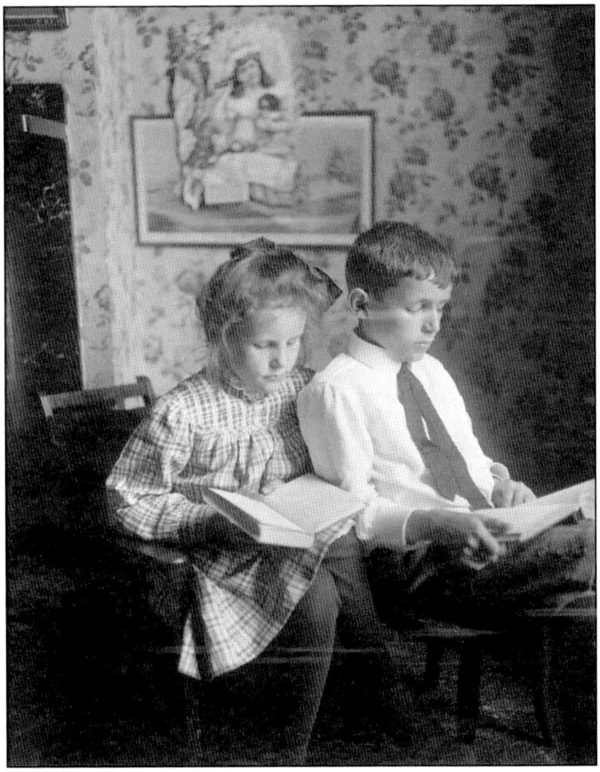

**MARY WILSON AND MARK SPENCER, MAY 1903.** Mary Wilson and Mark Spencer read in the Spencer home. Their father, Charles Hart Spencer, took the photograph using a Cooke Series III lens, according to his notes. (Courtesy of the University of Pittsburgh Archives Service Center.)

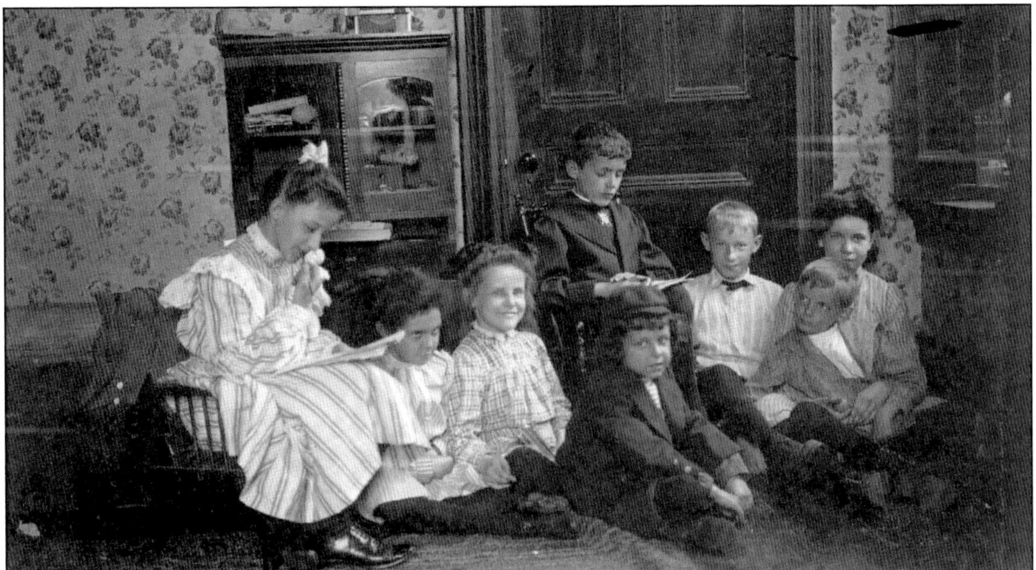

**PLAYING TOGETHER, JUNE 1903.** The Spencer and McClintock children were inseparable and often played at one or the other's house. The McClintock house was next to the Spencer home across Dahlia Street. From left to right are an unidentified girl, Madeline McClintock, Mary Wilson, Mark (sitting in the chair), Rodman McClintock (in front of Mark), an unidentified boy, Charles Spencer Jr., and Ethel Spencer. (Courtesy of the University of Pittsburgh Archives Service Center.)

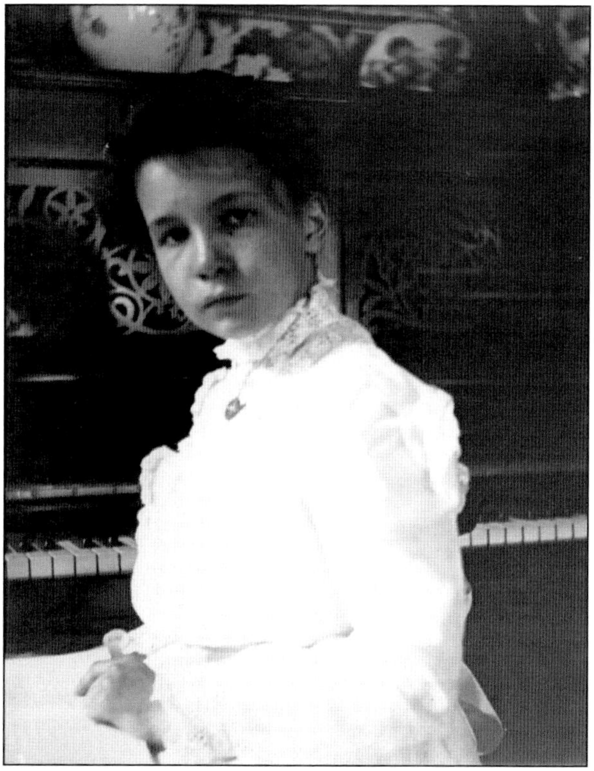

**ETHEL BY PIANO, MAY 1902.** Ethel sits by the family piano. (Courtesy of the University of Pittsburgh Archives Service Center.)

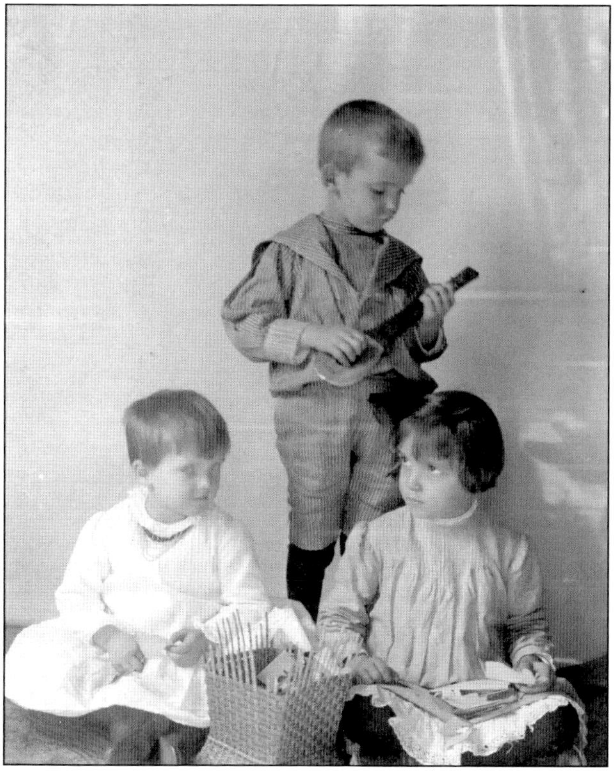

**MINIATURE GUITAR, OCTOBER 1901.** Charles Jr. strums a miniature guitar while an unidentified child at left and Elizabeth Spencer cut paper. (Courtesy of the University of Pittsburgh Archives Service Center.)

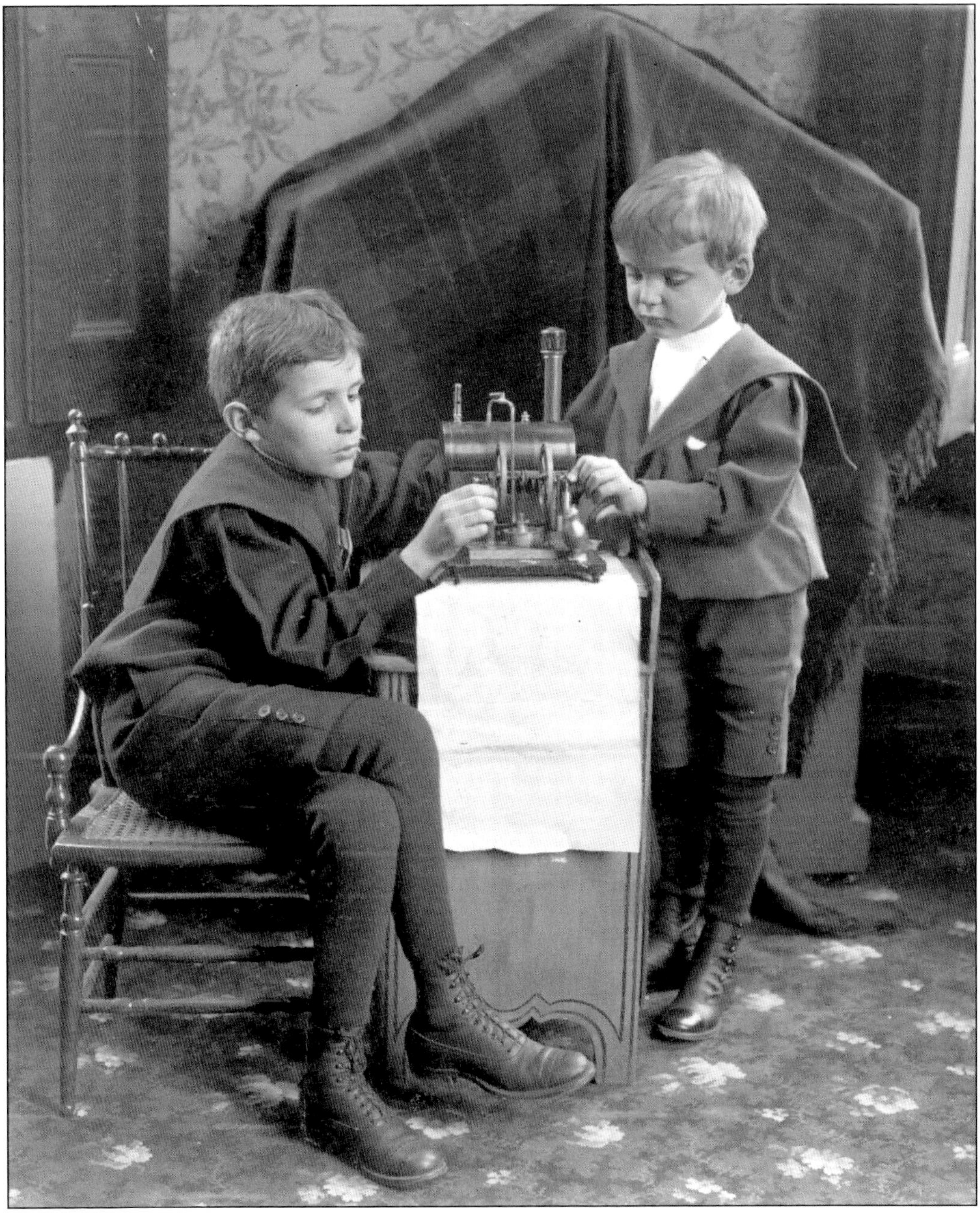

**STEAM ENGINE, MARCH 1902.** Mark Spencer and Charles Spencer Jr. play with a steam engine. (Courtesy of the University of Pittsburgh Archives Service Center.)

**Charles Hart Spencer, March 1905.** Charles Hart Spencer relaxes with a pet dog. He was a middle manager dealing with sales in the Henry Clay Frick concerns. (Courtesy of the University of Pittsburgh Archives Service Center.)

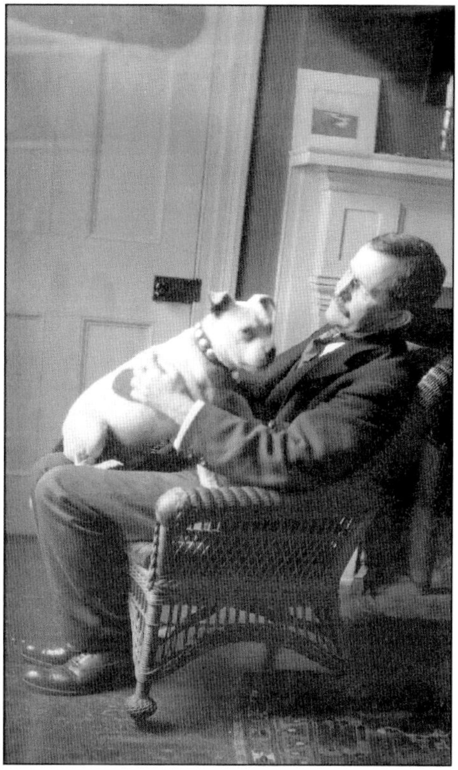

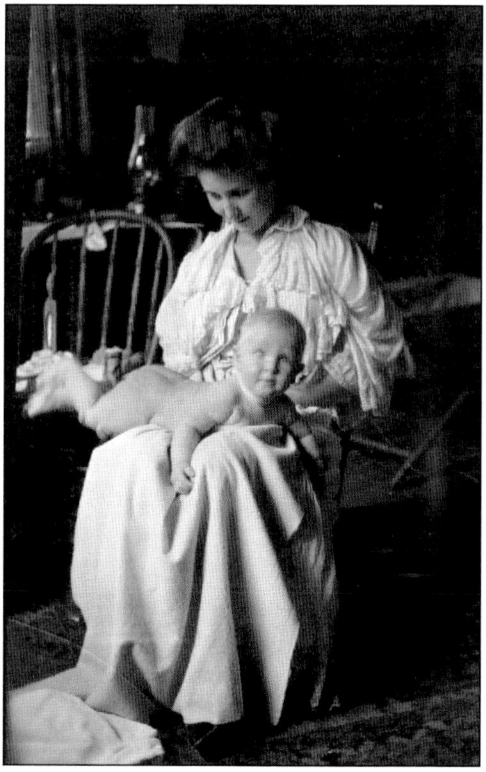

**Adeline Spencer's Baby, September 1906.** Adeline Spencer entered Bryn Mawr College in September 1902. By 1904, she and Chick Curry were asking permission from Charles Hart and Mary Spencer to get married. They married in June 1905. In 1906, Adeline had the first of eight children, who eventually made her the grandmother of 18. (Courtesy of the University of Pittsburgh Archives Service Center.)

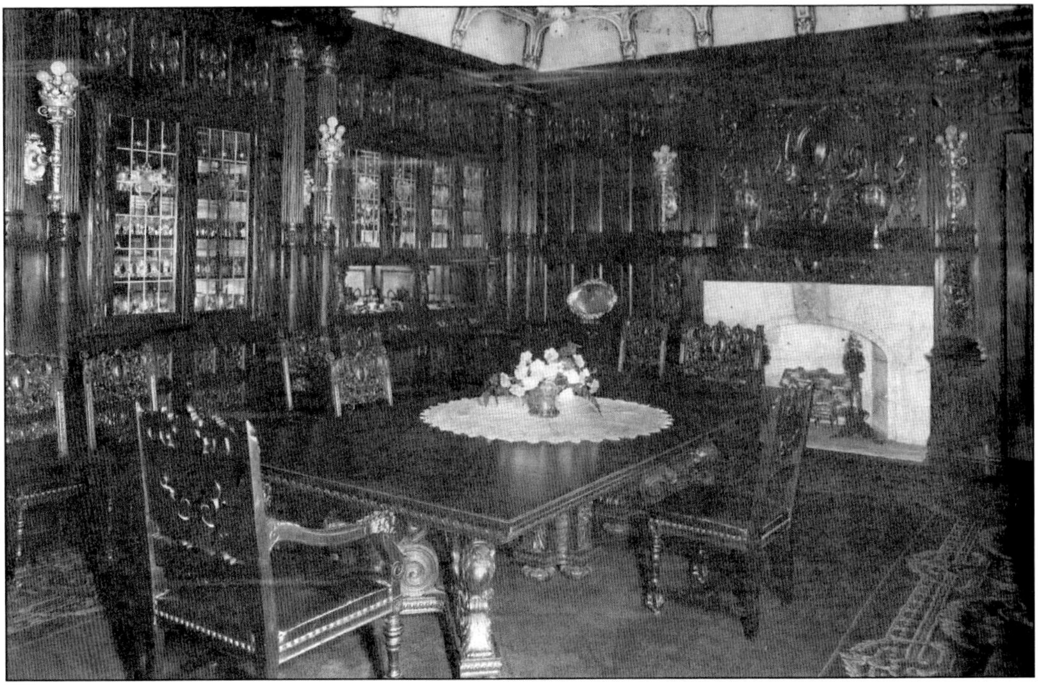

**McCook Dining Room, c. 1907.** The Willis F. McCook house was designed by architects Carpenter and Crocer in 1906. Its dining room included carved wood and a carved stone fireplace with a bacchante. (Courtesy of Martha Perego.)

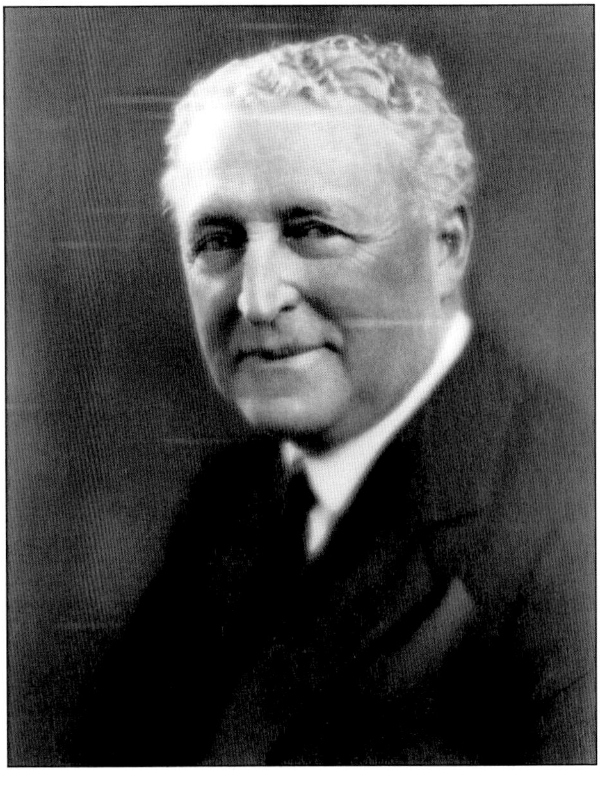

**Willis F. McCook, c. 1906.** McCook, born in 1851, was one of seven founders of Pittsburgh Steel Company in 1902. He became president of the company in 1921 and died in 1923. McCook was a prominent Catholic who converted to his wife's religion. (Courtesy of Martha Perego.)

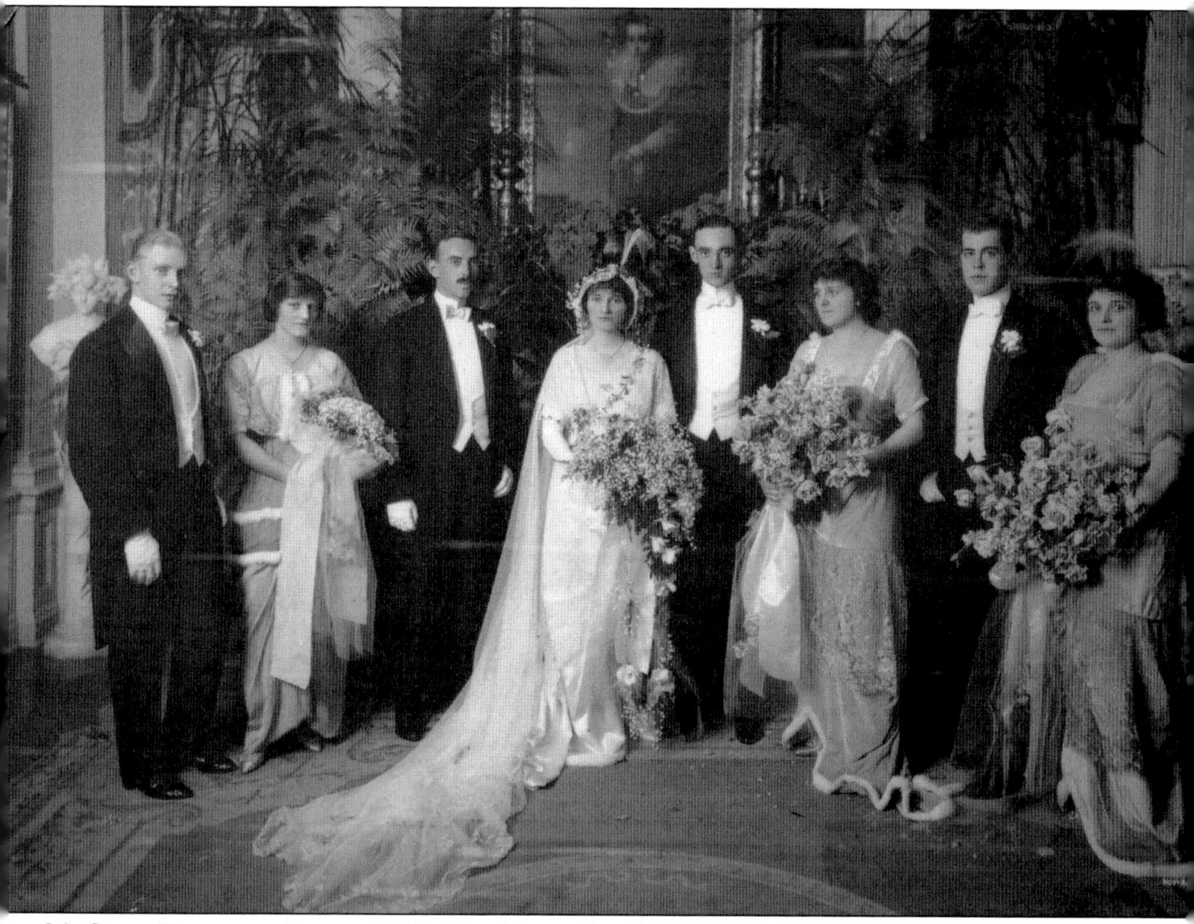

**McCook Drawing Room, 1913.** The Maxwell and McCook wedding party stands in the McCook house drawing room. Standing from left to right are an unidentified man, Margaret McCook, Allison Ripley Maxwell (groom), Eleanor M. McCook (bride), William Edgar Reed, Bessie Ahl Reed (née McCook), Harry J. Miller, and Katharine Miller (née McCook). Reed and his wife were given the house at 925 Amberson Avenue on the McCook property as their wedding gift from Mr. and Mrs. McCook. (Courtesy of Martha Perego.)

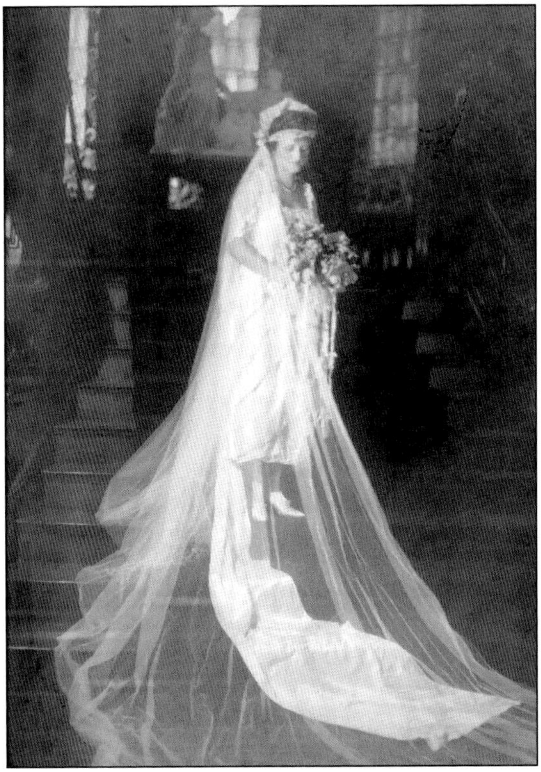

**Grand Staircase, 1920.** The grand staircase of the Willis F. McCook house was legendary for its beauty and as a perfect place for a bride to descend and present herself. This is Margaret McCook during her wedding to Dr. Edward McCague. (Courtesy of Martha Perego.)

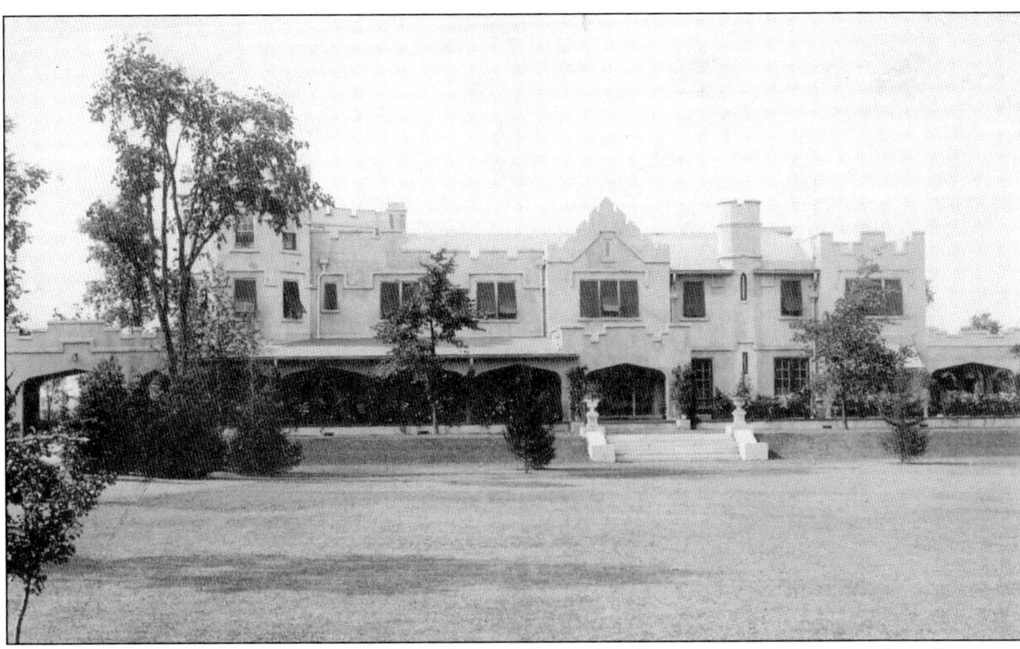

**McCook Summer House, c. 1910.** The McCook family spent summers at their house in Coburn, Canada. They had a constant stream of relatives and friends who stayed with them for various amounts of time. Coburn in Ontario, Canada, had a community of wealthy summer residents. (Courtesy of Martha Perego.)

**THE CHURCH OF THE ASCENSION, C. 1905.** The Church of Ascension was completed in 1898 for an Episcopal congregation at the corner of Ellsworth Avenue and Neville Street. The architect was William Halsey Wood.

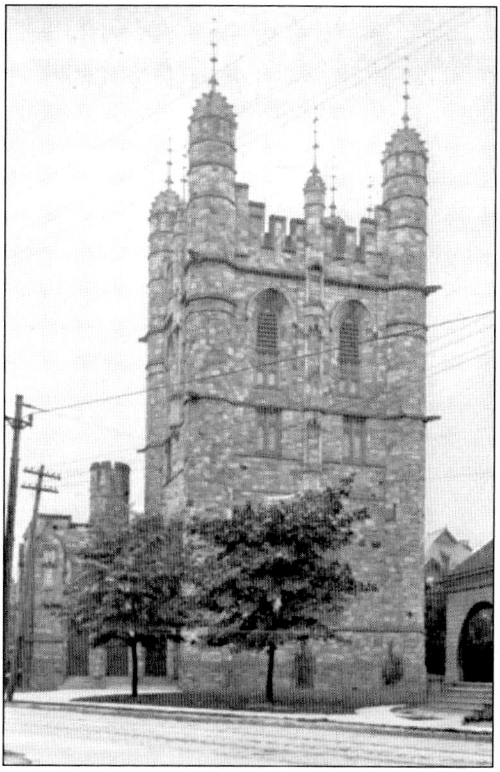

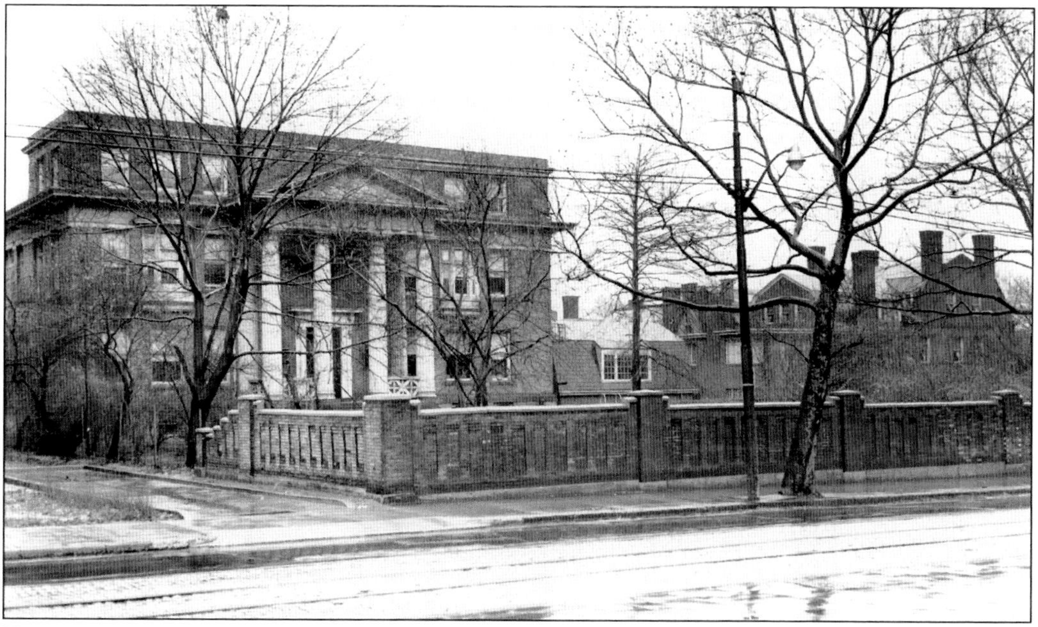

**THE WINCHESTER SCHOOL, C. 1912.** The Winchester School was a boys' and girls' school founded in 1902. In 1909, the school moved to the building at 4721 Fifth Avenue, and in 1935, it merged with the Winchester School and was renamed the Winchester-Thurston School. During the fall of 1962, it moved to new facilities where the Shadyside Academy was formerly located. (Courtesy of the Library and Archives Division, Senator John Heinz History Center.)

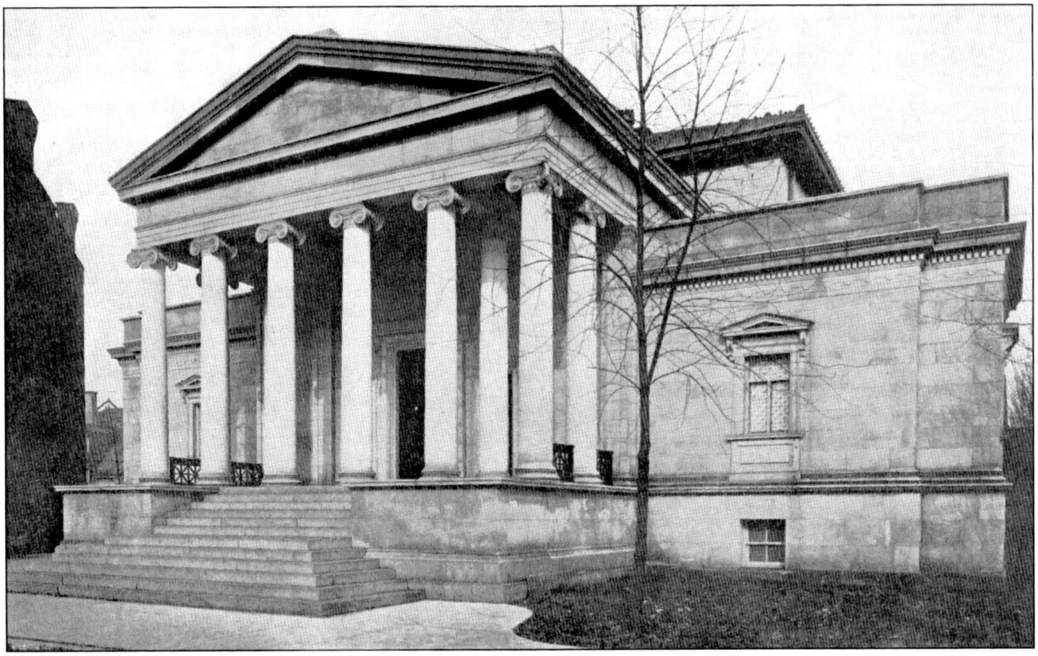

**FIRST CHURCH OF CHRIST SCIENTIST, 1907.** The Christian Scientists built this classical structure designed by architect Solon Spencer Beman at 623 Clyde Street in 1904 and 1905. (Courtesy of the Carnegie Mellon University Architecture Archives.)

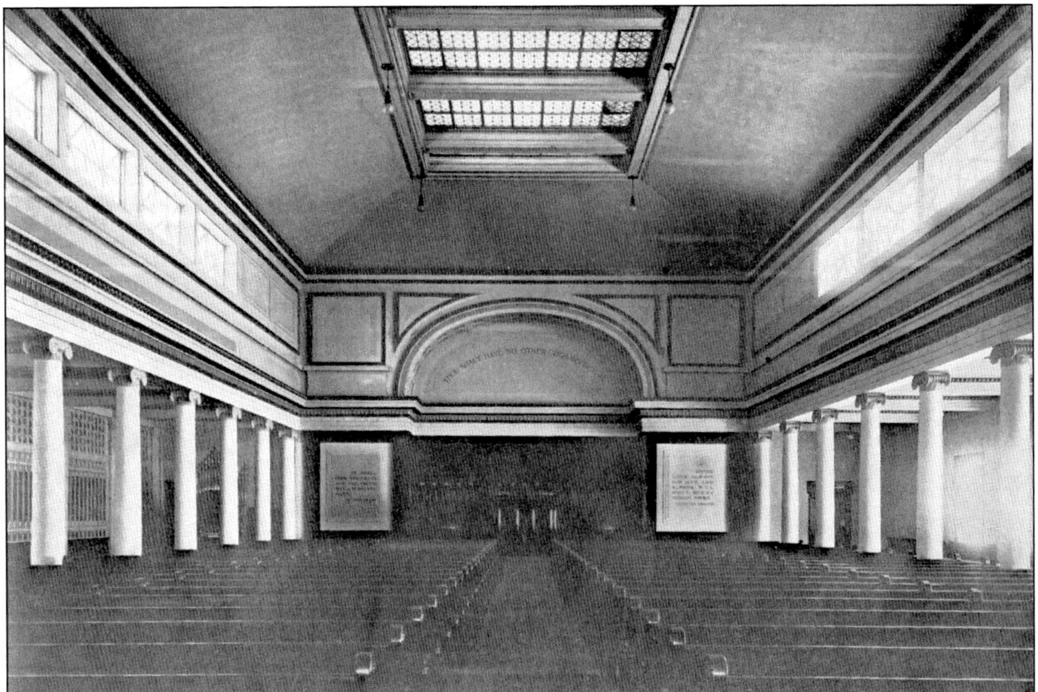

**FIRST CHURCH OF CHRIST SCIENTIST INTERIOR, 1907.** The interior of the First Church of Christ Scientist at 623 Clyde Street is a simple, classical expression of grandeur. (Courtesy of the Carnegie Mellon University Architecture Archives.)

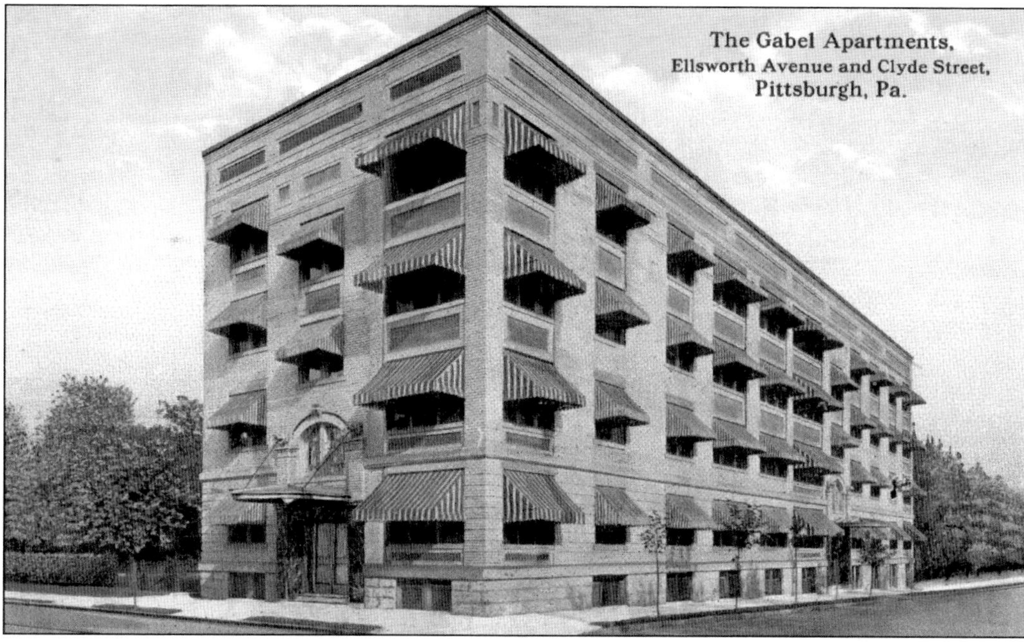


**THE GABEL APARTMENTS, C. 1917.** Mathilda Gabel was still living in her farmhouse, built in 1852, when she celebrated her 82nd birthday on January 9, 1910. The Gabel Apartments, set at the corner of Ellsworth Avenue and Clyde Street, were the first major development on the Gabel farm. General contractor John Grant Fullman was known for luxury apartments. The cathedral mansions now stand where Mathilda Gabel's home once stood.

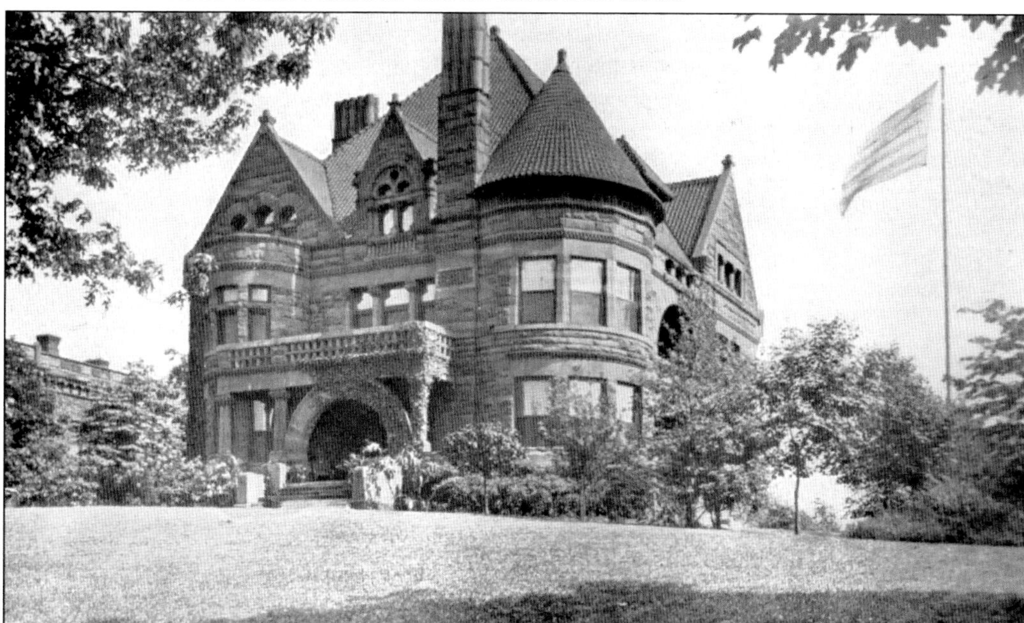

**RESIDENCE OF DAVID HERBERT HOSTETTER, C. 1905.** The residence of David Herbert Hostetter, his wife, Miriam Gerdes, and their four children, Miriam, Helene, Herbert Jr., and Frederick, was located at 4848 Fifth Avenue between Clyde Street and Bidwell Street (now Devonshire Street). Hostetter died on September 28, 1924, in Pasadena, California.

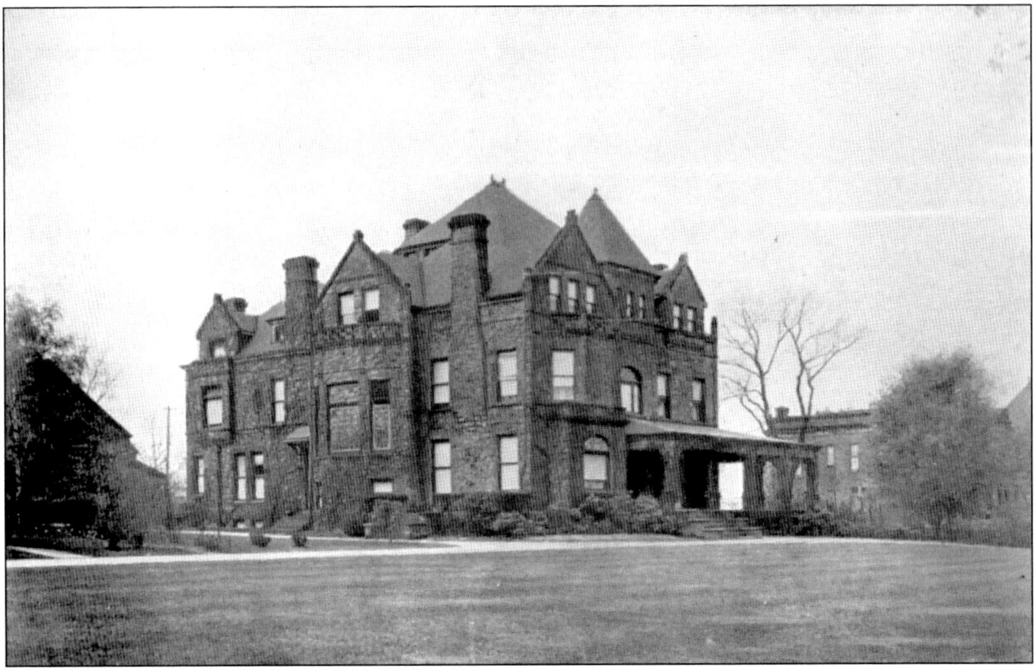

**Residence of Dr. William S. Huselton, c. 1905.** The Huselton home stood at 4936 Fifth Avenue close to Morewood Avenue and opposite the Rodef Shalom synagogue. The home at right in the background belonged to R. Miller.

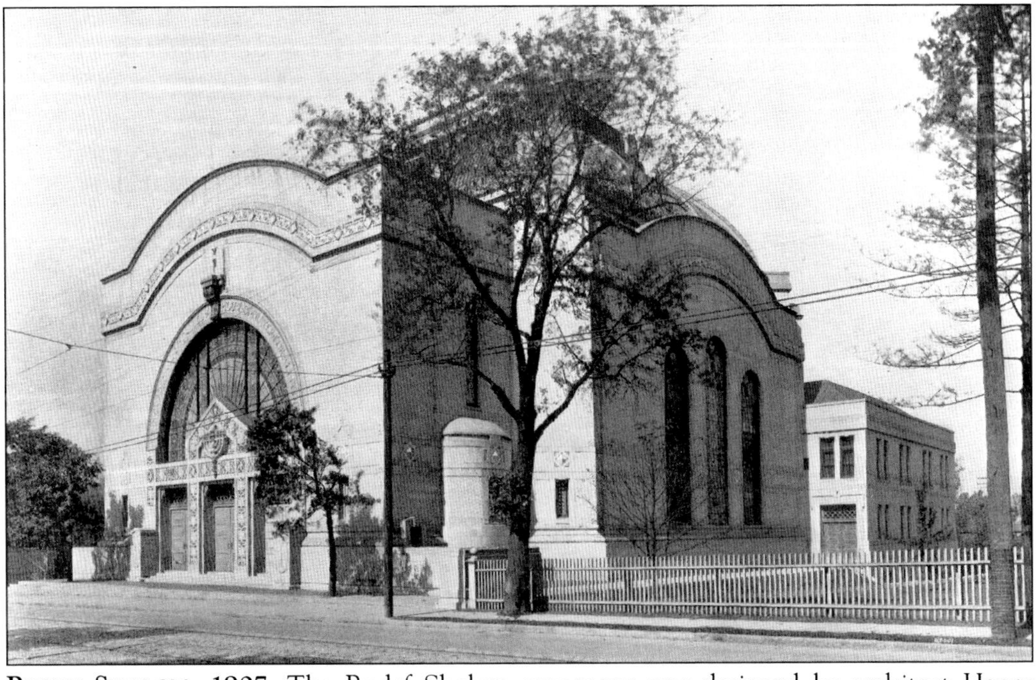

**Rodef Shalom, 1907.** The Rodef Shalom synagogue was designed by architect Henry Hornbostel of the firm Palmer and Hornbostel. It opened on Fifth Avenue between Morewood Avenue and Devonshire Road in 1907. (Courtesy of the Carnegie Mellon University Architecture Archives.)

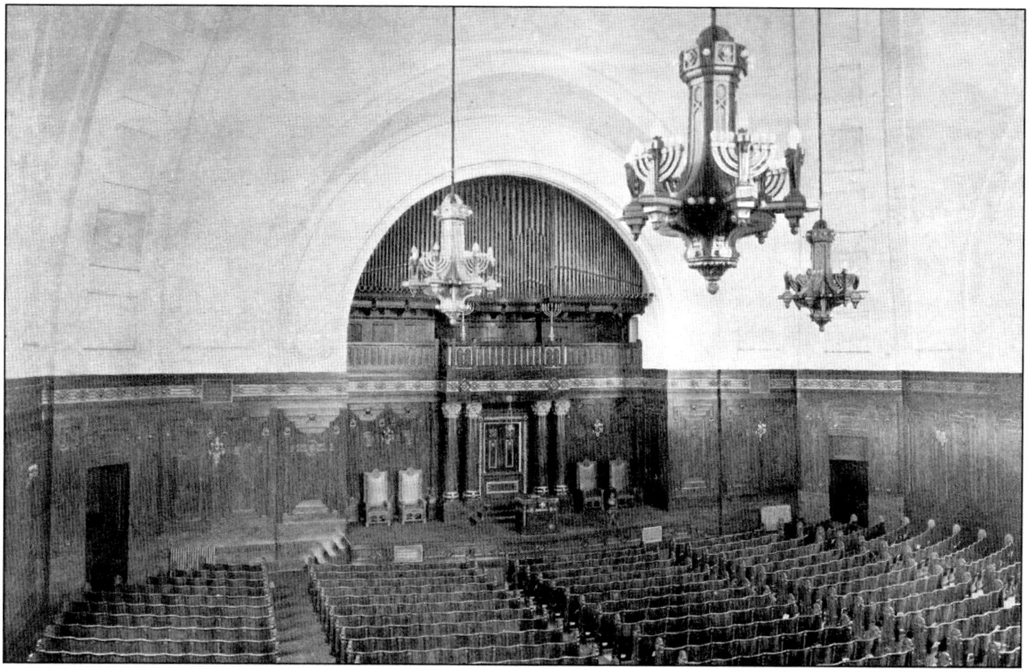

**RODEF SHALOM INTERIOR, 1907.** The interior space of the Rodef Shalom synagogue provides a sense of great vertical expanse. (Courtesy of the Carnegie Mellon University Architecture Archives.)

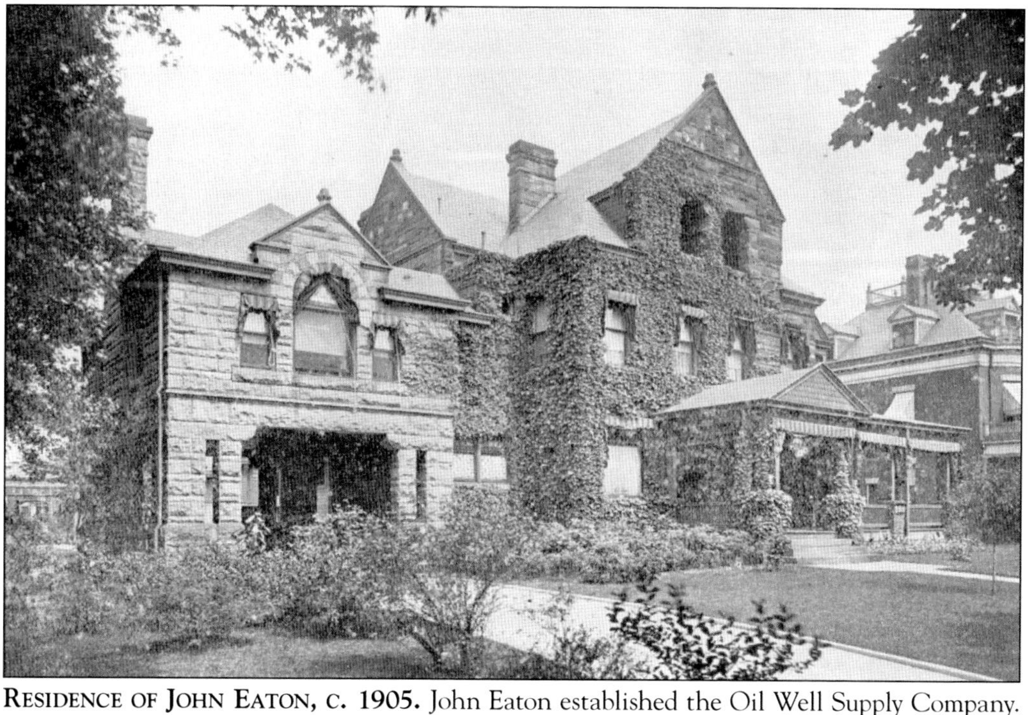

**RESIDENCE OF JOHN EATON, C. 1905.** John Eaton established the Oil Well Supply Company. He spent eight years in the New York militia and served a short time in the Civil War. He lived with his wife and two daughters at 705 Bidwell Street (now Devonshire).

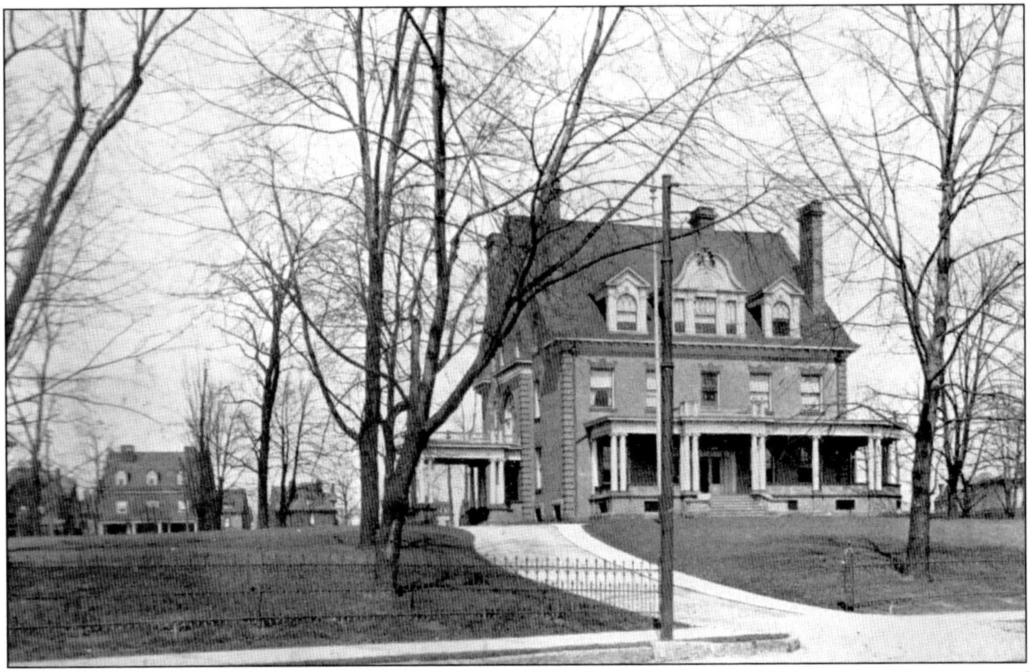

**RESIDENCE OF JAMES DAWSON CALLERY, C. 1905.** James Dawson Callery was chairman of the board of the Pittsburgh Railways Company. He lived with his wife and four children at 4875 Ellsworth Avenue near Bidwell Street (now Devonshire).

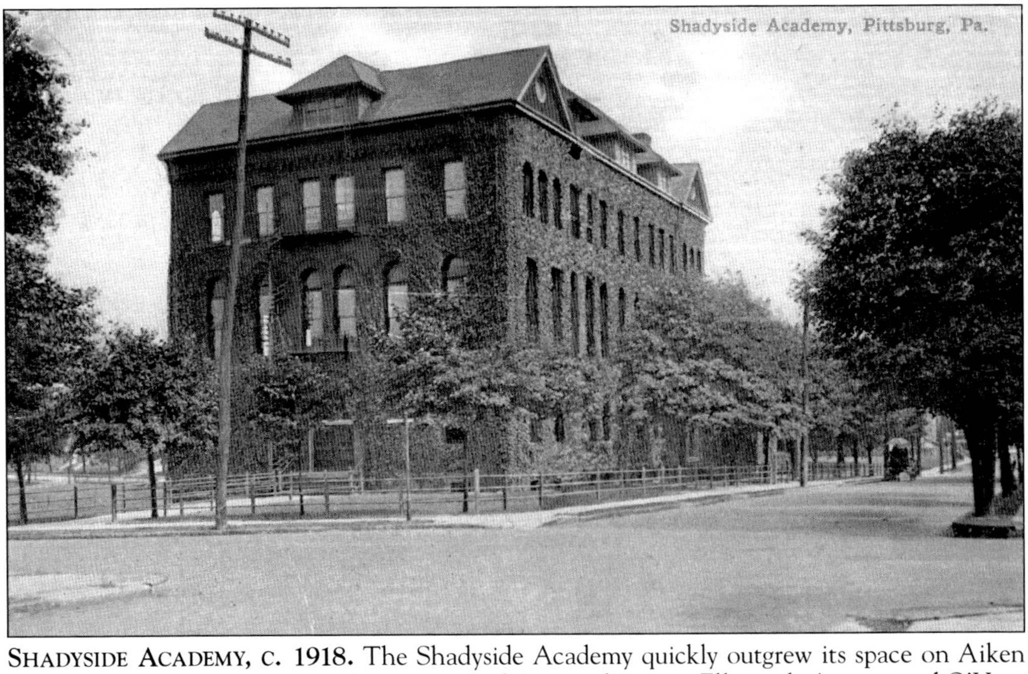


**SHADYSIDE ACADEMY, C. 1918.** The Shadyside Academy quickly outgrew its space on Aiken Avenue (see page 45) and moved to Morewood Avenue between Ellsworth Avenue and O'Hara Street (now Bayard Street). This view looks down Morewood Avenue toward Ellsworth Avenue with O'Hara Street crossing in the foreground.

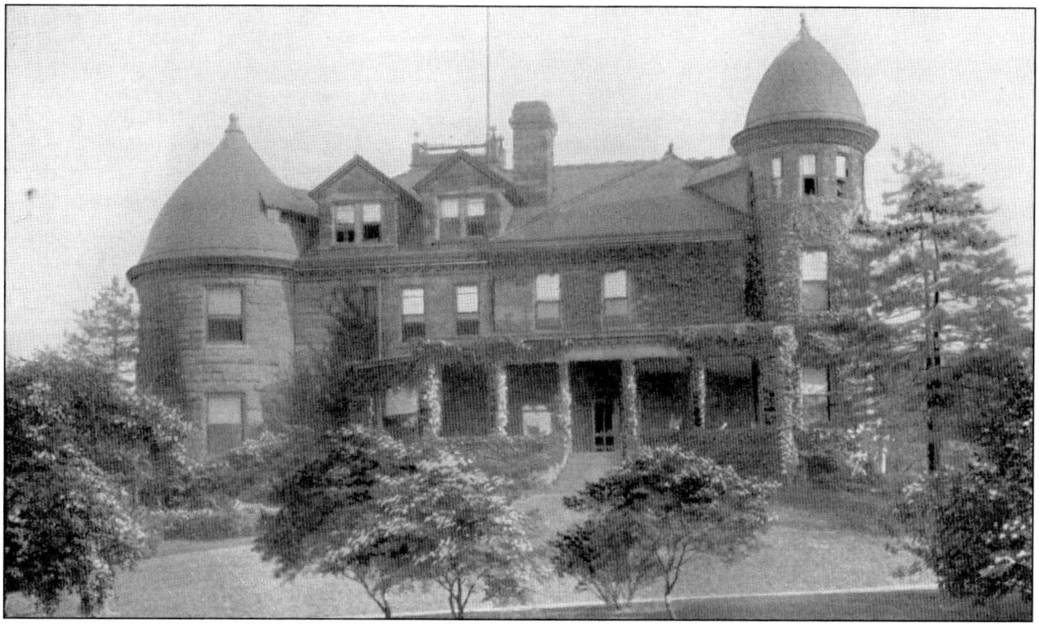

**RESIDENCE OF PHILANDER CHASE KNOX, C. 1901.** Philander Chase Knox was a nationally prominent Pittsburgh lawyer. He was appointed attorney general of the United States by Pres. William McKinley and also served under Pres. Theodore Roosevelt. He served as secretary of state under Pres. William Howard Taft and was elected a U.S. senator. Knox lived with his wife and four children at 5044 Ellsworth Avenue near Amberson Avenue.

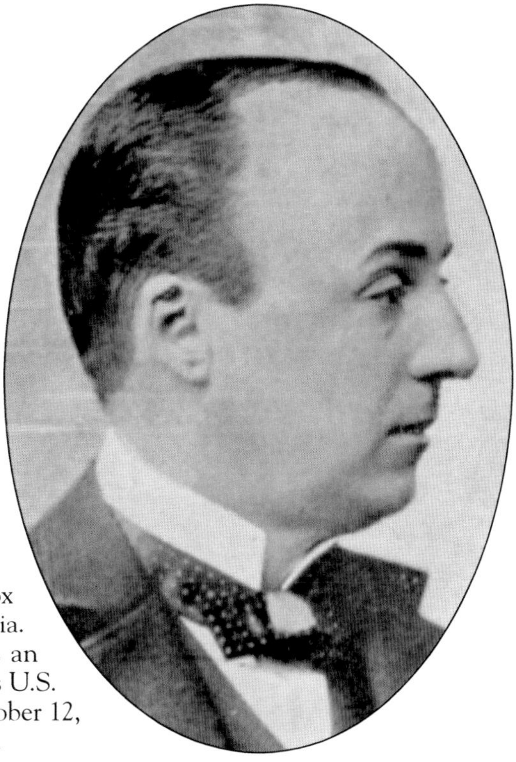

**HON. PHILANDER CHASE KNOX, C. 1901.** Knox was elected a U.S. senator from Pennsylvania. He was most proud of his accomplishments as an attorney on international law but also served as U.S. attorney general and secretary of state. On October 12, 1921, he died in his library in Washington, D.C.

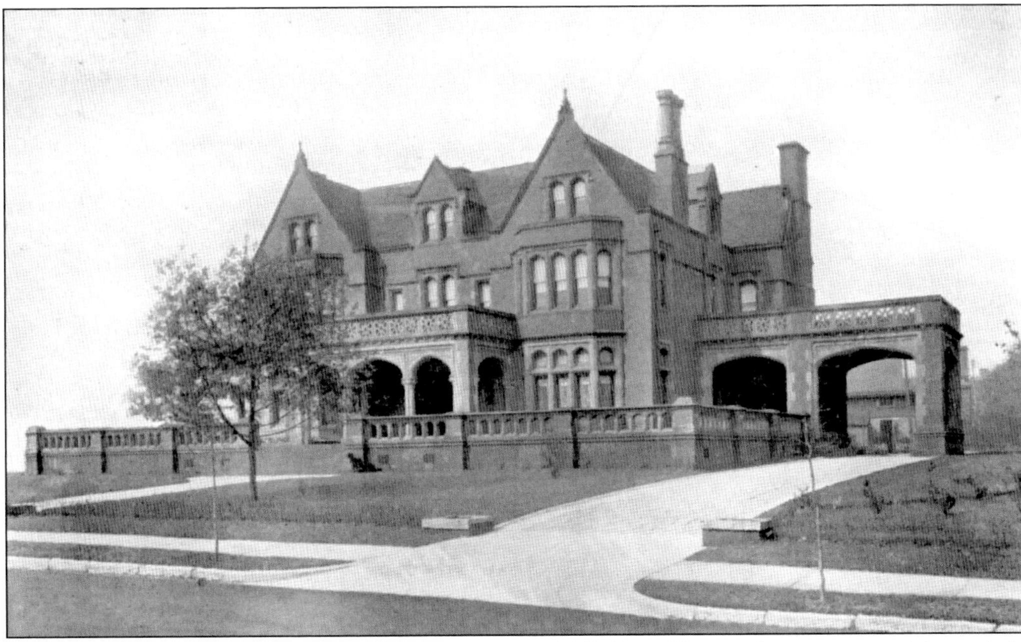

**Residence of Wallace Hurtte Rowe, c. 1905.** Wallace Hurtte Rowe was president of the Pittsburgh Steel Company and lived at 624 Morewood Avenue, a home designed by architects Rutan and Russel. The Rowe family had a summer home known as Cottesmore Hall in Cobourg, Ontario, Canada.

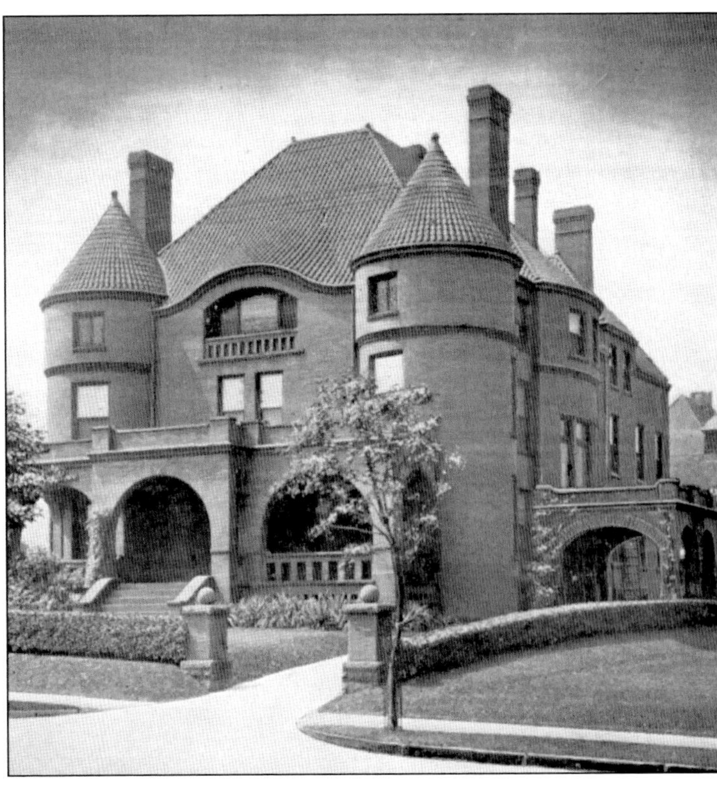

**Residence of William Latham Abbott, c. 1905.** William Latham Abbot was a partner of Andrew Carnegie and an office holder in many of his companies. He was chairman of Carnegie Steel Company. Abbot was considered a leader in the U.S. steel industry. He lived with his wife and seven children at 808 Morewood Avenue.

**RESIDENCE OF HENRY S. ATWOOD STEWART, C. 1905.** Henry S. Atwood Stewart was vice president and director of Fidelity Title and Trust Company and was officially connected with other leading monetary institutions and great manufacturing concerns. He lived at 800 Morewood Avenue.

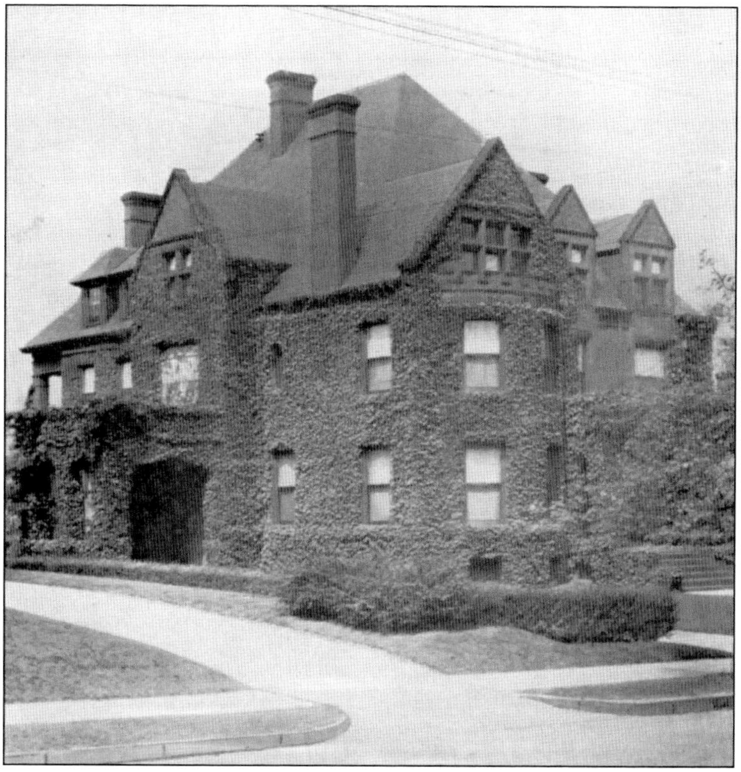

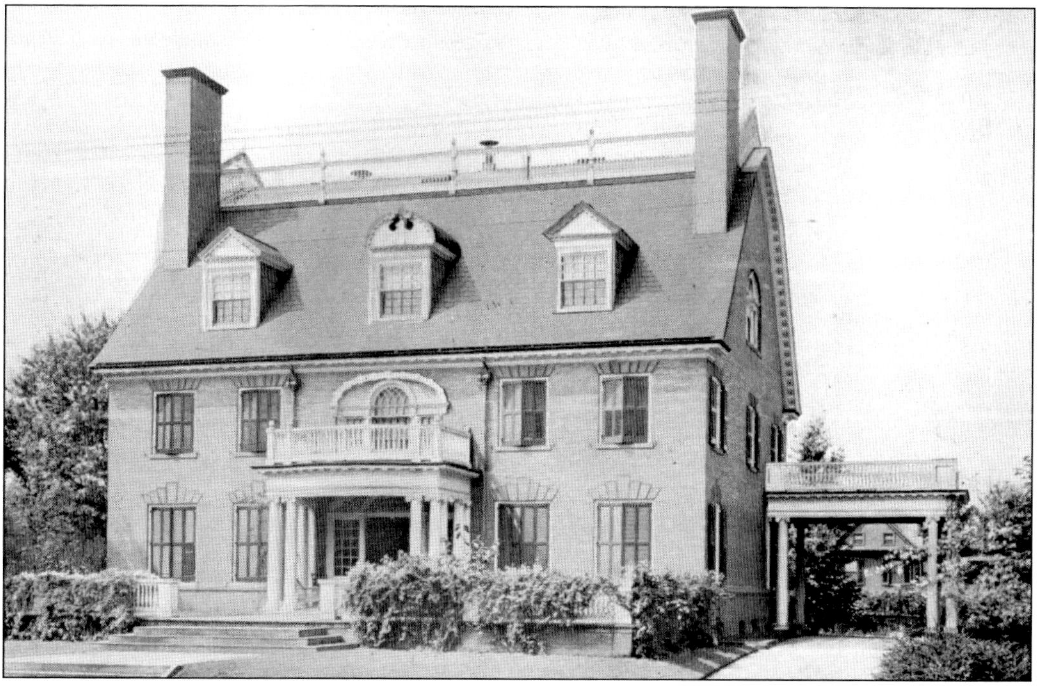

**RESIDENCE OF NATHANIEL HOLMES, C. 1905.** Nathaniel Holmes was a prominent banker who was an officer in many of the banking institutions in Pittsburgh. Early in the 20th century there were many such institutions in the city. He lived at Fifth and Morewood Avenues.

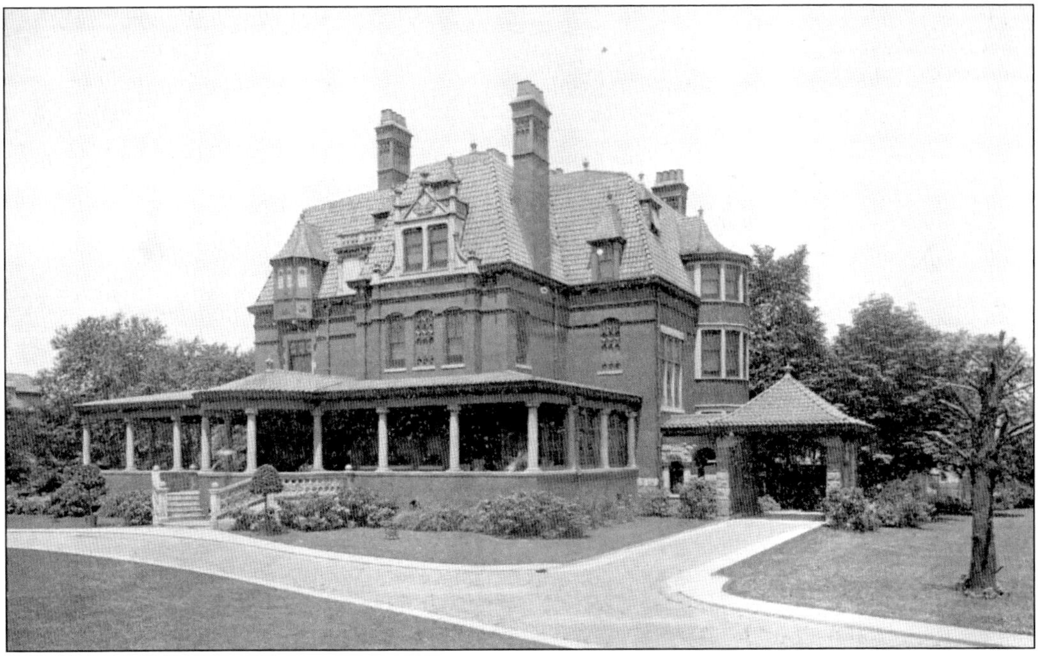

**RESIDENCE OF COL. JAMES MCCLURG GUFFEY, C. 1905.** Col. James McClurg Guffey began as a railroad clerk but became a pioneer in the oil and natural gas development of Pennsylvania. For 50 years, he was a democratic leader in the state. He lived with his wife and three children at 5025 Fifth Avenue.

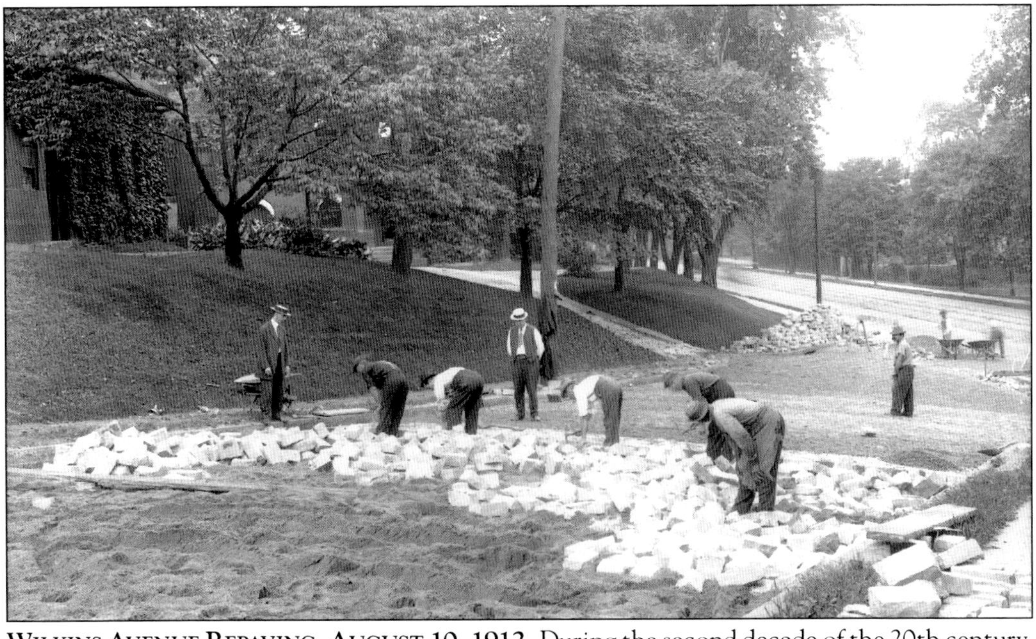

**WILKINS AVENUE REPAVING, AUGUST 10, 1912.** During the second decade of the 20th century, paving new roads or repaving was common in Shadyside. The men working to repave Wilkins Avenue are above Fifth Avenue. Dr. James H. McClelland's home, Sunnyledge, is behind the trees at center left. The McCook house is just out of view on the other side of Fifth Avenue. (Courtesy of the University of Pittsburgh Archives Service Center.)

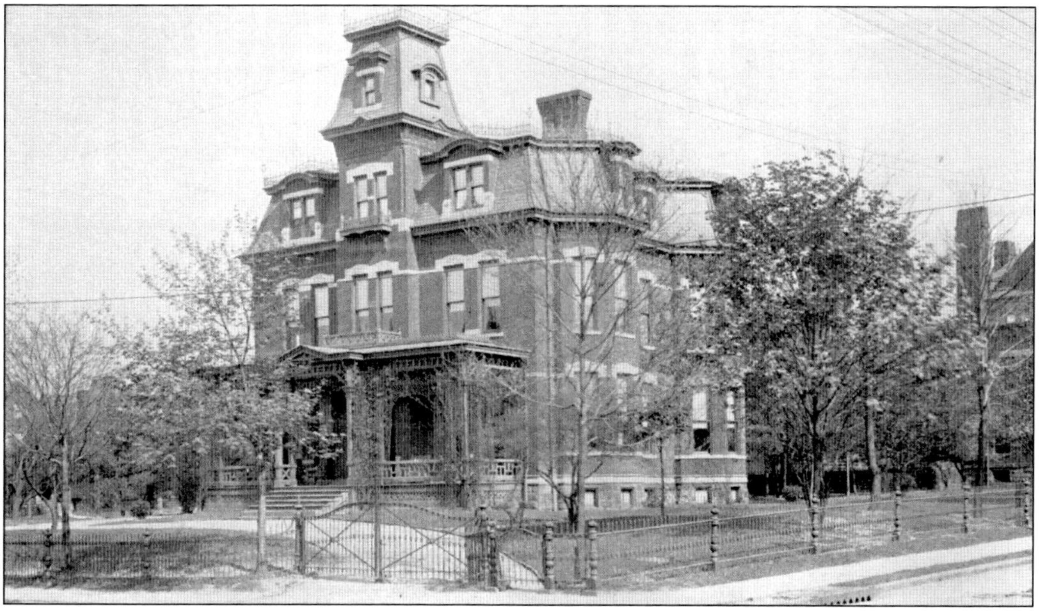

**RESIDENCE OF AUGUST E. SUCCOP, C. 1905.** August E. Succop ran his father's grocery business and later worked in the general merchandise business. Around 1880, he associated himself with E. H. Myers and Company in the pork packing and banking businesses. Succop became president of the Germania Savings Bank of Pittsburgh and other financial institutions. He lived at 5700 Ellsworth Avenue. The road to the right is South Negley Avenue.

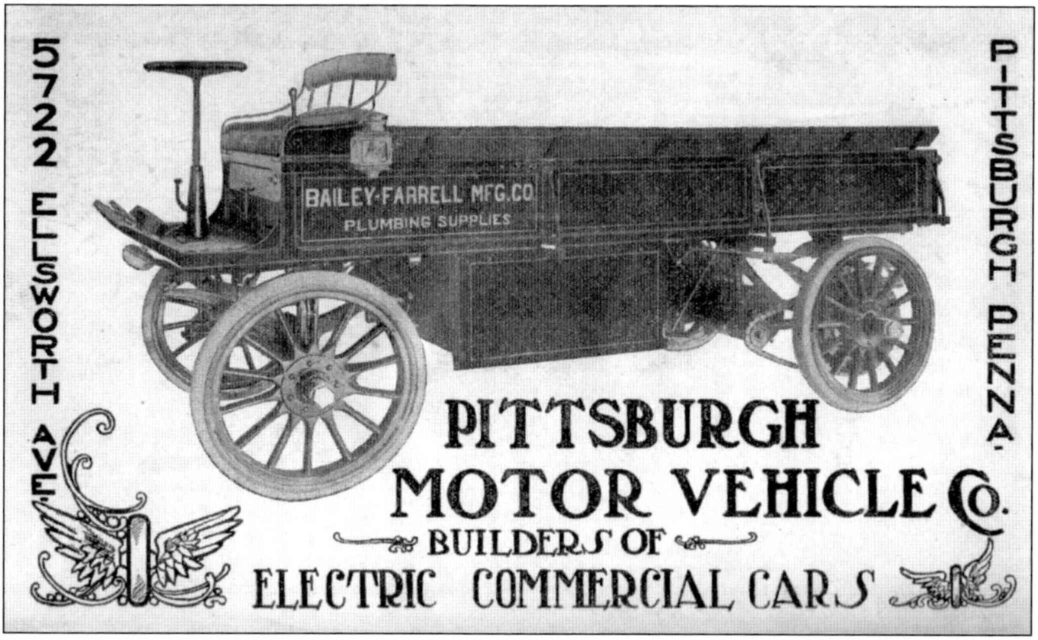


**PITTSBURGH MOTOR VEHICLE COMPANY, 1907.** Establishments dealing with motor vehicles appeared in and close to Shadyside very early on because of the large number of affluent automobile enthusiasts in the neighborhood. The Pittsburgh Motor Vehicle Company was one of several homegrown makers of motorized vehicles. The company was built at Ellsworth Avenue and Summerlea Street, almost right next to the Succop house.

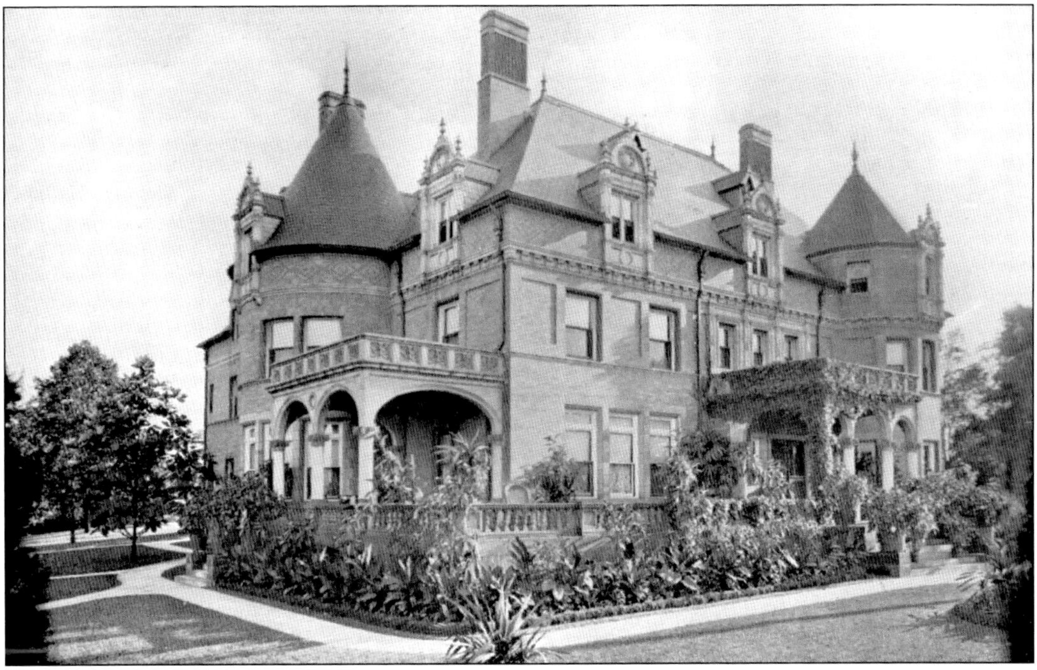

**RESIDENCE OF DANIEL M. CLEMSON, C. 1905.** Daniel M. Clemson was active in the steel industry for more than half a century and was one of the Andrew Carnegie partners who helped build the steel empire that became the United States Steel Corporation. He lived at Highmont on Fifth Avenue near Shady Avenue.

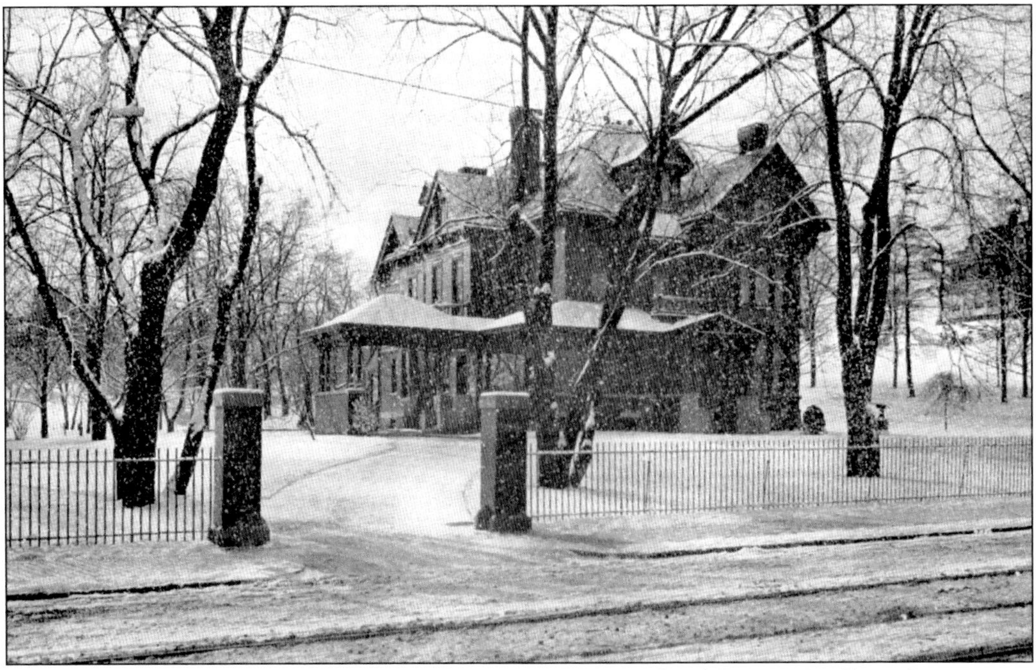

**RESIDENCE OF RICHARD BEATTY MELLON, C. 1905.** Richard Beatty Mellon, the younger brother of Andrew Mellon, was a great industrialist and banker. His home at 6500 Fifth Avenue near Beechwood Boulevard was next door to his brother's.

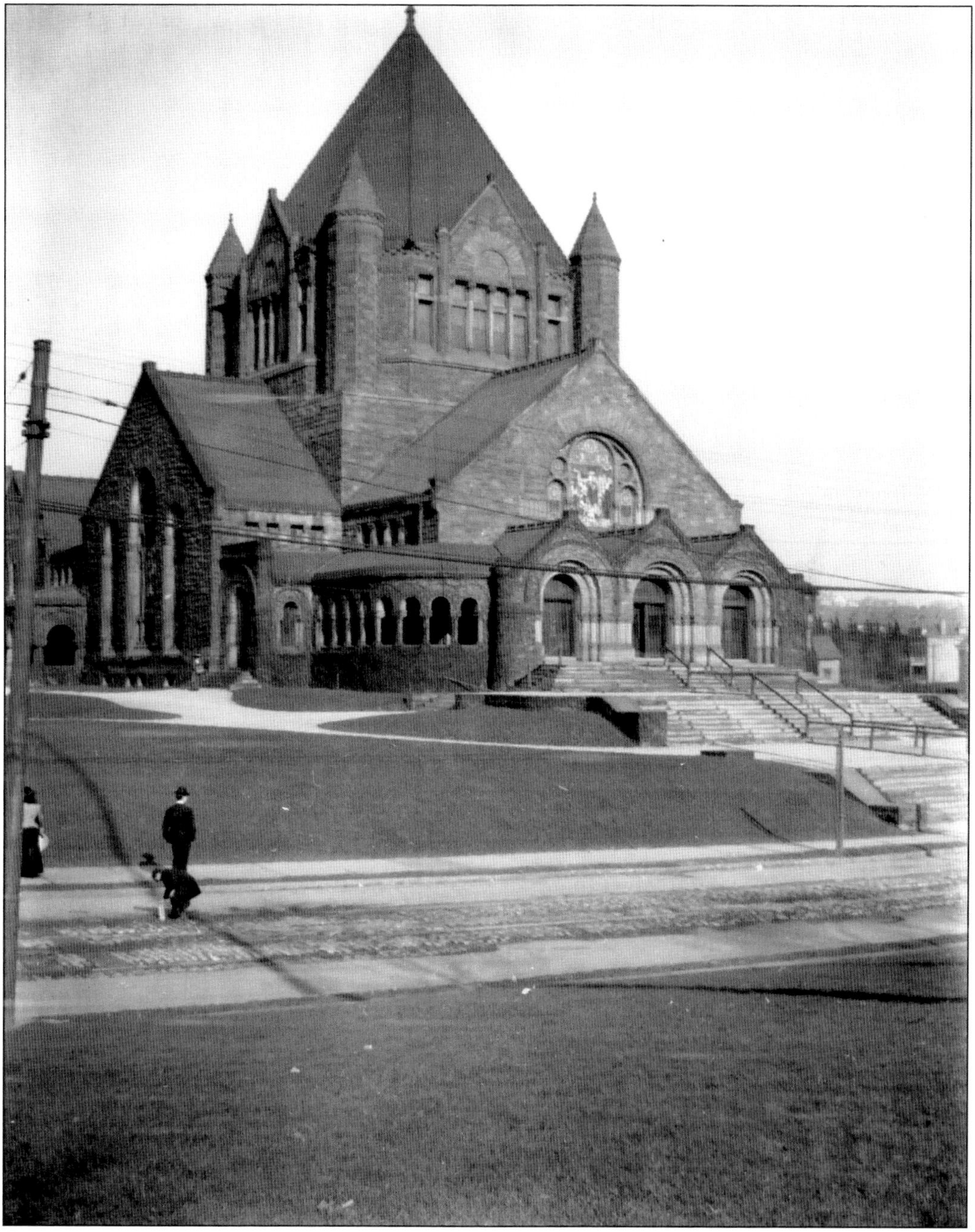

**CHRIST METHODIST EPISCOPAL CHURCH, C. 1904–1905.** Many architectural experts considered Christ Methodist Episcopal Church on Centre Avenue at South Aiken Avenue to be a masterpiece by the firm of Weary and Kramer. The placement of the church was said to be outside the area of Shadyside. However, residents across the street on Centre Avenue clearly considered themselves a part of the Shadyside neighborhood and the church's congregation was composed of a large number of prominent Shadyside residents. (Courtesy of the Georgetown University Library.)

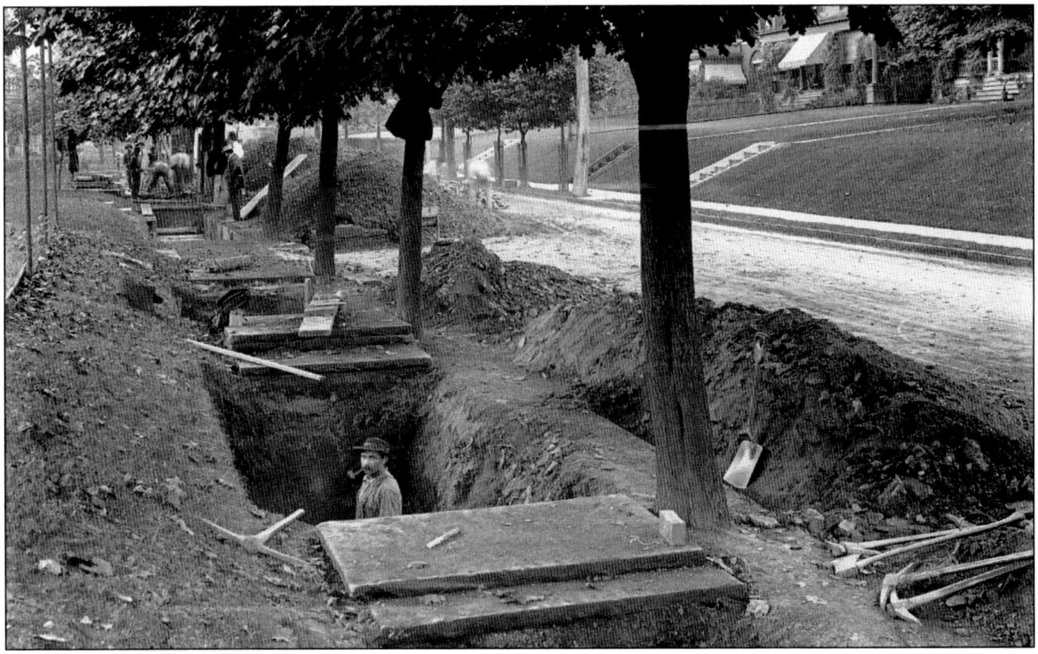

**SEWER WORK, SEPTEMBER 10, 1907.** A lot of new infrastructure was built up in Shadyside during the first two decades of the 20th century. Sewer work was very common, as seen here on Aiken Avenue looking from Centre Avenue toward Claybourne Street. (Courtesy of the University of Pittsburgh Archives Service Center.)

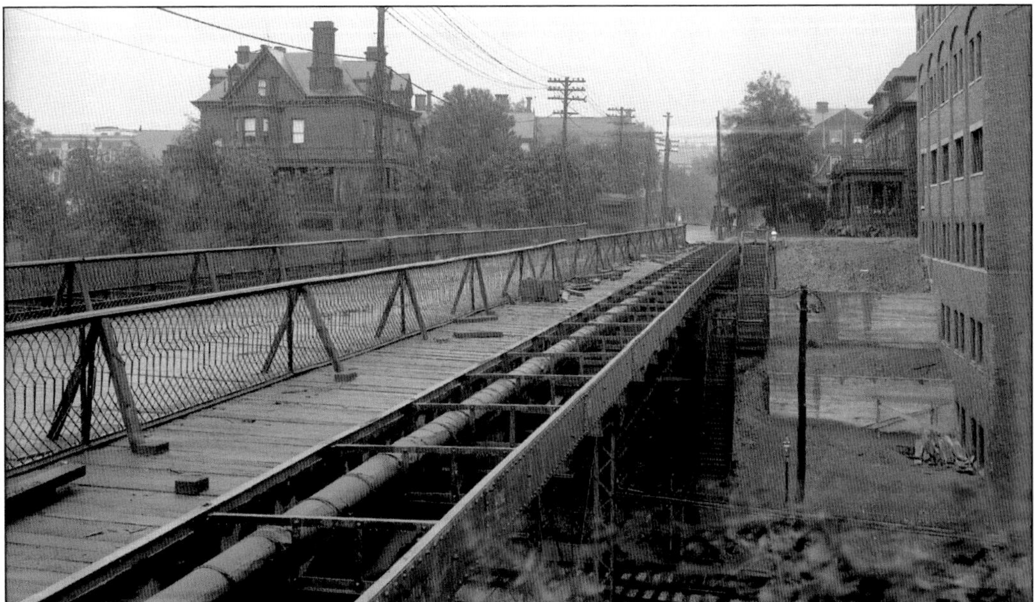

**AIKEN BRIDGE, SEPTEMBER 23, 1909.** The Aiken Bridge (now South Aiken Bridge) over the Pennsylvania Railroad tracks and gully connects the early-20th-century commercial activities of the Centre Avenue and Baum Boulevard corridor with residential streets. The widowed Mrs. Gripp lived in the home to the left. In the right foreground is the Manufacturers Power Company building. (Courtesy of the University of Pittsburgh Archives Service Center.)

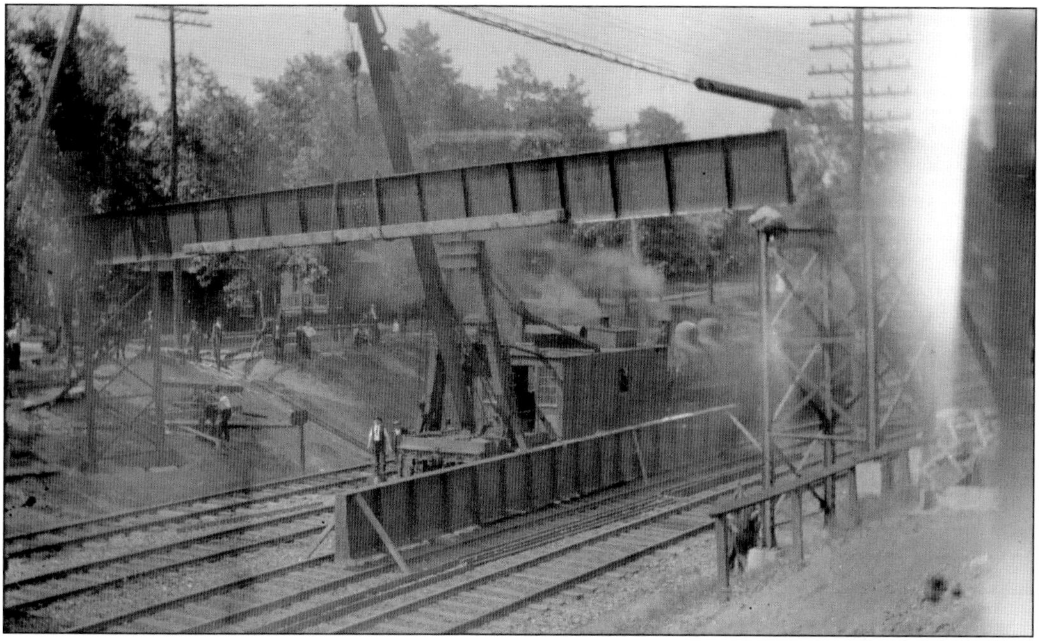

**FOOTBRIDGE CONSTRUCTION, 1908.** Construction of a footbridge over the Pennsylvania Railroad tracks at Graham Street resulted in residents being able to safely cross the tracks. The increasingly heavy train traffic made it impossible to cross the tracks without a bridge. (Courtesy of the University of Pittsburgh Archives Service Center.)

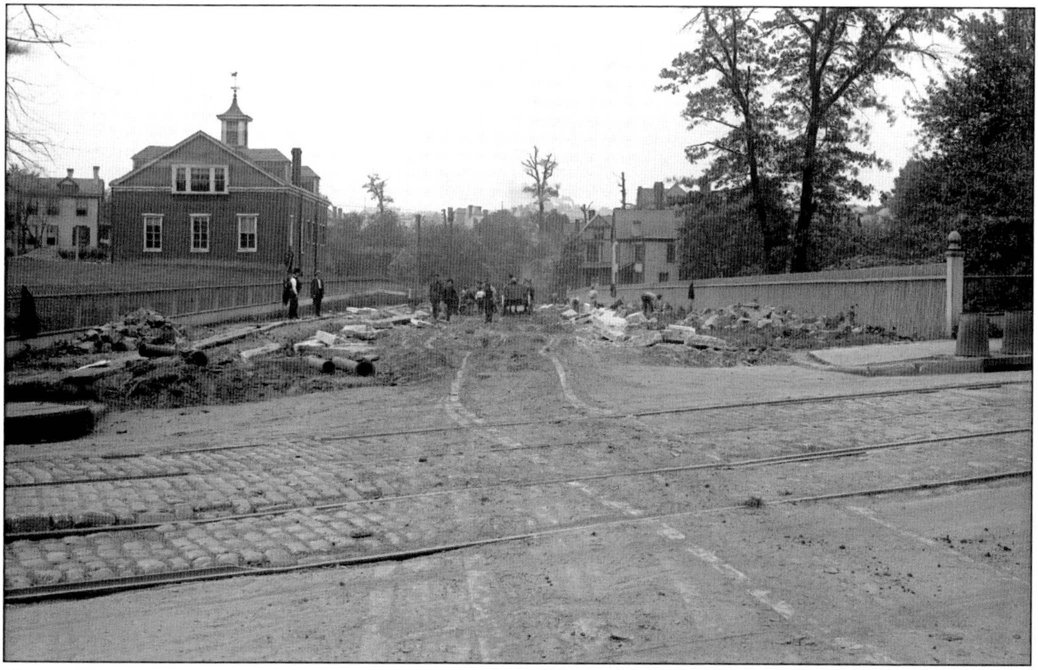

**ROAD CONSTRUCTION FROM ELLSWORTH AVENUE, JUNE 22, 1910.** Streetcar tracks are visible in Ellsworth Avenue looking down Summerlea Street toward the Pennsylvania Railroad tracks. (Courtesy of the University of Pittsburgh Archives Service Center.)

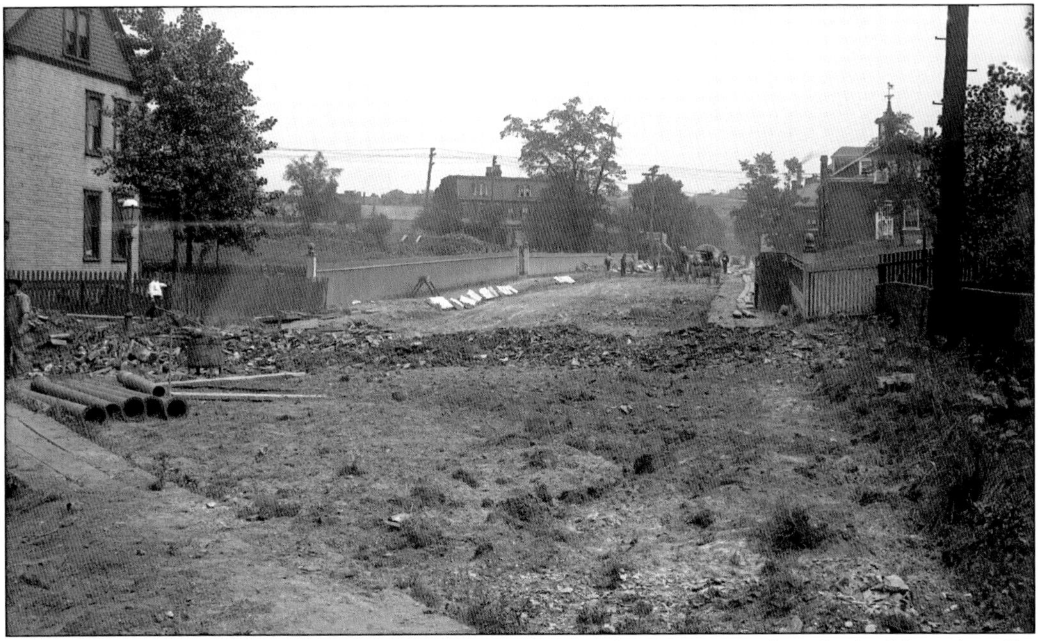

**ROAD CONSTRUCTION FROM TRACKS, JUNE 22, 1910.** Flagstone is ready to be laid for sidewalks along Summerlea Street in this view from the Pennsylvania Railroad tracks toward Ellsworth Avenue. (Courtesy of the University of Pittsburgh Archives Service Center.)

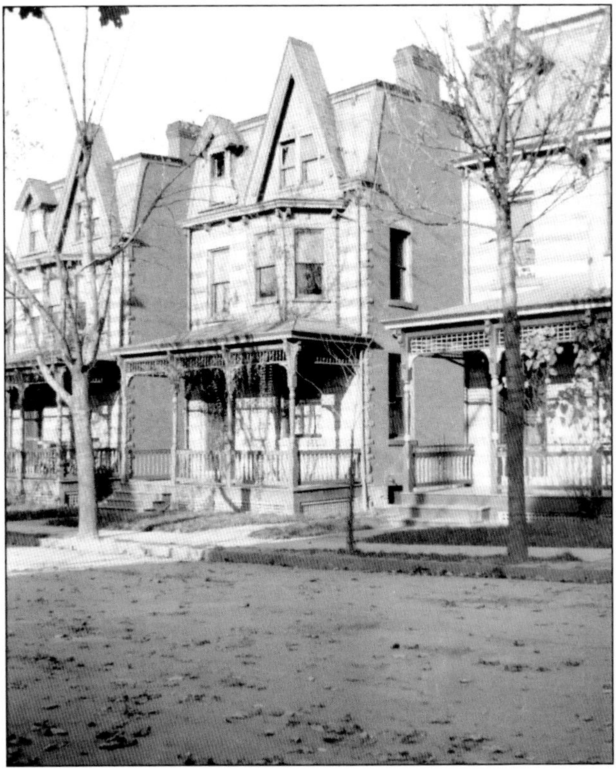

**THREE HOUSES ON MARYLAND AVENUE, C. 1904–1905.** During the first two decades of the 20th century, Shadyside experienced a sharp growth in speculative housing on a more modest scale than was typical during the previous century. These three homes, from left to right, are 817, 819, and 823 Maryland Avenue. (Courtesy of the Georgetown University Library.)

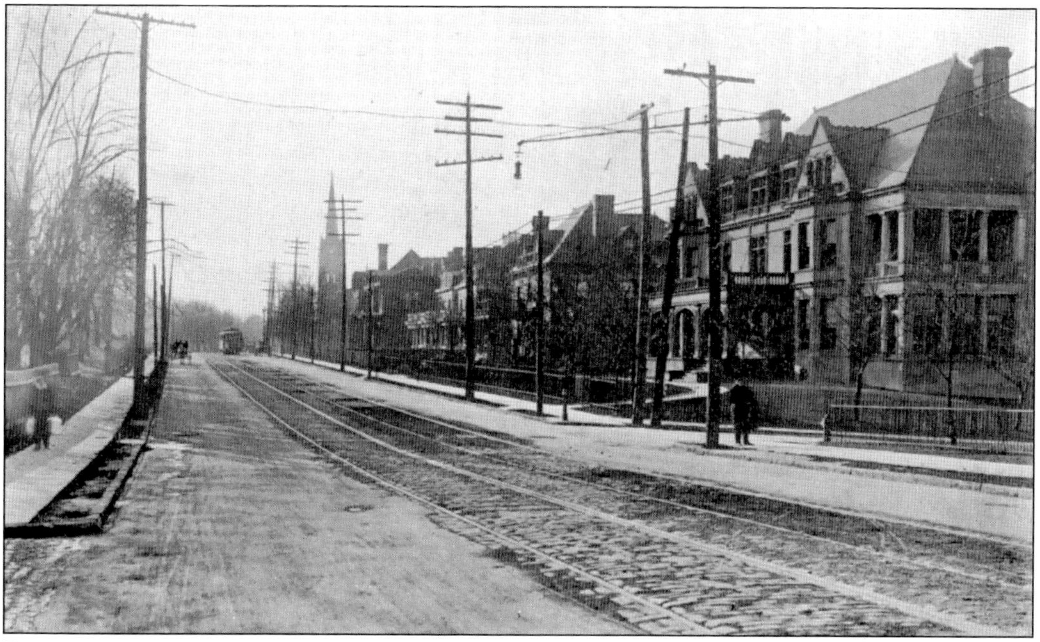

**Fifth Avenue at Woodland Road, 1904.** Looking toward the Third Presbyterian Church, a streetcar and horse and buggy are visible in the distance on Fifth Avenue. The man across the street stands on the corner of College Avenue. Behind him is the Lockhart home and then the Hartley house. (Courtesy of the Chatham College Archives.)

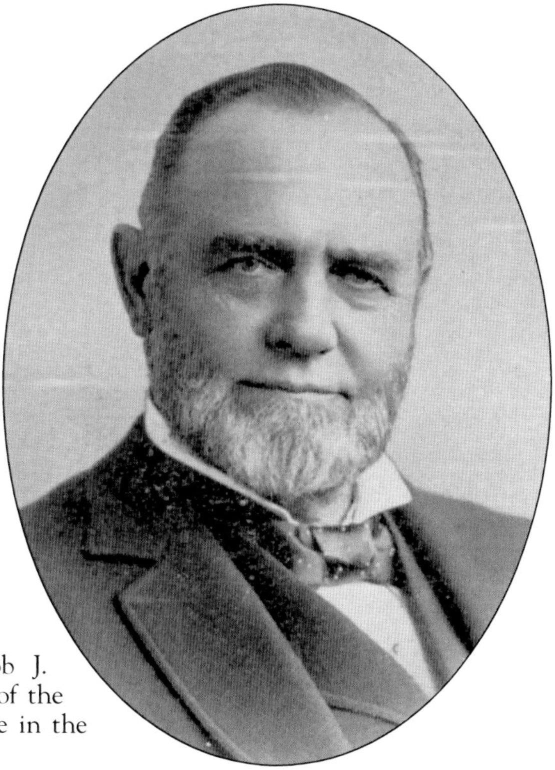

**Jacob J. Vandergrift, c. 1905.** Jacob J. Vandergrift was considered the "oil king" of the Standard Oil Company. He was also active in the steel and banking businesses.

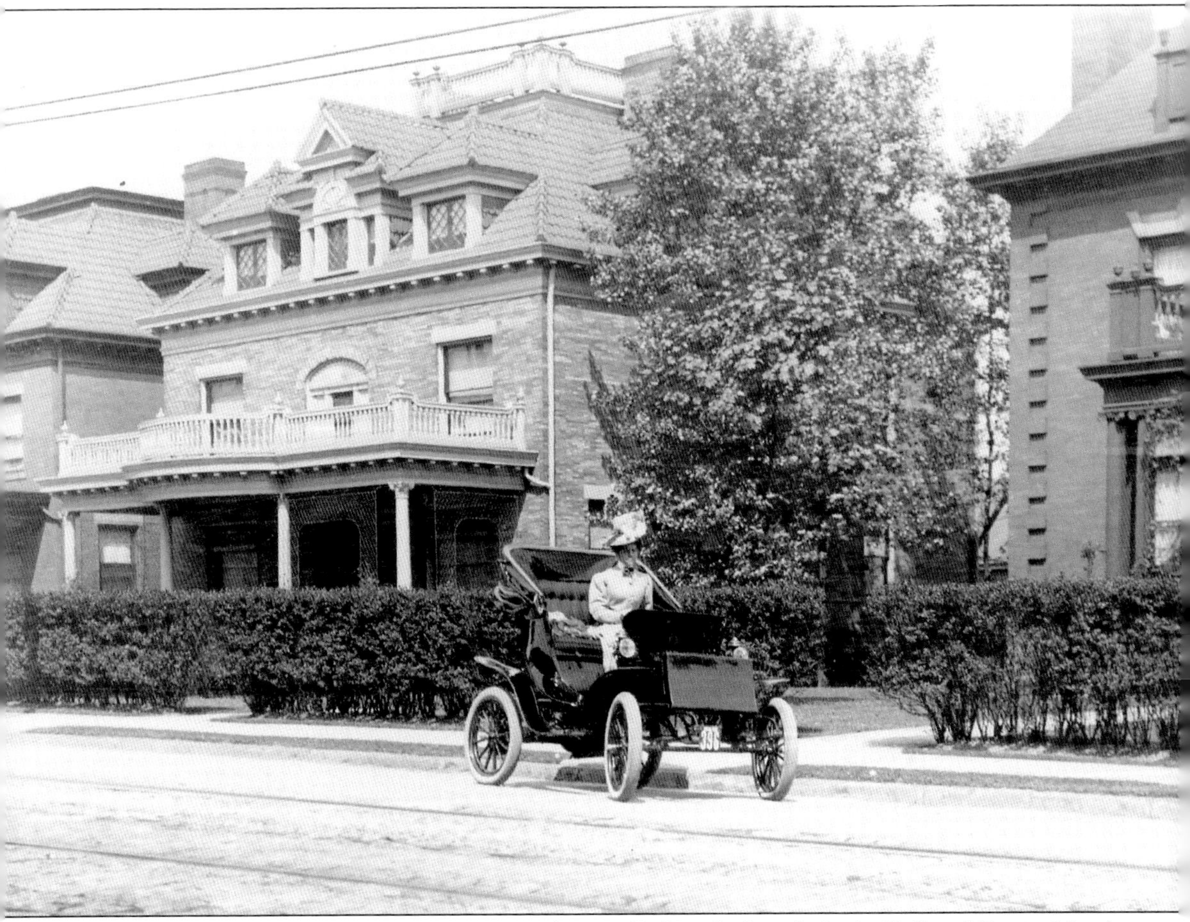

**MOTORING ON FIFTH AVENUE, 1902.** Thomas R. Hartley's wife, Lyde Holland Davitt Hartley, is driving one of his motorized vehicles in front of their house (far right) at 5825 Fifth Avenue. Mr. Edsall, a speculator, built the two homes next to the Hartley house and sold them in 1902 for $26,000 each. He sold the one at center, 5818 Fifth Avenue, to Mr. Wilson and the one at left, 5815 Fifth Avenue, to Mr. Kirk. (Courtesy of the Library and Archives Division, Senator John Heinz History Center.)

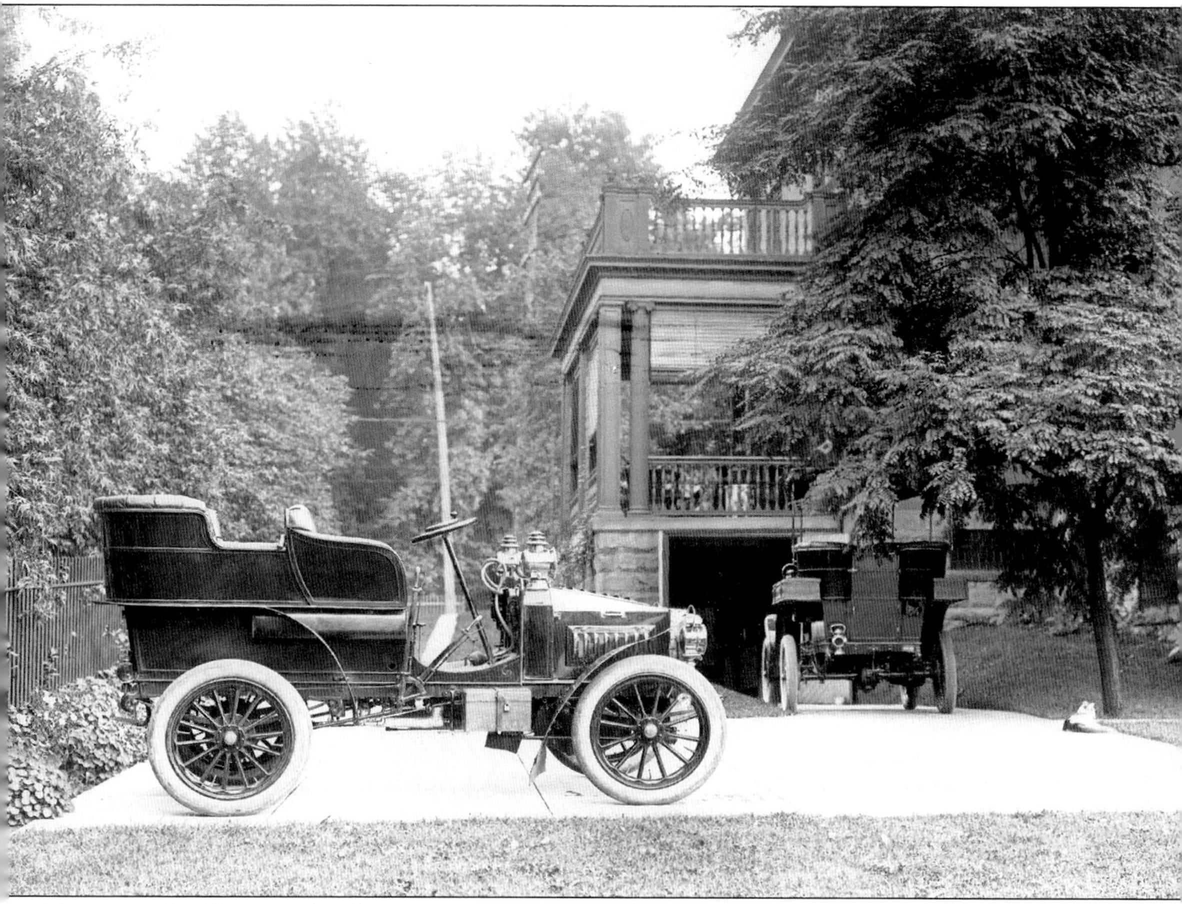

**THOMAS R. HARTLEY'S AUTOMOBILES, 1902.** Thomas R. Hartley was an automobile enthusiast. He lived with his wife, Lyde Holland Davitt Hartley, and mother-in-law, Frances G. Vandergrift, at 5825 Fifth Avenue, shown here with two steam-powered automobiles. The home was purchased by Vandergrift in 1900 from S. E. Logan for $52,500. (Courtesy of the Library and Archives Division, Senator John Heinz History Center.)

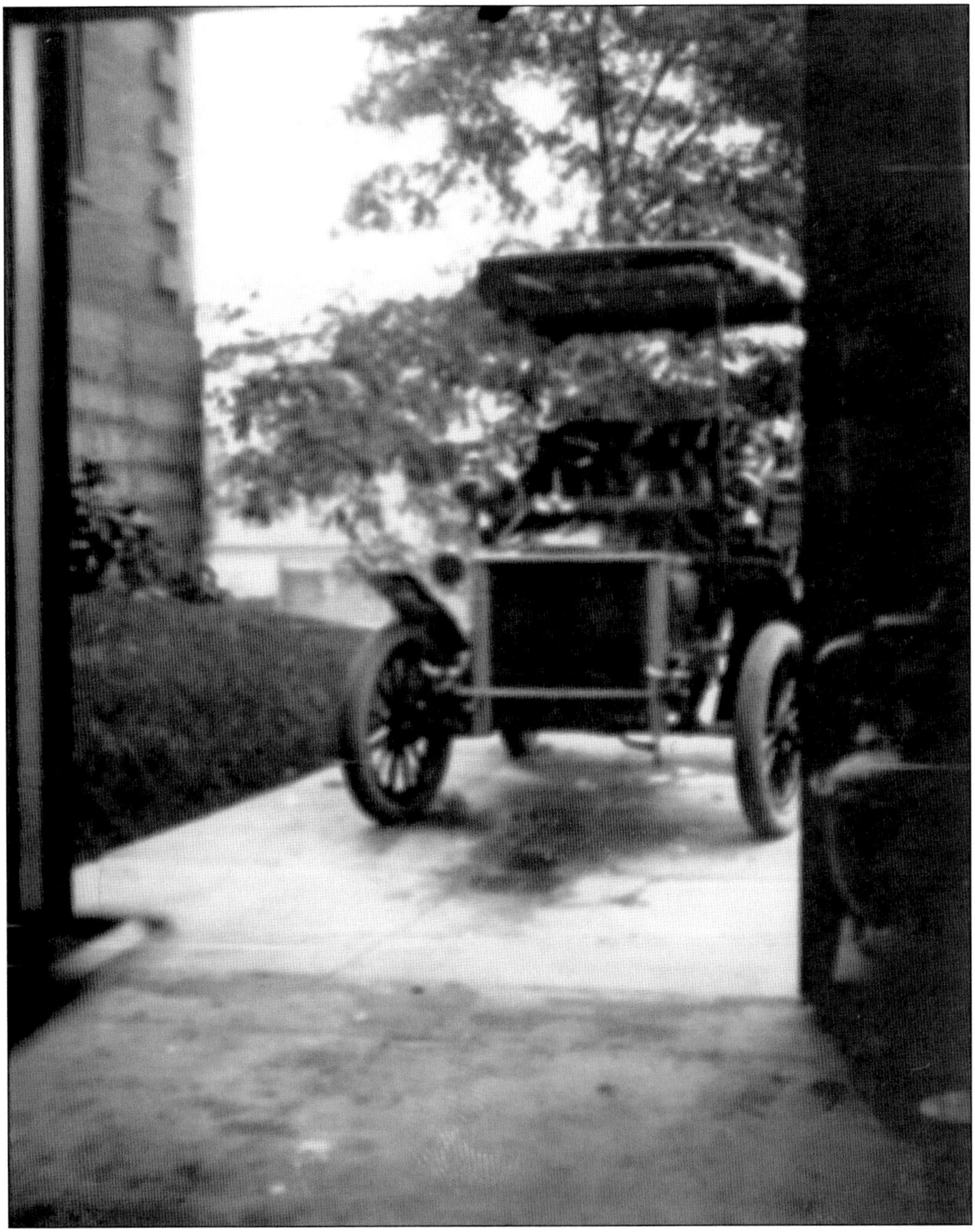

**AUTOMOBILE STORAGE, 1902.** Hartley had a garage for his automobiles under the porch of his home on Fifth Avenue. (Courtesy of the Library and Archives Division, Senator John Heinz History Center.)

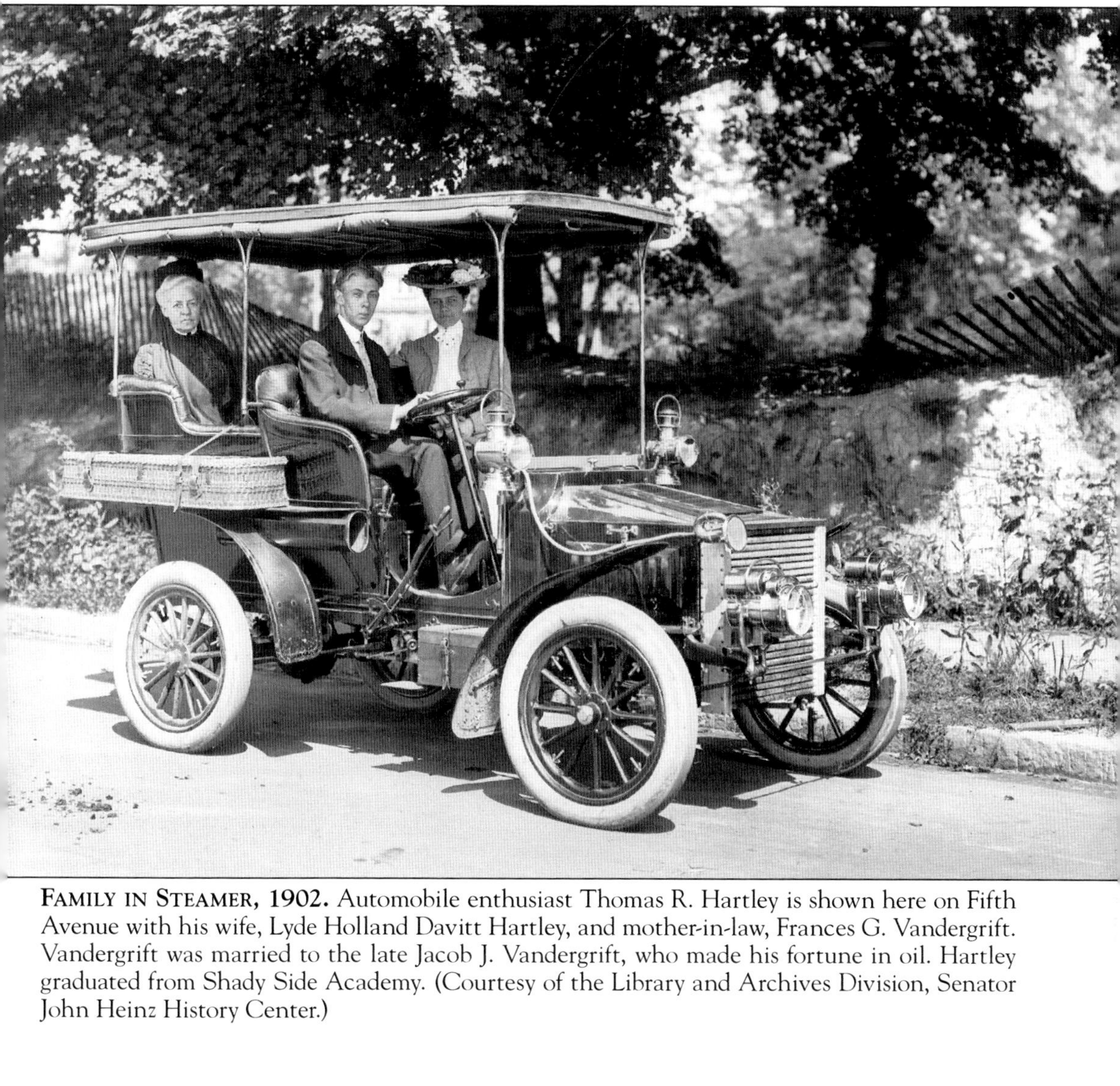

**FAMILY IN STEAMER, 1902.** Automobile enthusiast Thomas R. Hartley is shown here on Fifth Avenue with his wife, Lyde Holland Davitt Hartley, and mother-in-law, Frances G. Vandergrift. Vandergrift was married to the late Jacob J. Vandergrift, who made his fortune in oil. Hartley graduated from Shady Side Academy. (Courtesy of the Library and Archives Division, Senator John Heinz History Center.)

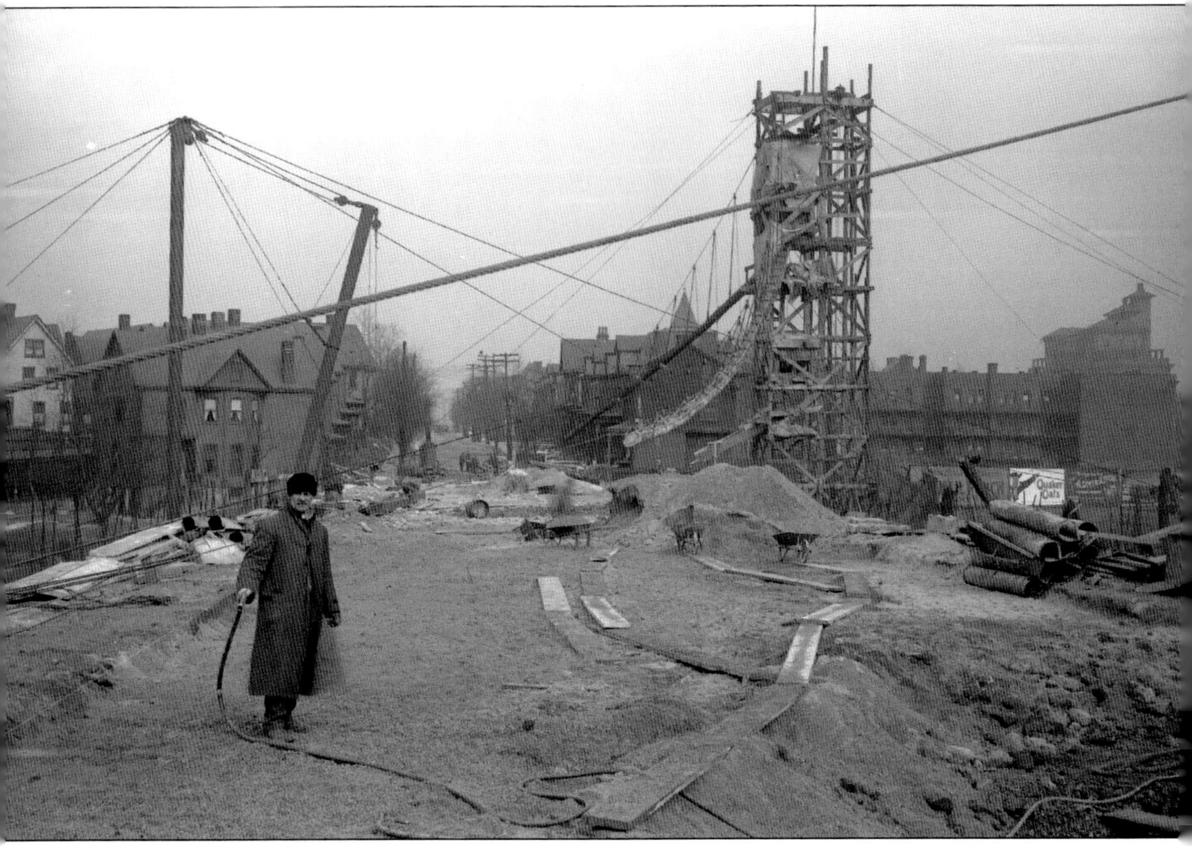

**ATHERTON AVENUE BRIDGE, FEBRUARY 14, 1913.** Here is a view of the Atherton Avenue bridge construction and slag fill looking east from where the Alexander Bradley estate once stood. The bridge crossed over the Pennsylvania Railroad. The name of Atherton Avenue was later changed to Baum Boulevard, and a few years later, the Ford Motor Company built an assembly plant to the right of this side of the bridge. (Courtesy of the University of Pittsburgh Archives Service Center.)

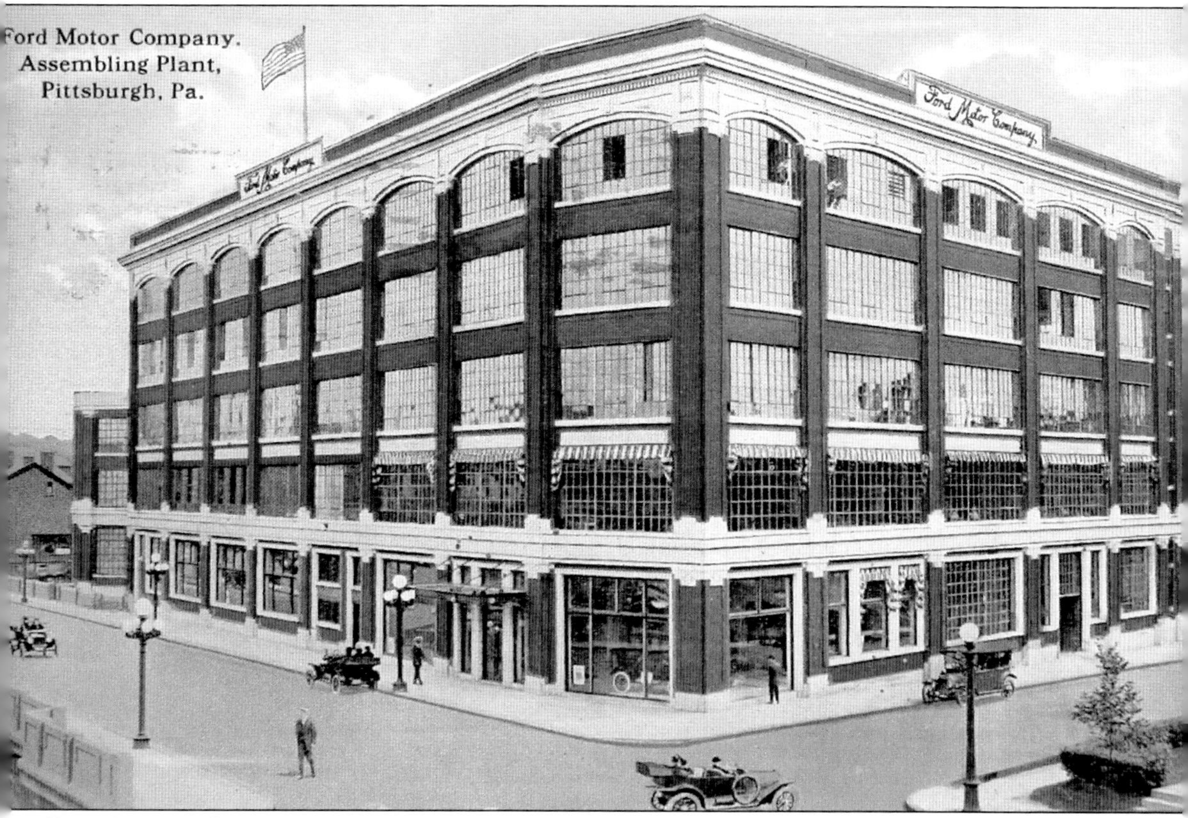


**FORD MOTOR COMPANY ASSEMBLY PLANT, 1916.** Ford Motor Company constructed a building of the most modern design that was eight stories in height, measured 219 by 167 feet, and contained over 180,000 square feet of floor space at the corner of Baum Boulevard and Morewood Avenue in 1915. The building was made of pressed brick and reinforced concrete, and the plant was the sixth largest in the chain of Ford assembling plants in the country at the time. The plant had a capacity for building 100 automobiles per day, which were distributed throughout Pennsylvania, Ohio, West Virginia, and Maryland, and it employed about 350 people. Now everyone could afford to buy a car from Automobile Row.

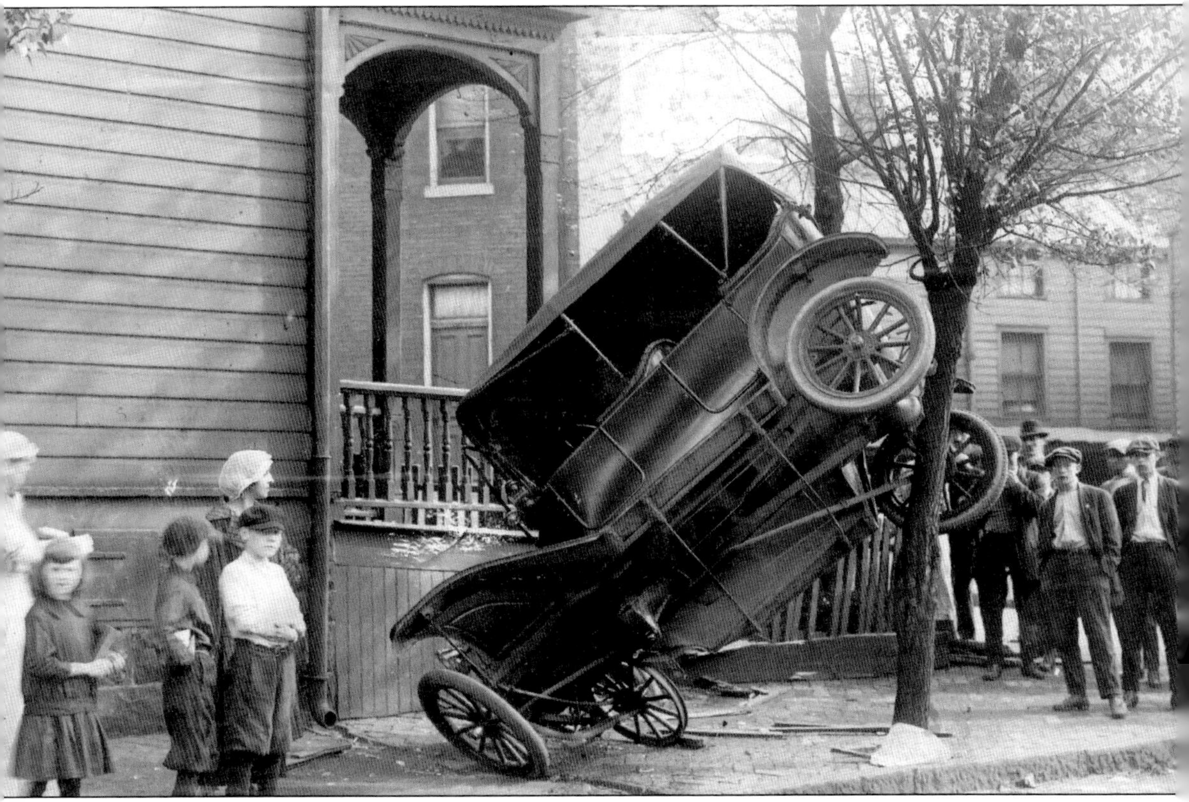

**FORD WRECK, MAY 20, 1916.** The Pittsburgh Ford Motor Company's shop foreman M. P. Smith wrote to his father that he had repaired this car during the previous week.

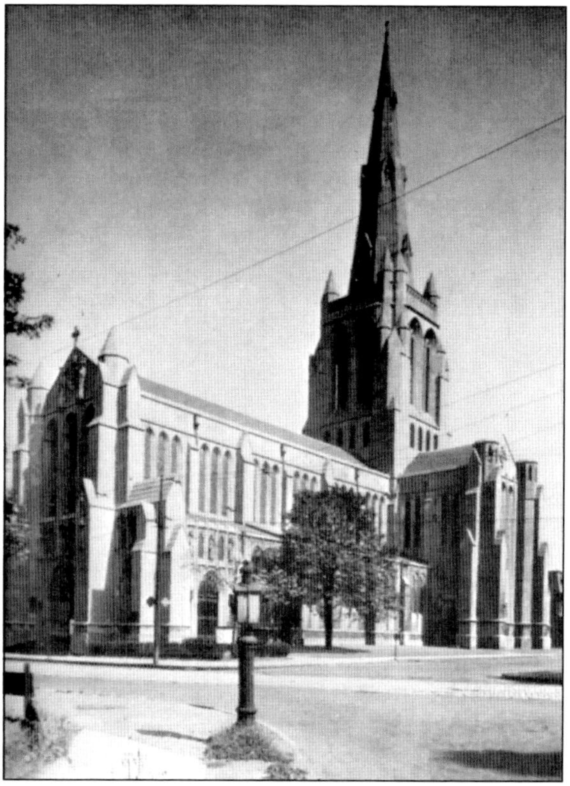

**CALVARY EPISCOPAL CHURCH, C. 1910.** The Calvary Episcopal Church at Shady Avenue and Walnut Street was designed by Ralph Adams Cram of the Cram, Goodhue and Ferguson firm in 1906 and 1907. Henry Clay Frick was in the congregation along with many prominent Shadyside residents.

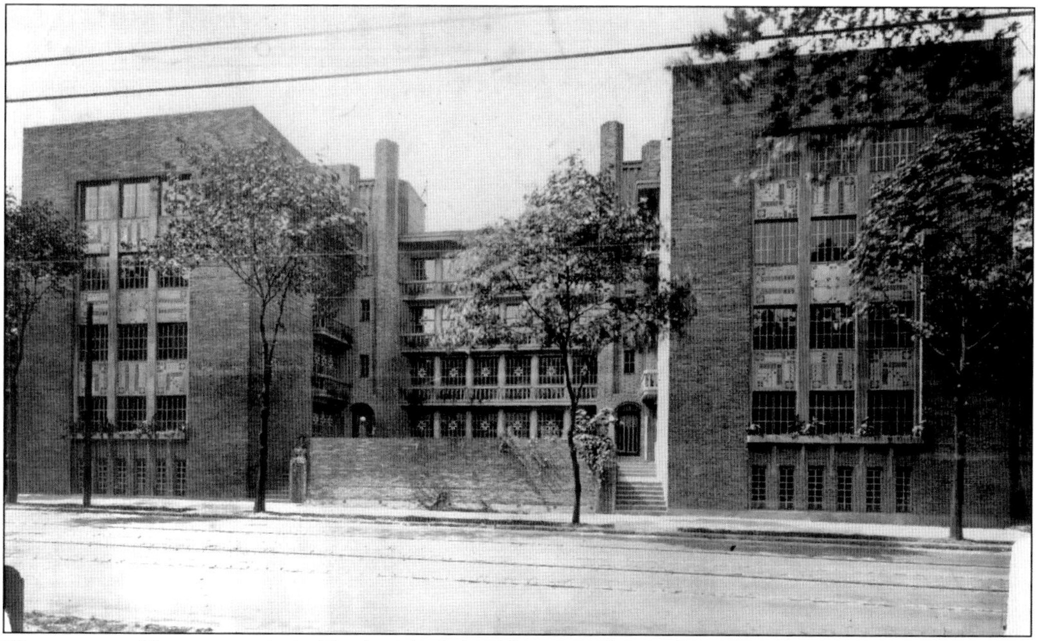

**HIGHLAND TOWERS, 1913.** Frederick Scheibler was the architect of this strikingly modern building at 340 South Highland Avenue. (Courtesy of the Carnegie Mellon University Architecture Archives.)

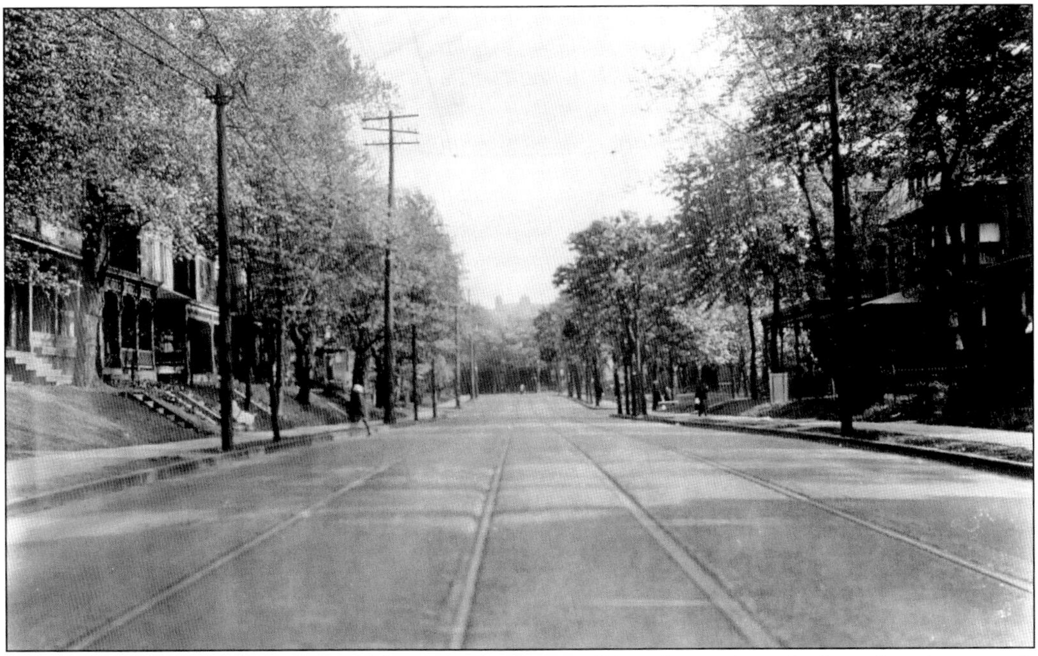

**HIGHLAND AVENUE C. 1906.** Highland Avenue was still largely residential when this photograph was taken. The Pennsylvania College for Women is seen on the hill in the distance. (Courtesy of the Chatham College Archives.)

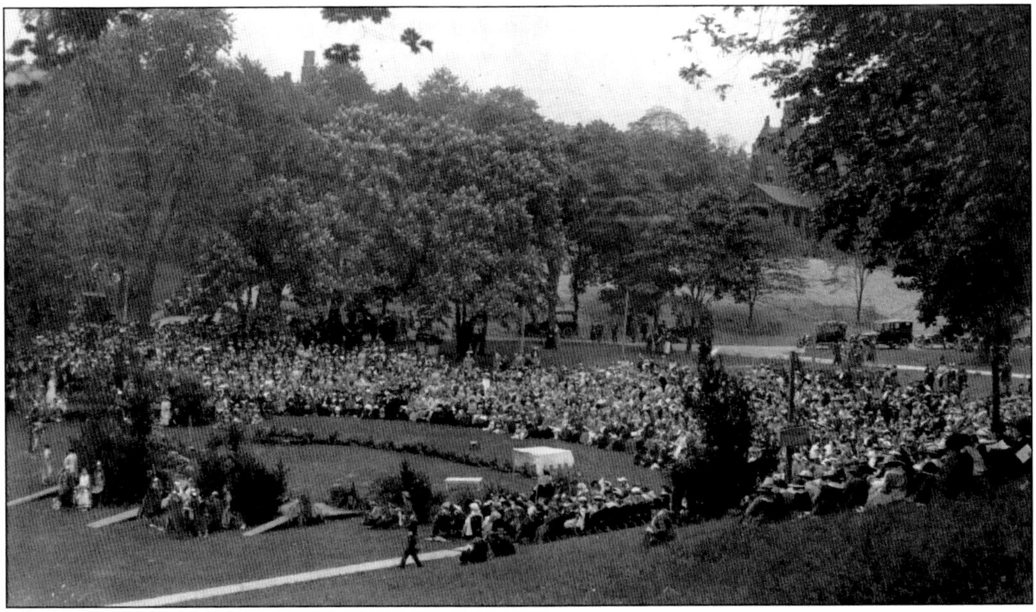

**MAY DAY, 1918.** Spectators gather on the Pennsylvania College for Women green for May Day celebrations. (Courtesy of the Chatham College Archives.)

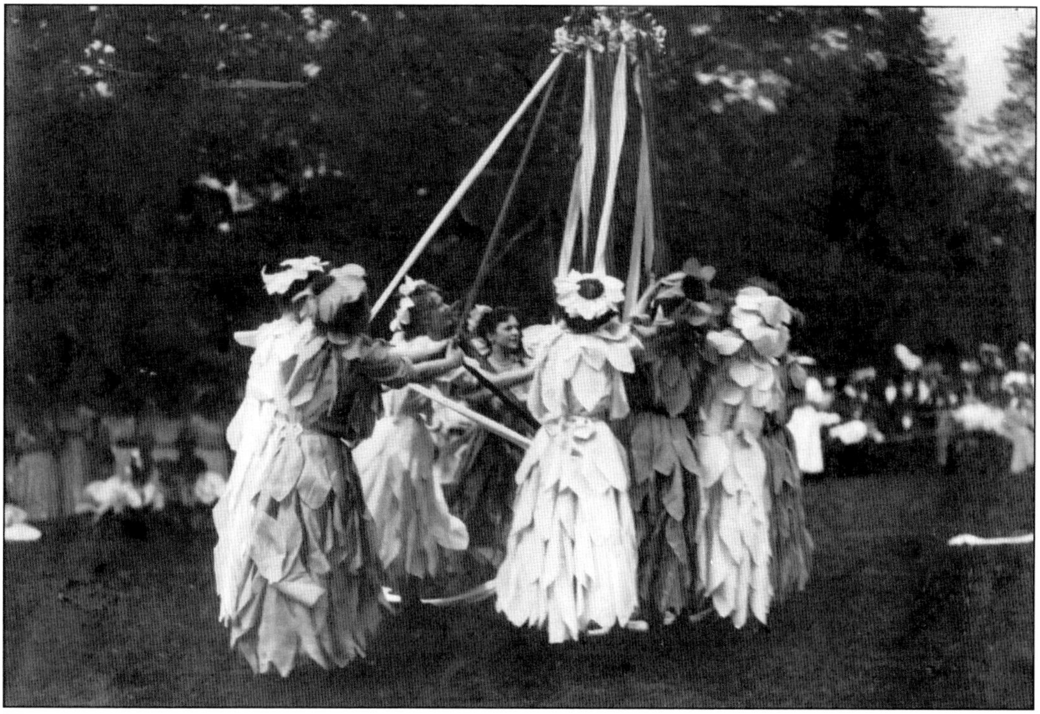

**THE MAYPOLE, MAY 18, 1907.** Dancing around the maypole is a tradition to welcome springtime. (Courtesy of the Chatham College Archives.)

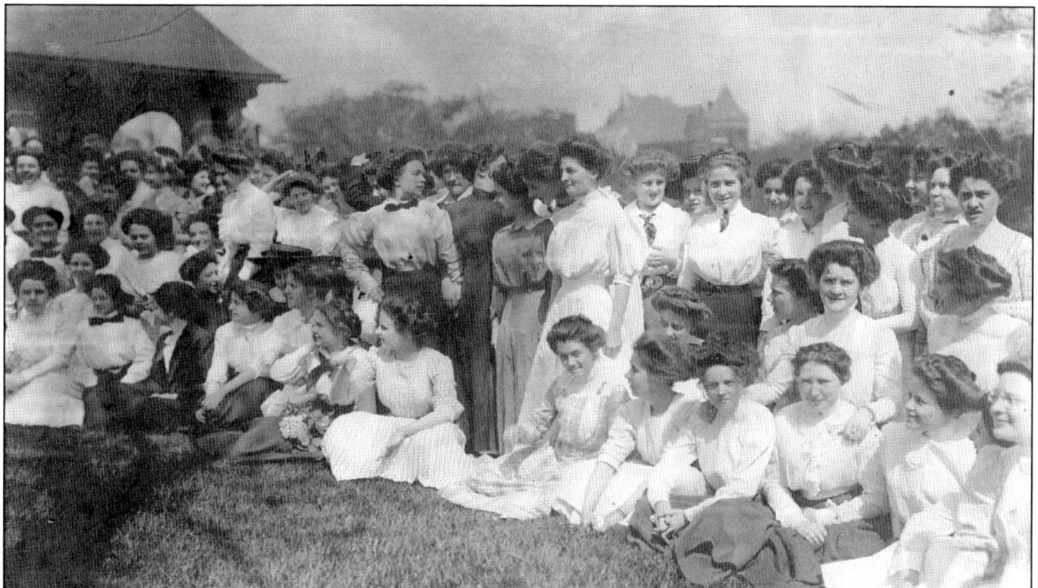

**WAITING FOR TAFT, 1910.** The women at the Pennsylvania College for Women waited in anticipation for Pres. William Howard Taft to speak. By 1908, the annual average enrollment was 200, including both the preparatory school and college. There were 22 faculty members. Preparatory school tuition was $175 per year. The college cost $125 per year, and the rate for room and board was $275 per year. (Courtesy of the Chatham College Archives.)

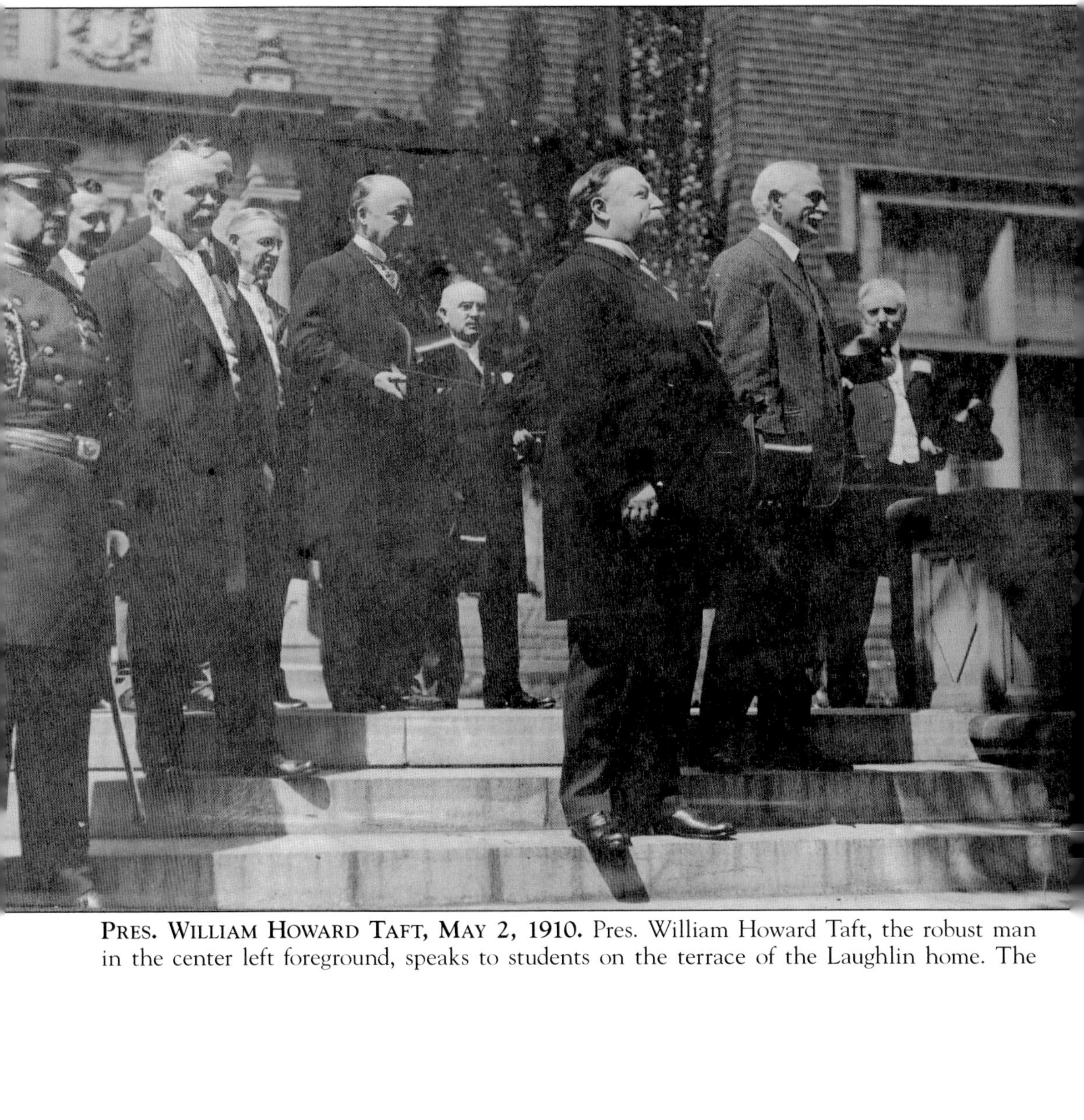

**PRES. WILLIAM HOWARD TAFT, MAY 2, 1910.** Pres. William Howard Taft, the robust man in the center left foreground, speaks to students on the terrace of the Laughlin home. The

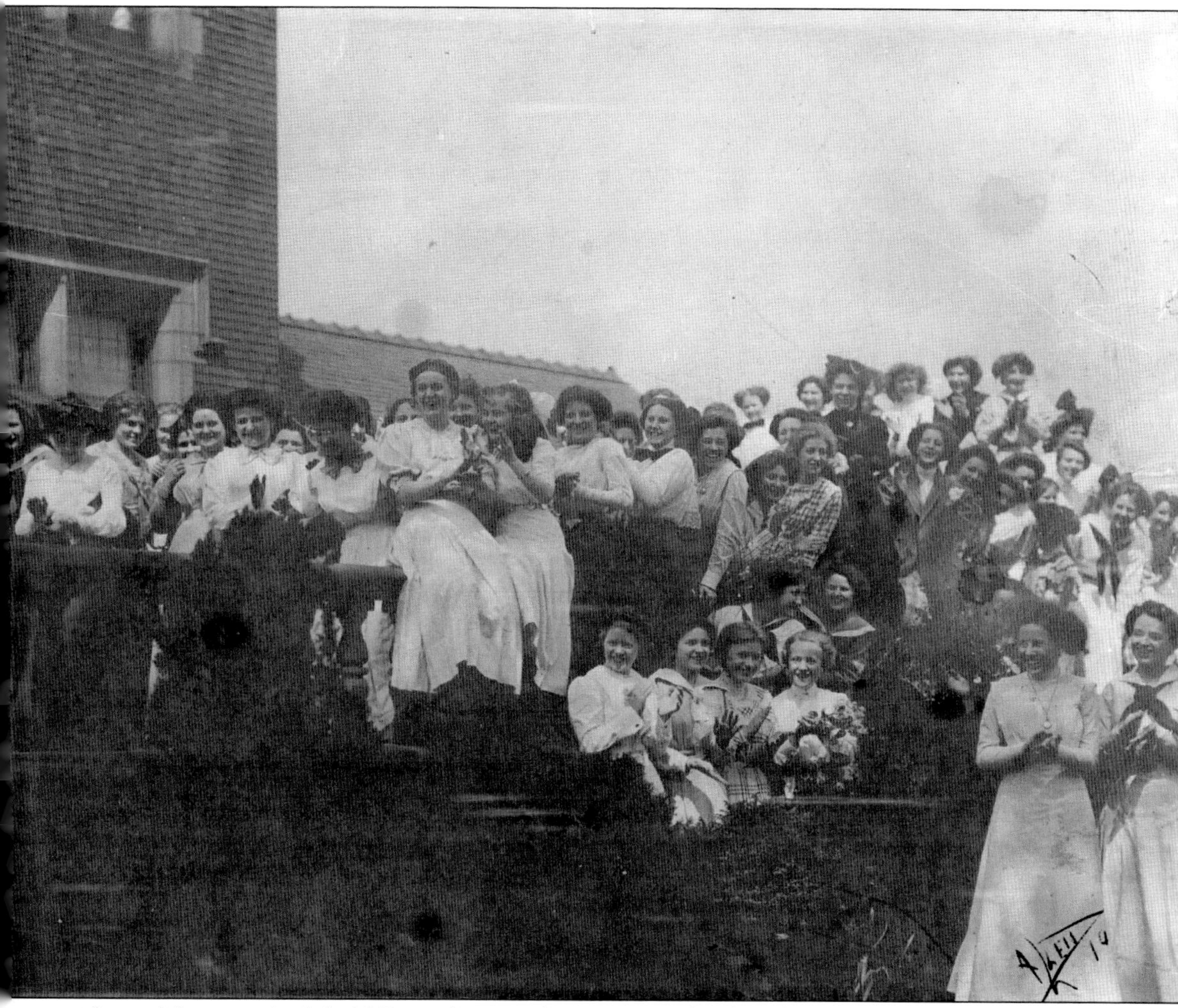

uniformed figure is Archibald Butt, the president's personal aide. The Pennsylvania College for Women was renamed Chatham College in 1955. (Courtesy of the Chatham College Archives.)

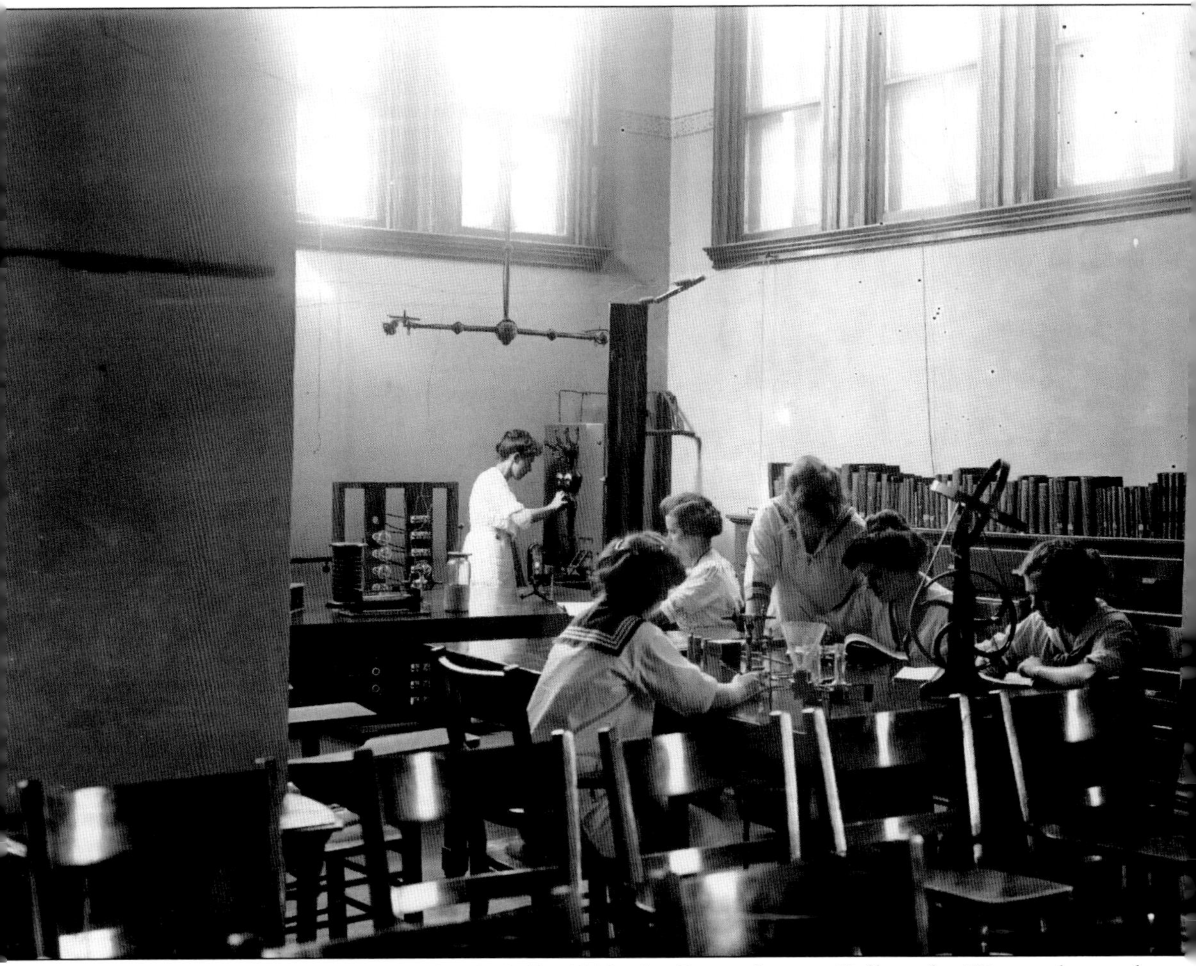

**SCIENTIFIC PRINCIPLES, 1915–1916.** By 1908, the Pennsylvania College for Women boasted that its science department included a lecture room and chemical and biological laboratories supplied with all modern apparatuses. The chemical laboratory was equipped with accurate chemical balances, boiling and freezing point apparatuses, and other facilities for careful, quantitative work. (Courtesy of the Chatham College Archives.)

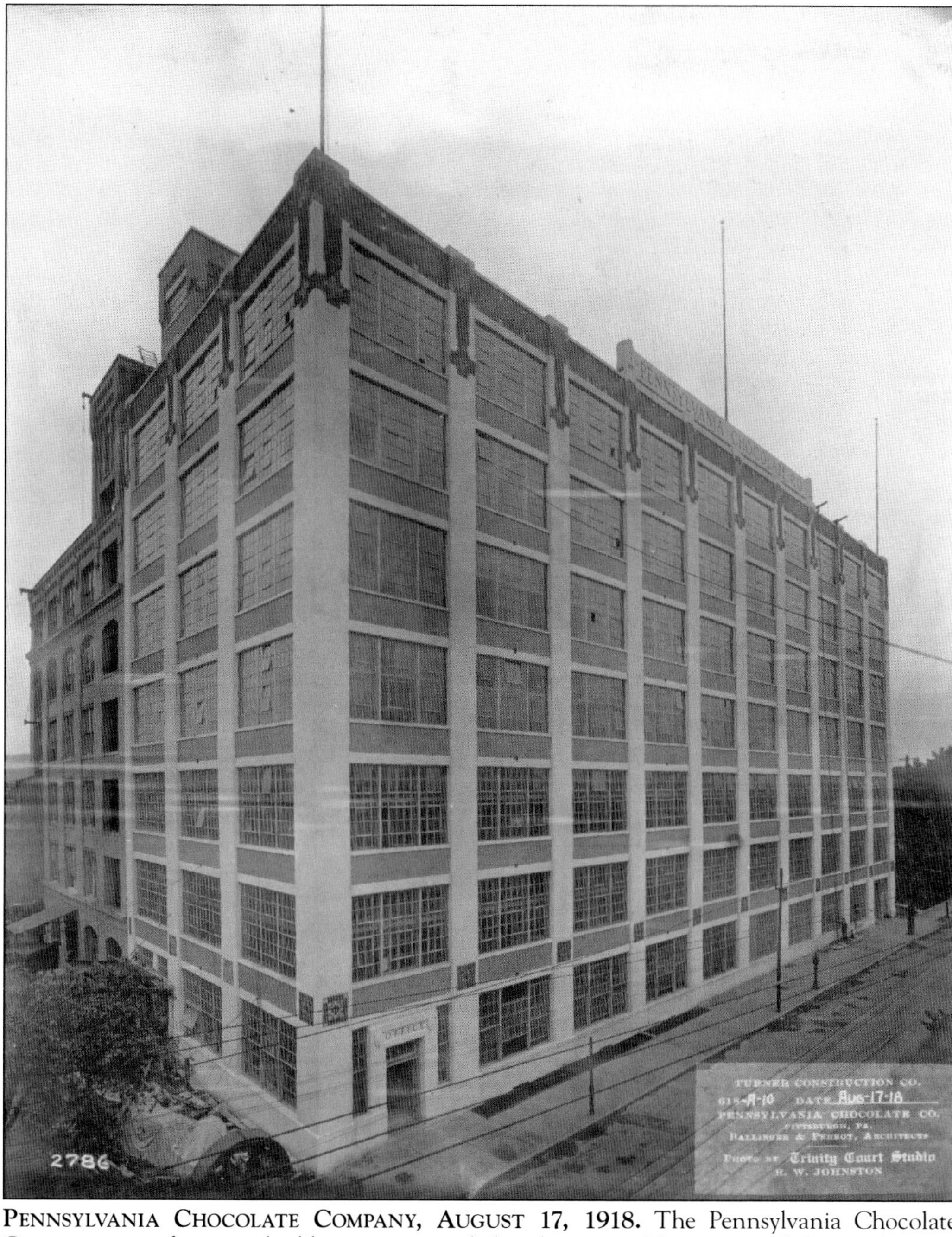


**PENNSYLVANIA CHOCOLATE COMPANY, AUGUST 17, 1918.** The Pennsylvania Chocolate Company manufacturing building was expanded with a new addition toward Centre Avenue. Seen at left, the existing structure was darker and all brick along the Pennsylvania Railroad tracks. The streetcar tracks are visible on Centre Avenue. Hallinger and Perrot were the architects for the expansion. (Courtesy of the Athenaeum of Philadelphia.)

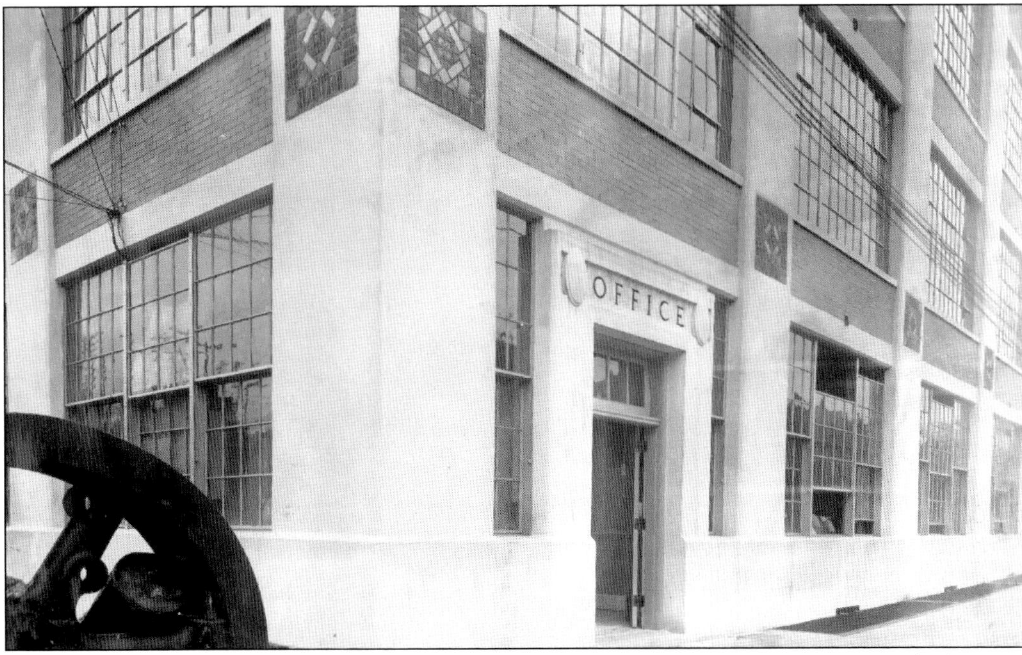


**OFFICE, AUGUST 17, 1918.** The Pennsylvania Chocolate Company was known as "the home of Zatek cocoa and chocolate." (Courtesy of the Athenaeum of Philadelphia.)

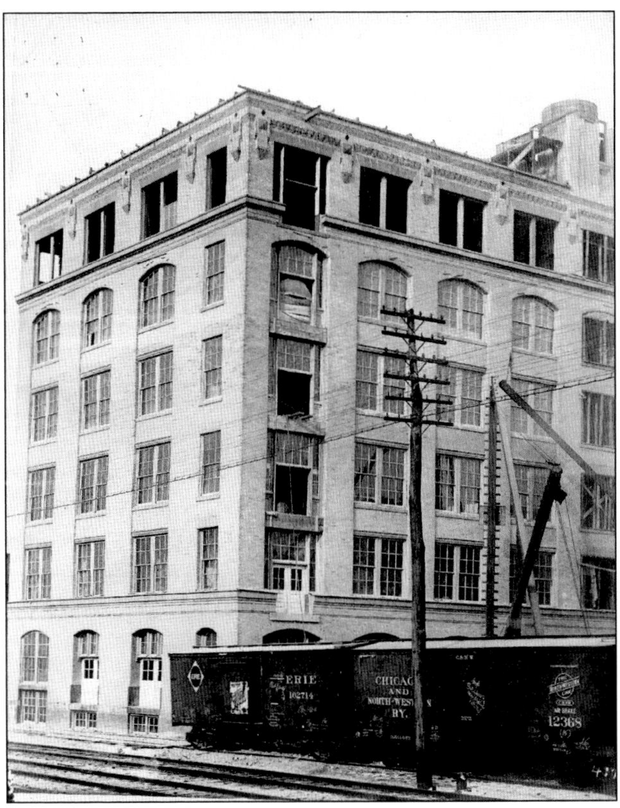


**OLD MANUFACTURING BUILDING, AUGUST 17, 1918.** The Pennsylvania Chocolate Company manufacturing building sat next to the Pennsylvania Railroad tracks for easy loading and unloading of goods. (Courtesy of the Athenaeum of Philadelphia.)

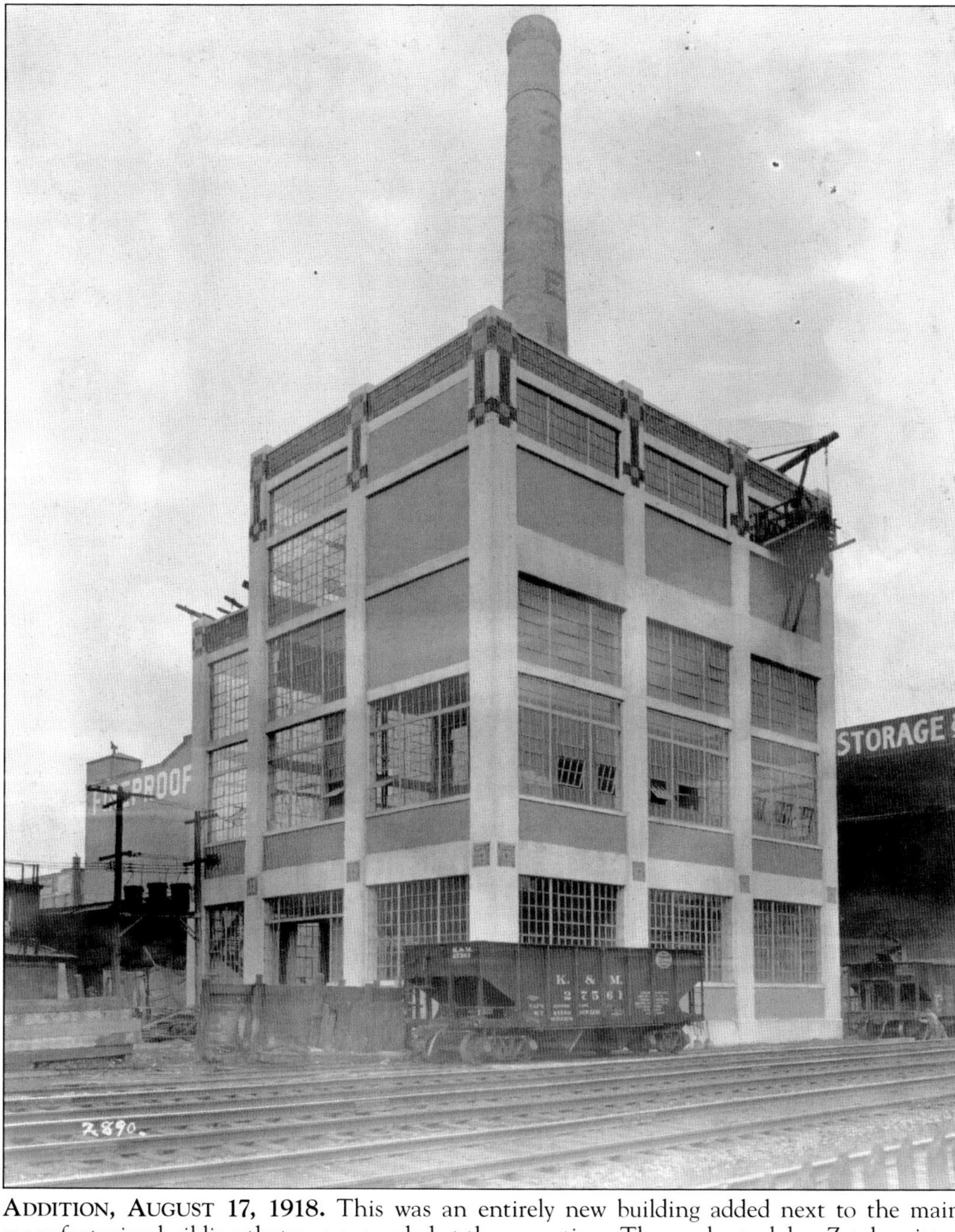


**ADDITION, AUGUST 17, 1918.** This was an entirely new building added next to the main manufacturing building that was expanded at the same time. The smokestack has Zatek written on it, which was a brand name of the Pennsylvania Chocolate Company. (Courtesy of the Athenaeum of Philadelphia.)

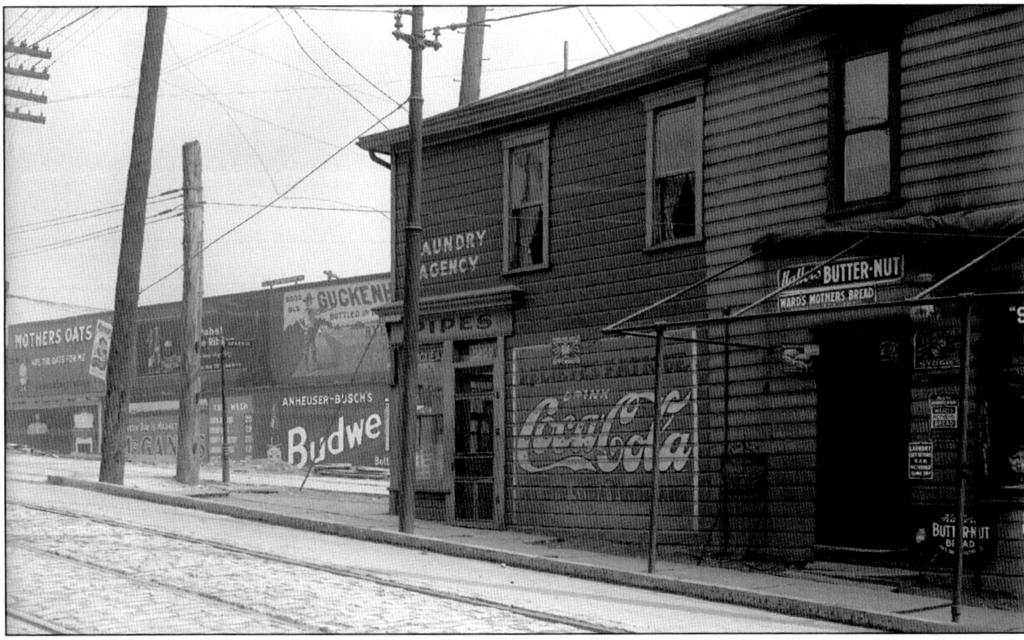


**BILLBOARDS, SEPTEMBER 18, 1908.** This building at the corner of Ellsworth Avenue and Spahr Street sits just before the bridge that leads to Centre Avenue and East Liberty. Advertisers take advantage of both automobile and railroad traffic with the positioning of the billboards at left. (Courtesy of the University of Pittsburgh Archives Service Center.)

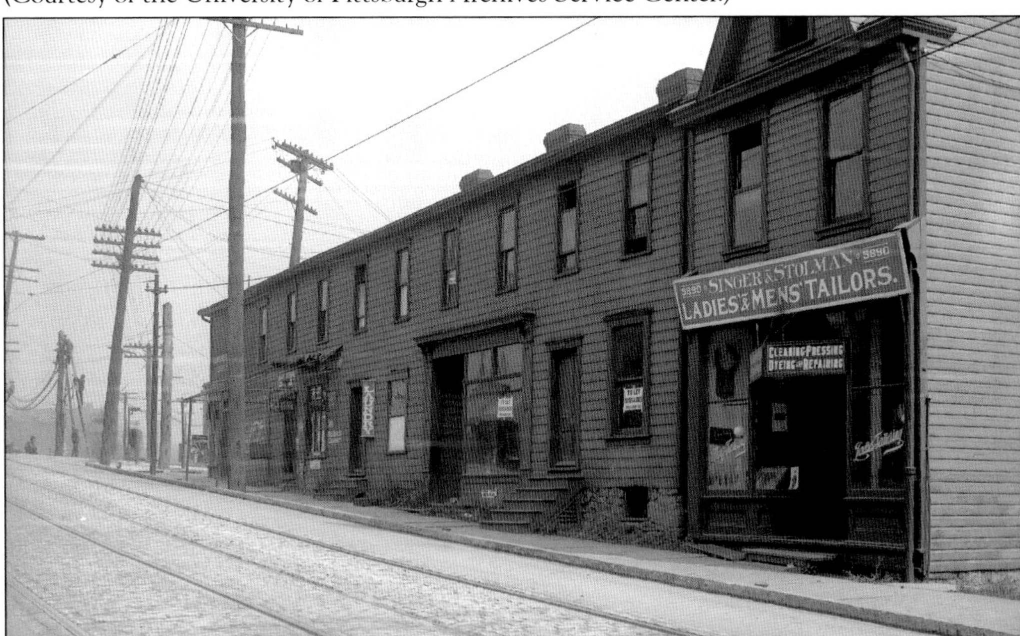


**TAILORS FOR LADIES AND MEN, SEPTEMBER 18, 1908.** The building in the right foreground houses the tailor at 5890 Ellsworth Avenue. A wooden footbridge crosses the Pennsylvania Railroad tracks to the left, and Ellsworth Avenue continues as a wooden bridge at East Liberty. (Courtesy of the University of Pittsburgh Archives Service Center.)

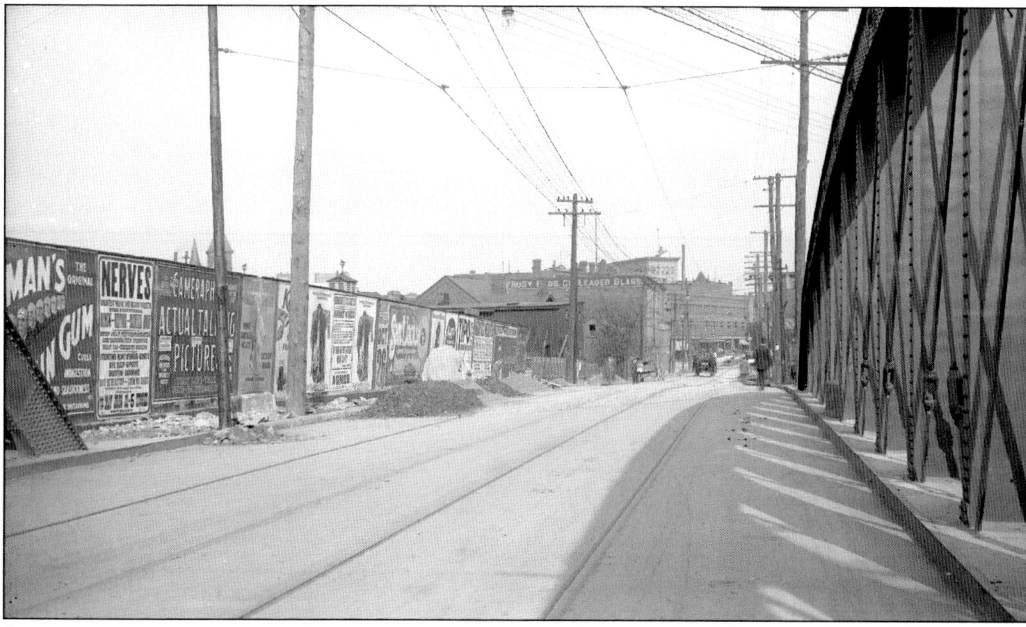


**SHADYSIDE ADVERTISING, OCTOBER 27, 1908.** The Ellsworth Avenue bridge into East Liberty is plastered with advertising. At the left side of the road and on the far end of the bridge is the Rudy Brothers building. It was clearly in East Liberty at the time, but today it is officially in Shadyside because it sits south of Centre Avenue. (Courtesy of the University of Pittsburgh Archives Service Center.)

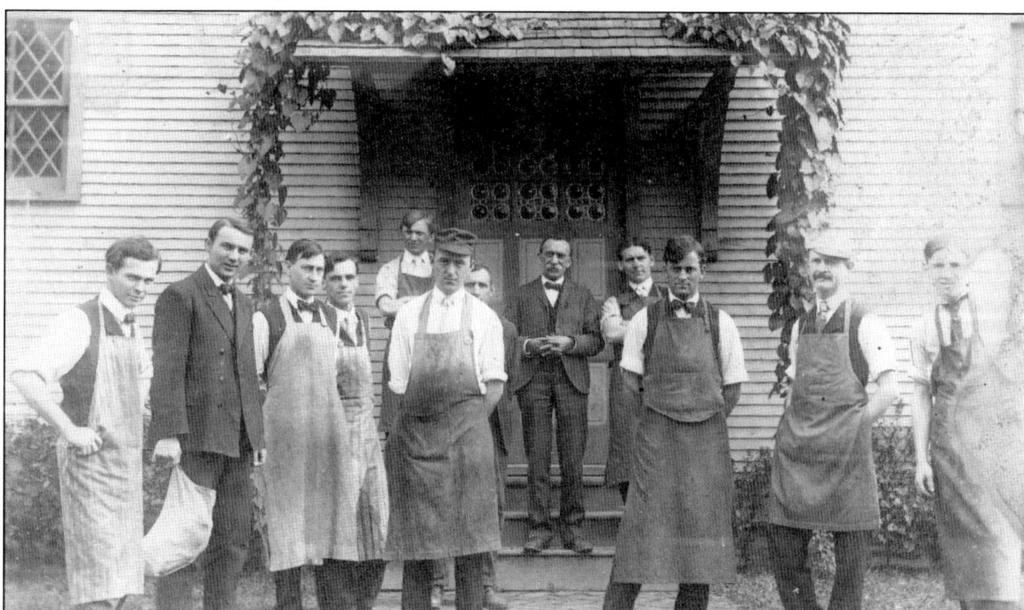

**RUDY BROTHERS, C. 1900.** The Rudy Brothers contributed a number of magnificent windows to Shadyside homes and churches. From left to right are unidentified, Isaiah Rudy, unidentified, unidentified, Chas Schmidt, Harry McNaulty, Chas Connich, Oldman Rudy, Leo Sotter, unidentified, Jesse Rudy, and ? Lobengier. (Courtesy of the Library and Archives Division, Senator John Heinz History Center.)

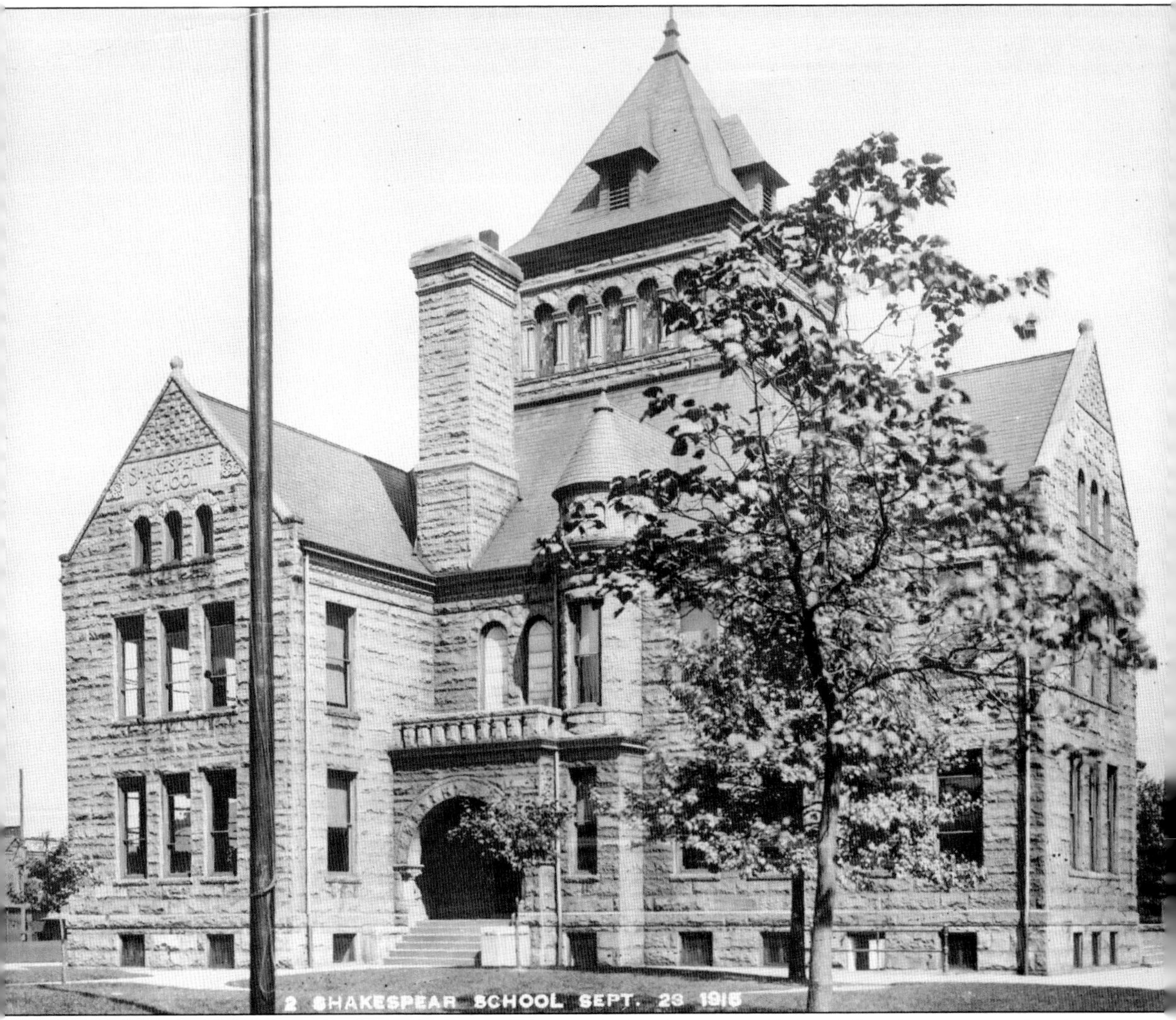


**SHAKESPEARE SCHOOL, SEPTEMBER 23, 1915.** Shakespeare School (no longer standing) was named for a country inn or roadhouse, the Shakespeare Hotel, which occupied the site in the pioneer days. The school, located on 6322 Shakespeare Street, was built in 1844 and closed in 1956. (Courtesy of the Library and Archives Division, Senator John Heinz History Center.)

# *Three*

# CITY NEIGHBORHOOD 1920–1930

By the 1920s, Shadyside was a city neighborhood. Industry built up around the Pennsylvania Railroad tracks, and large estates gave way to developments of smaller and more closely spaced homes. With all the transitions, two areas in Shadyside retained much of their 19th-century character, the west part of Shadyside between Aiken Avenue and Neville Street, where the original suburb began, and the area around Woodland Road, including Chatham College.

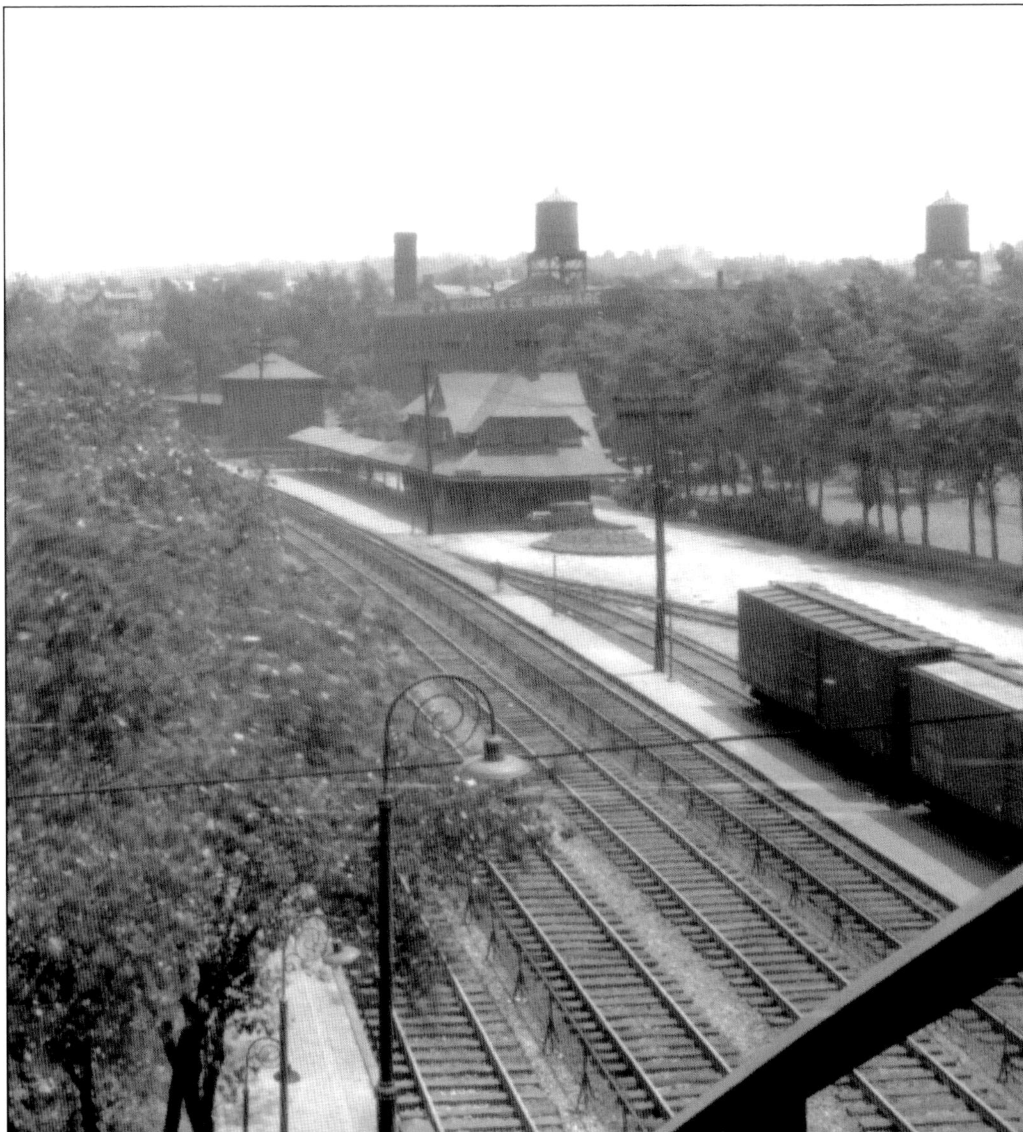

**SHADYSIDE TRAIN STATION, JULY 24, 1928.** The Shadyside train station is visible to the right of the Pennsylvania Railroad tracks. The photograph was taken from the Centre Avenue Bridge. The J. A. Williams Company warehouse is directly behind the station. (Courtesy of the University of Pittsburgh Archives Service Center.)

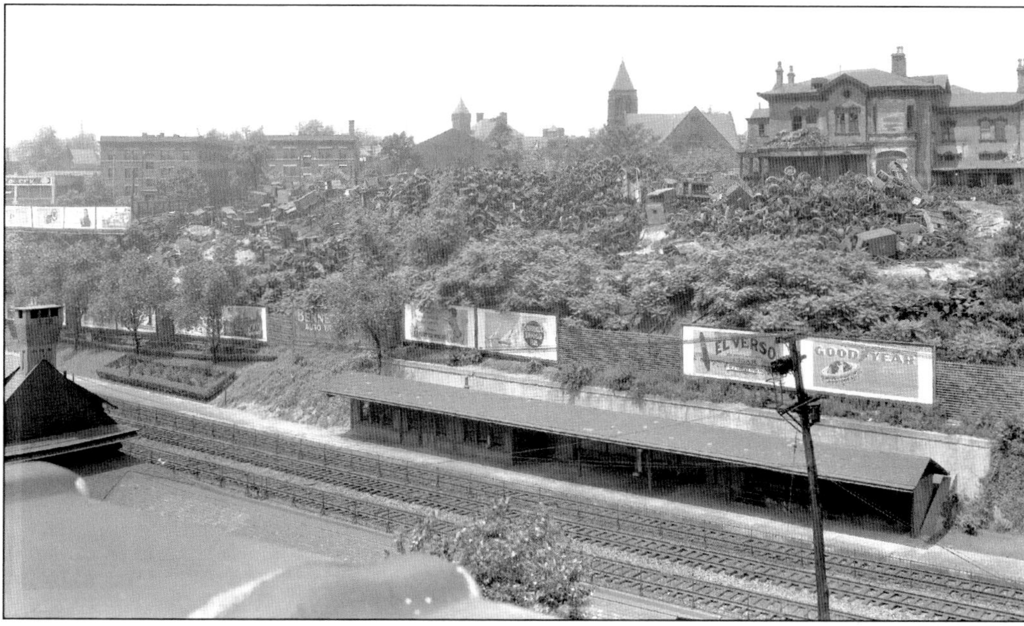


**BENNETT BROTHERS AUTO WRECKERS, JULY 24, 1928.** Bennett Brothers Auto Wreckers junk dump and part of the Shadyside station are visible from the roof of the J. A. Williams and Company warehouse. The home at right is the ruins of the Edward H. Alsop estate at 5200 Centre Avenue, which was considered to be in Shadyside. (Courtesy of the University of Pittsburgh Archives Service Center.)

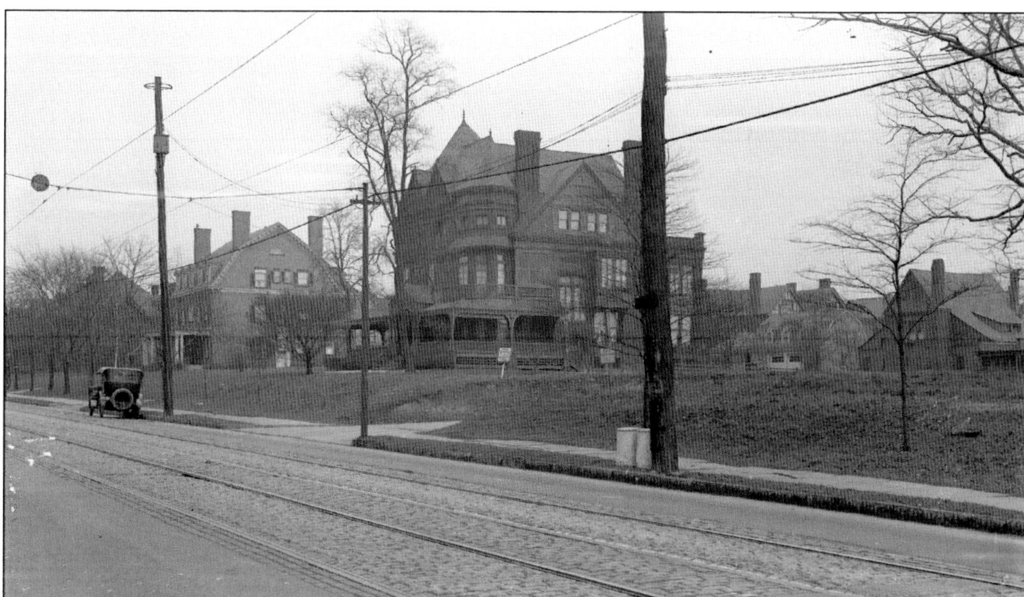

**ELLSWORTH AVENUE, APRIL 9, 1920.** This view down Ellsworth Avenue is from Colonial Place looking toward St. James Street. The closer home at center, 5220 Ellsworth Avenue, belonged to James McCrea. The Dutch Colonial house in the distance at 5238 Ellsworth Avenue on the corner of St. James Street belonged to the Smith family. (Courtesy of the University of Pittsburgh Archives Service Center.)

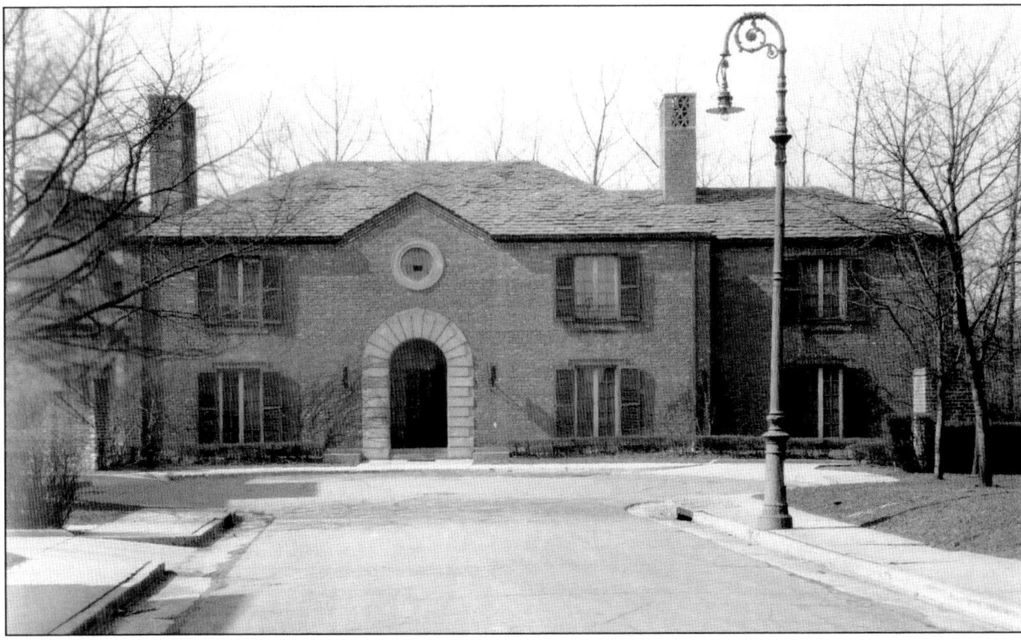

**LEE L. CHANDLER HOUSE, 1924.** The Lee L. Chandler house at 5016 Amberson Place is prominent at the end of the cul-de-sac. The home, designed by architect Benno Janssen, clearly displays a new aesthetic for the Shadyside neighborhood in the early 20th century. (Courtesy of the Carnegie Mellon University Architecture Archives.)

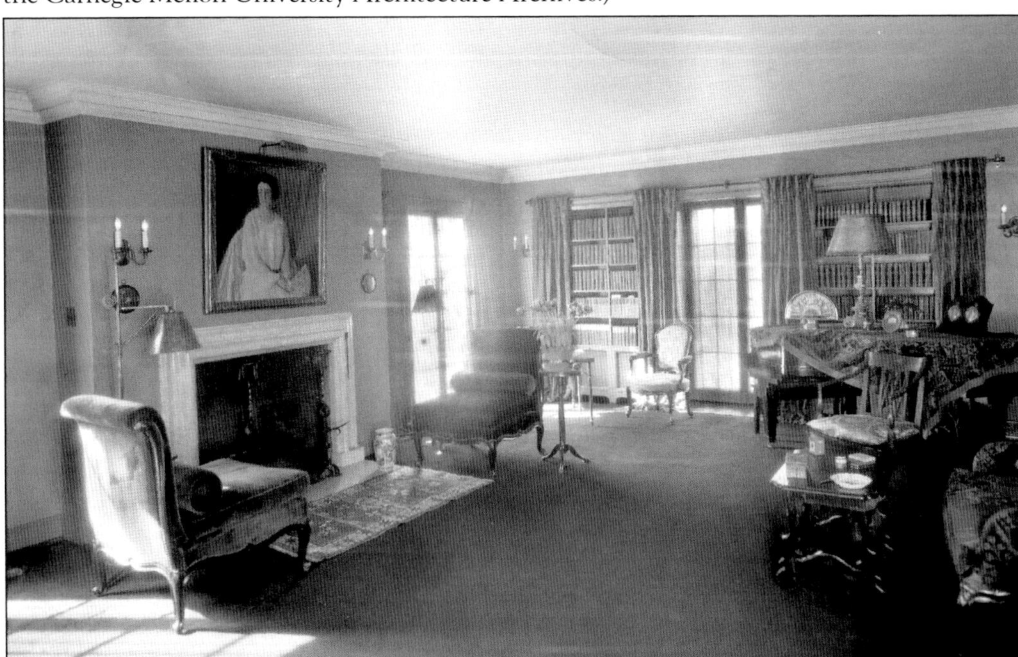

**LIVING ROOM, 1924.** The Lee L. Chandler house living room retains some of the classic grandeur of the old estates while providing a more modern look. (Courtesy of the Carnegie Mellon University Architecture Archives.)

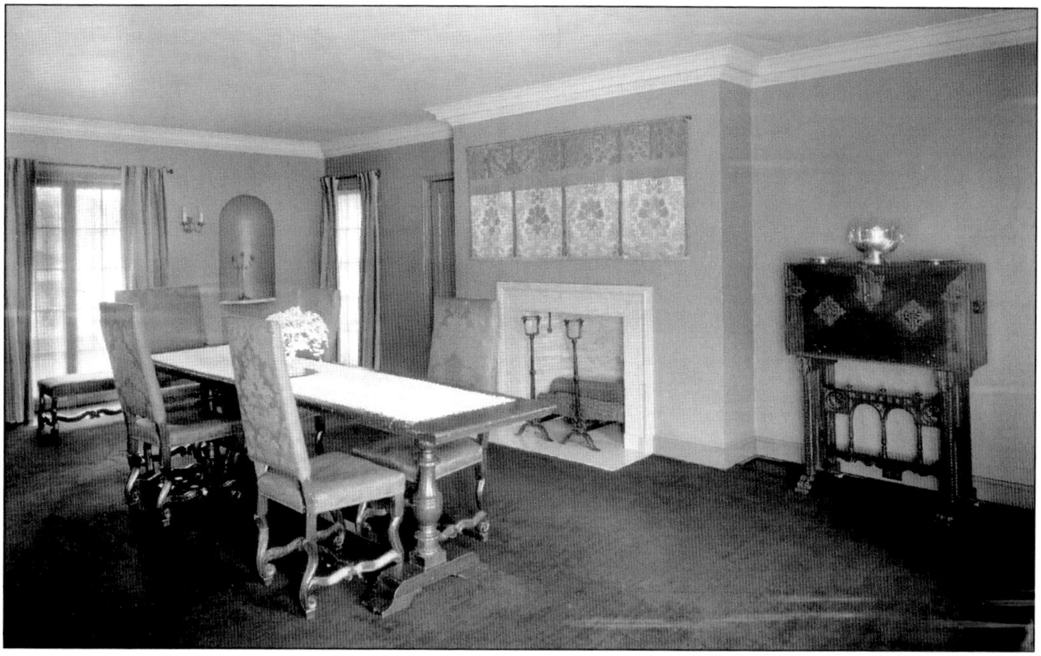

**Dining Room, 1924.** The Lee L. Chandler house dining room is a big break from the typical 19th-century Shadyside dining room, which, like the McCooks' or even the Dennistons' dining rooms, was ornately decorated. (Courtesy of the Carnegie Mellon University Architecture Archives.)

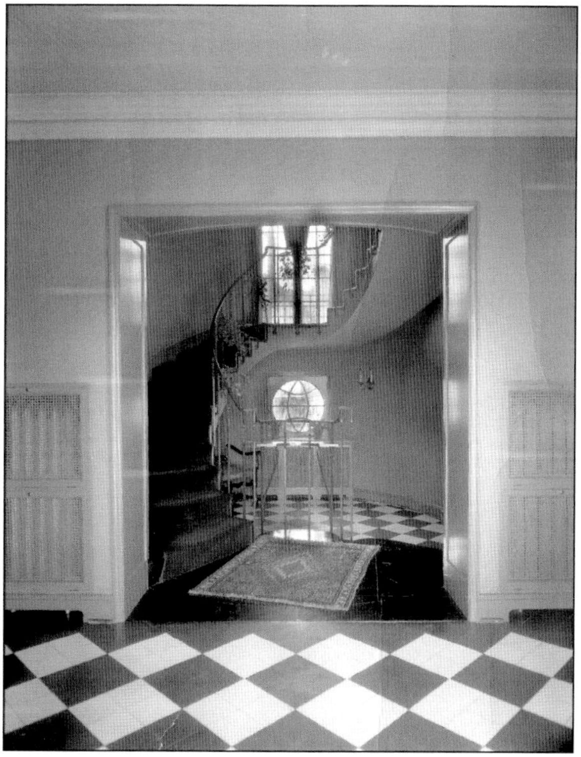

**Flying Stairway, 1924.** This flying stairway is a striking Lee L. Chandler house feature. (Courtesy of the Carnegie Mellon University Architecture Archives.)

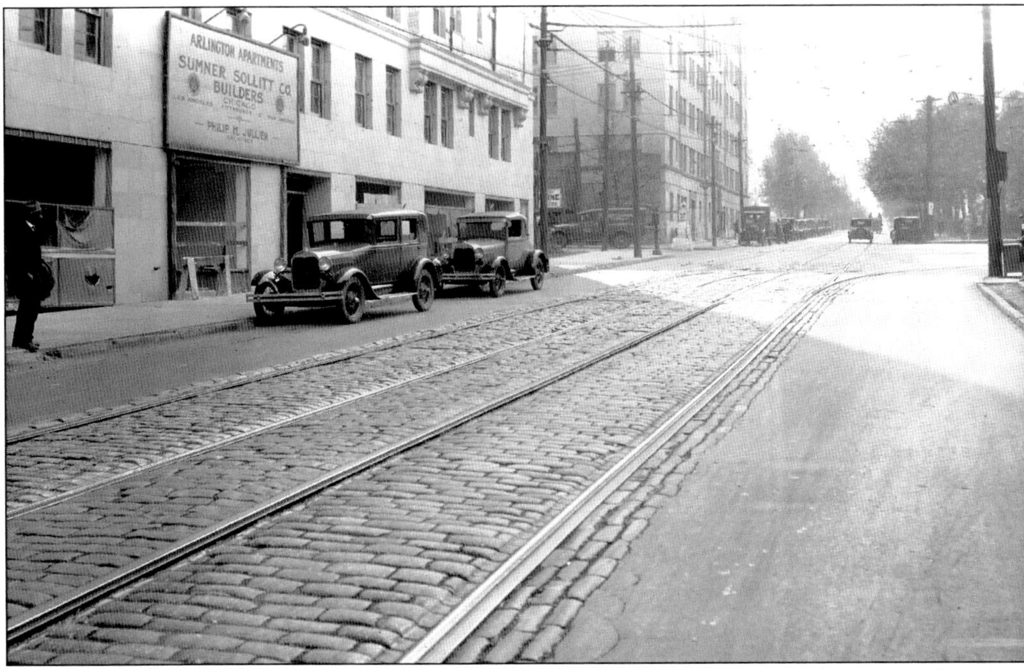


**ARLINGTON APARTMENTS, SEPTEMBER 24, 1929.** Standing on Centre Avenue and looking toward South Aiken Avenue, the new, larger buildings along Shadyside's perimeter are as apparent as the automobiles. (Courtesy of the University of Pittsburgh Archives Service Center.)

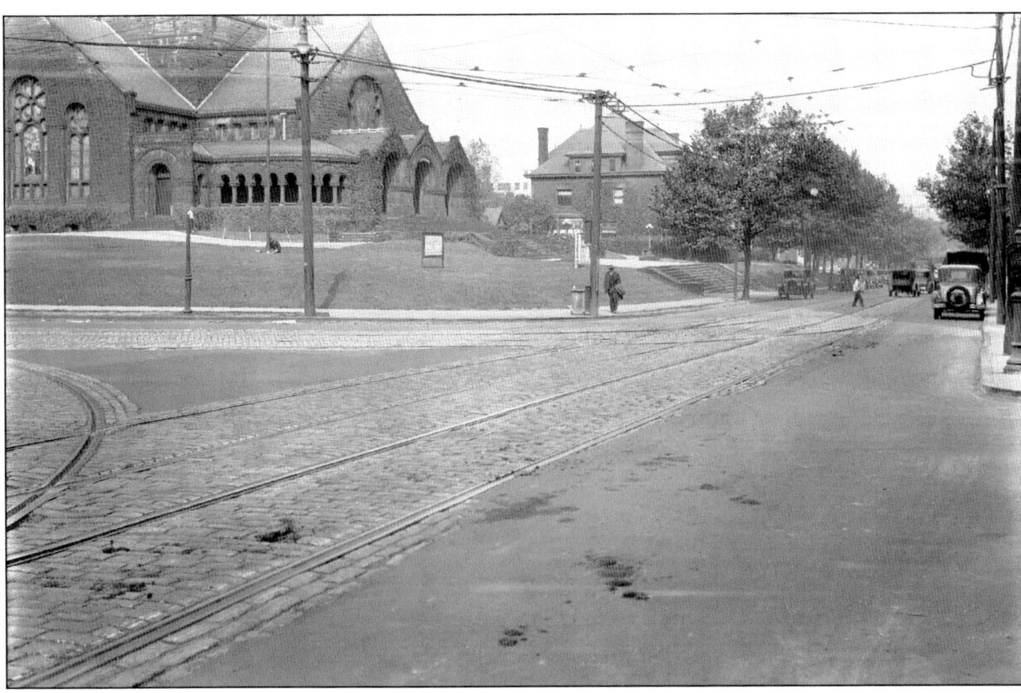

**CHRIST METHODIST CHURCH, SEPTEMBER 24, 1929.** This photograph was taken standing in the intersection of South Aiken and Centre Avenues looking toward the Christ Methodist Church. (Courtesy of the University of Pittsburgh Archives Service Center.)

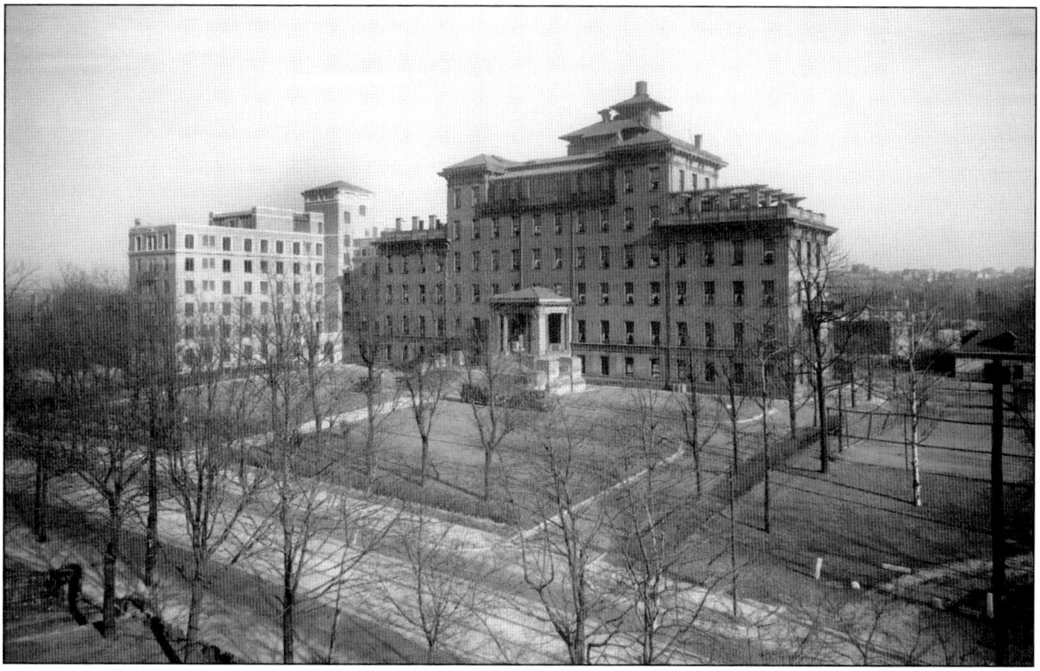

**SHADYSIDE HOSPITAL, C. 1927.** The Homeopathic Hospital opened a new state-of-the-art building in Shadyside on Centre Avenue west of the intersection with South Aiken Avenue. (Courtesy of the Shadyside Hospital Archives.)

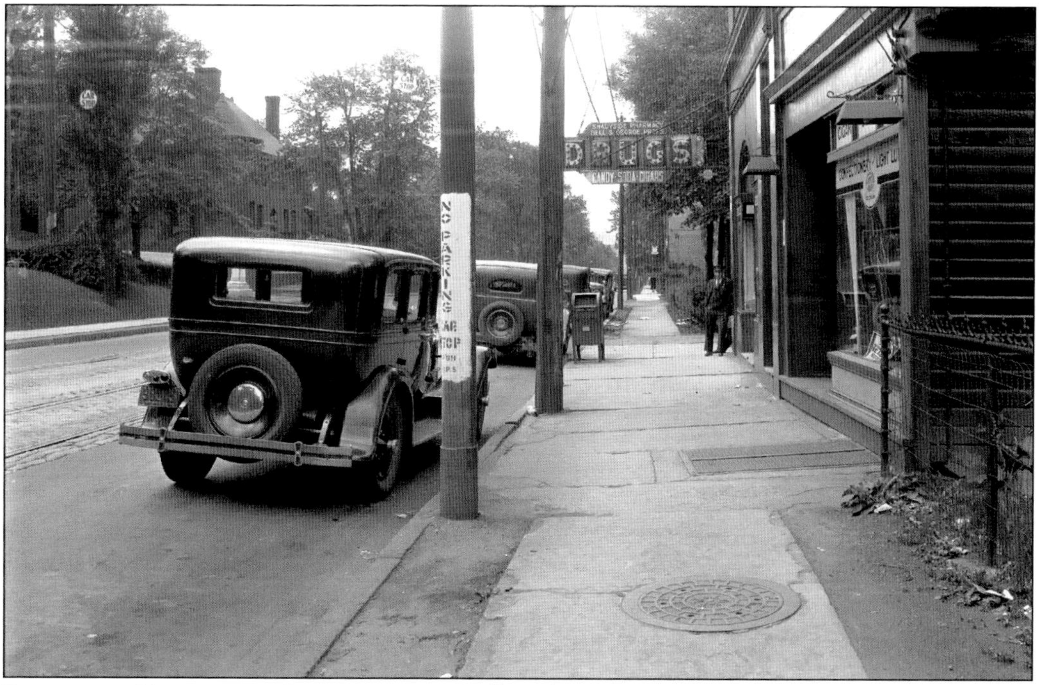


**SHADYSIDE PHARMACY, JUNE 8, 1931.** Bell and George were the proprietors of Shadyside Pharmacy at 5213 Fifth Avenue. Looking west on the left is Sunnyledge, the home of Dr. James H. McClelland. (Courtesy of the University of Pittsburgh Archives Service Center.)

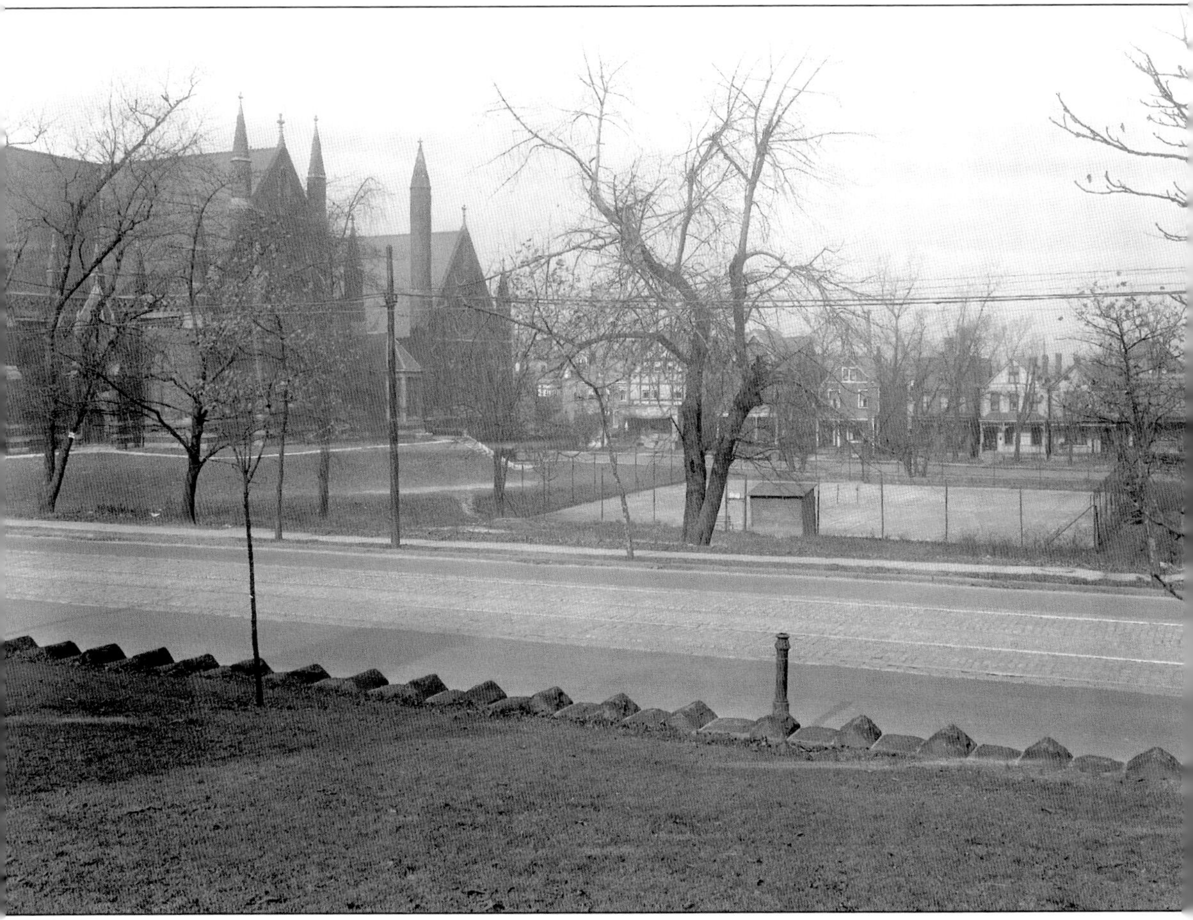

**THIRD PRESBYTERIAN CHURCH, NOVEMBER 2, 1927.** The Third Presbyterian Church is left of the tennis courts, and the homes lining Kentucky Avenue are clearly visible. (Courtesy of the University of Pittsburgh Archives Service Center.)

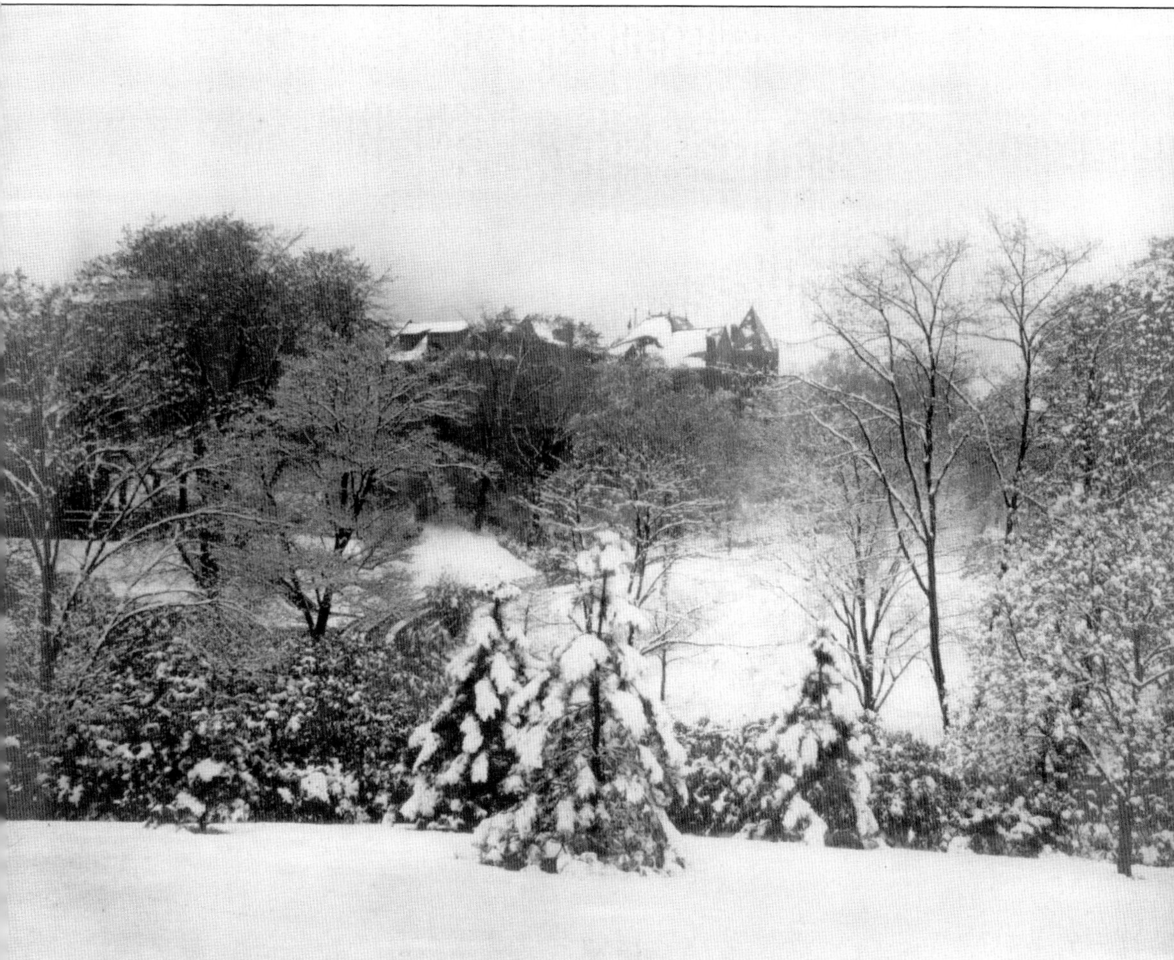

**CAMPUS DURING WINTER, 1923–1924.** Pictured here is the beautiful campus of the Pennsylvania College for Women during winter. (Courtesy of the Chatham College Archives.)

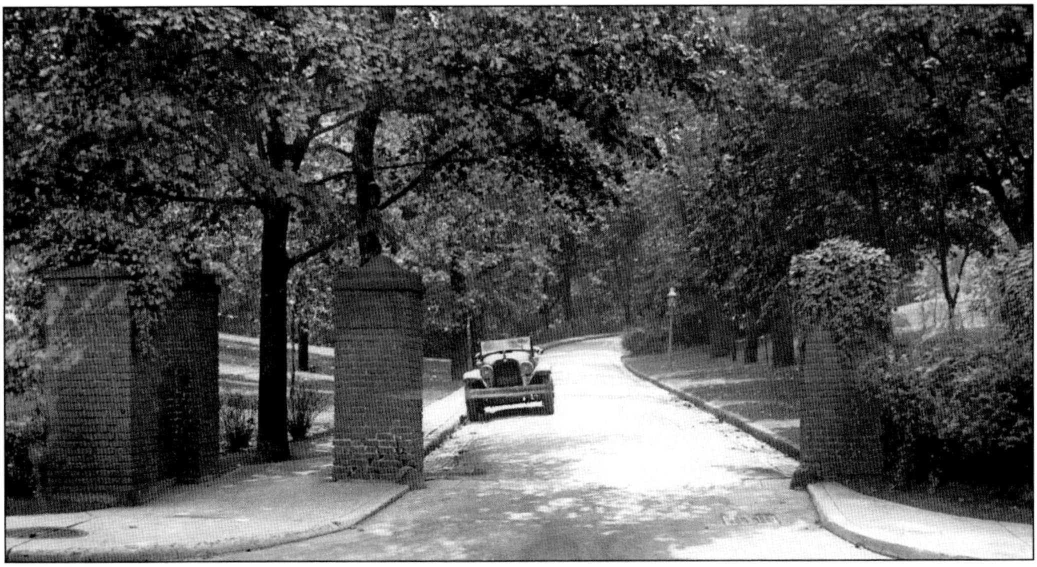

**WOODLAND ROAD GATE, 1926.** The Pennsylvania College for Women campus changed very little over the years. (Courtesy of the Chatham College Archives.)

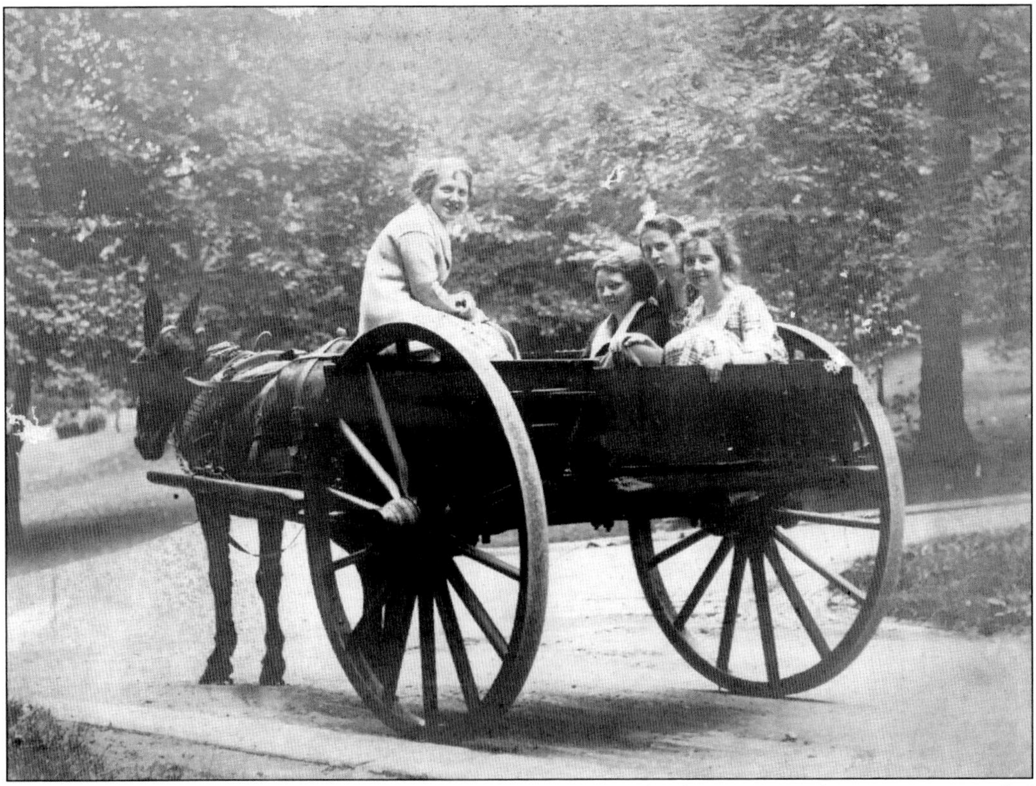

**THE WAGONETTE, 1920–1925.** Several generations of phaetons and wagons provided transportation and insured deliveries at the Pennsylvania College for Women. This is the wagonette as it appeared in the early 1920s during a regular run from Fifth Avenue to the top of college hill. (Courtesy of the Chatham College Archives.)

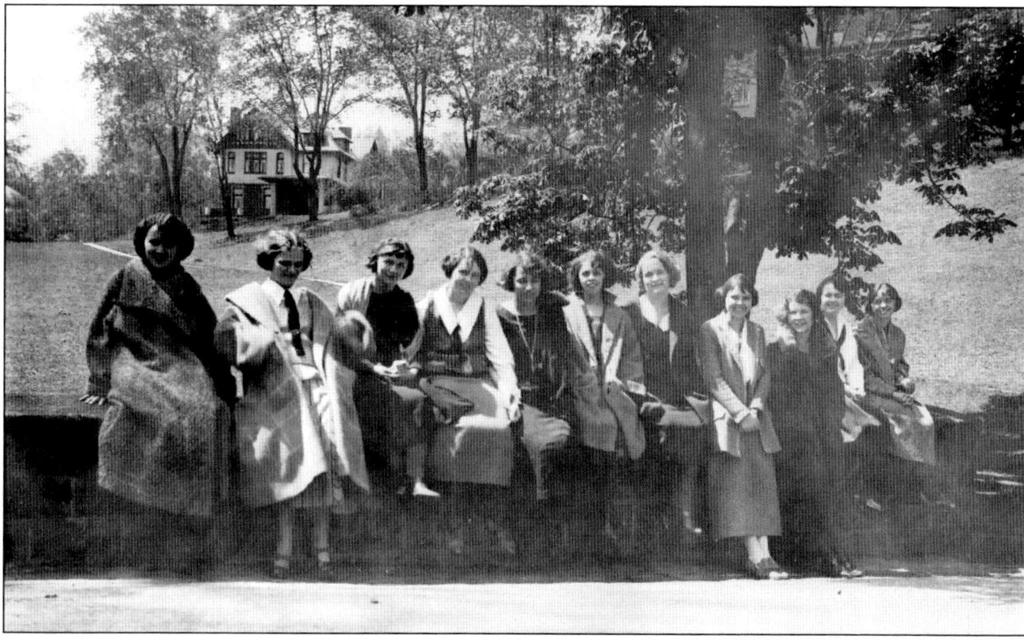

**BIRTHDAY PARTY, 1923–1925.** The Pennsylvania College for Women green has remained very much the same over the years. (Courtesy of the Chatham College Archives.)

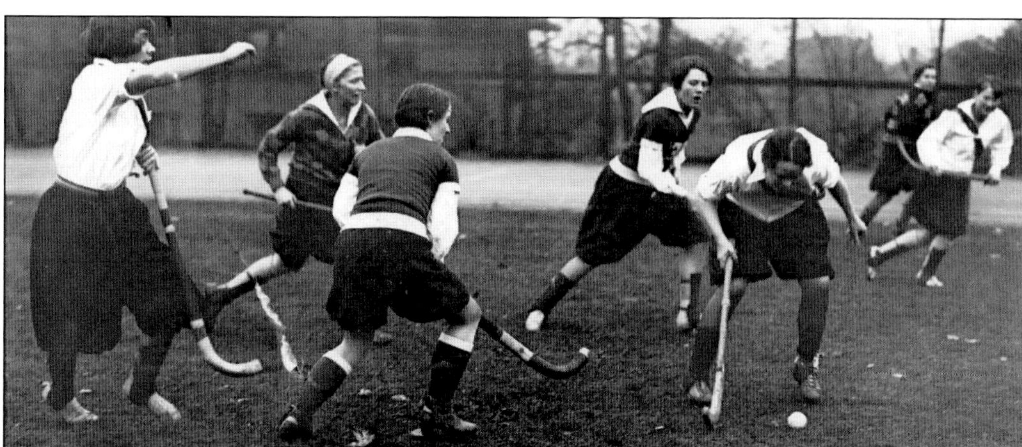

**FIELD HOCKEY TEAM, 1928–1930.** The women at the Pennsylvania College for Women are active in a number of sports. (Courtesy of the Chatham College Archives.)

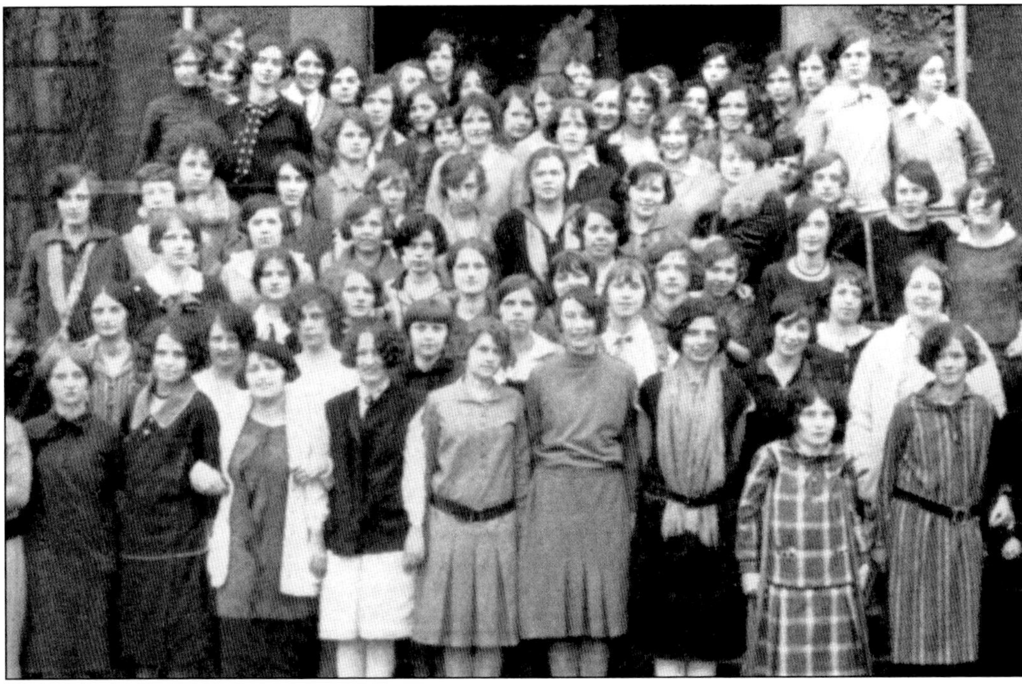

**FRESHMAN CLASS OF 1925.** The class size grew substantially since the graduating class of 1888 shown on page 49. The Pennsylvania College for Women freshman class of 1925 included Rachel Carson. (Courtesy of the Chatham College Archives.)

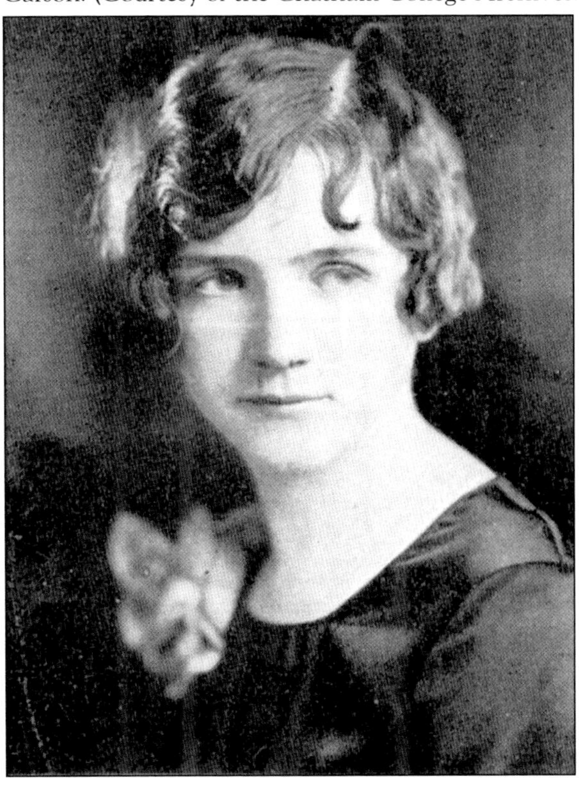

**RACHEL CARSON, 1928.** This is the senior photograph of Carson when she graduated from the Pennsylvania College for Women. She became famous for her book on the dangers of pollution and destroying the environment, *Silent Spring.* (Courtesy of the Chatham College Archives.)

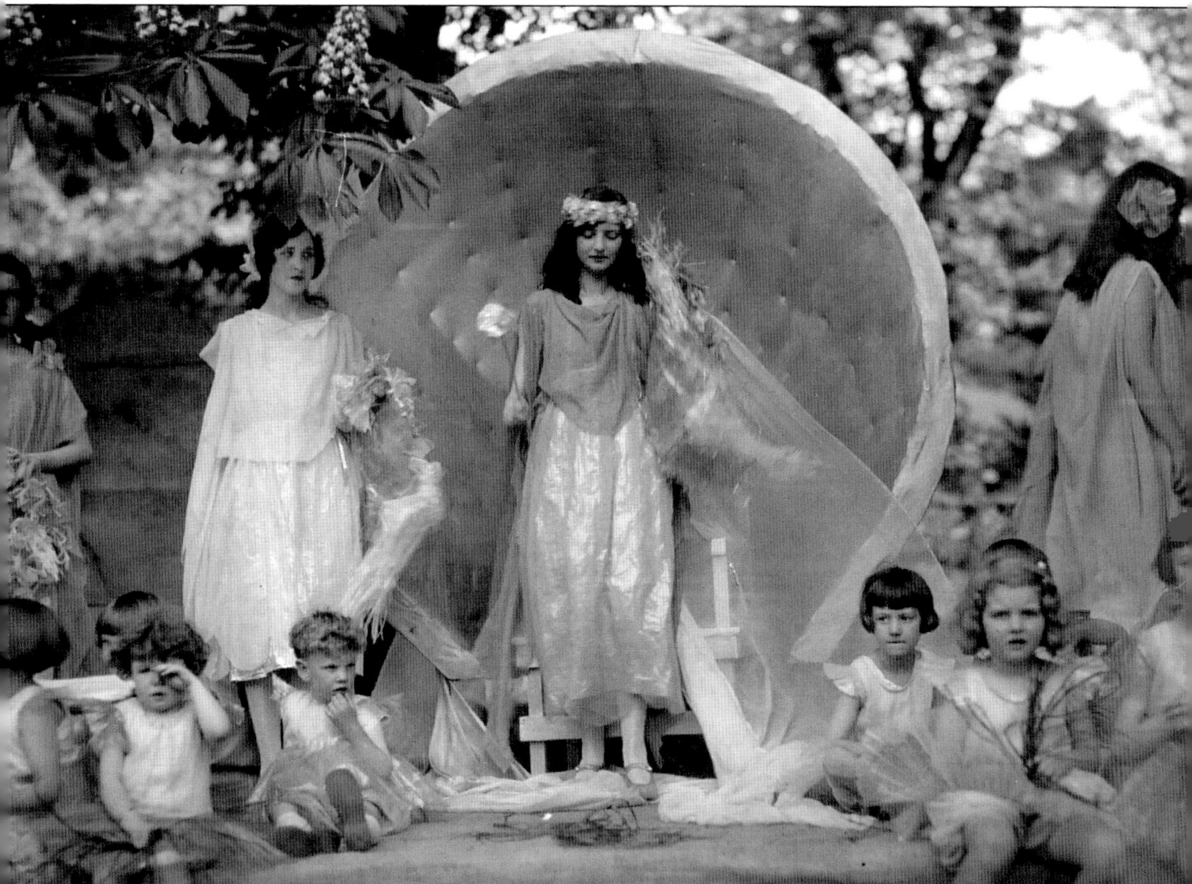

**MAY DAY, 1927.** Anne Negley is the May Queen (center, in shell) and acts in the *Deep Sea Caverns* play. The Pennsylvania College for Women made lavish sets and costumes for its May Day celebration. The celebration was popular with the community and turned a profit every year. (Courtesy of the Chatham College Archives.)

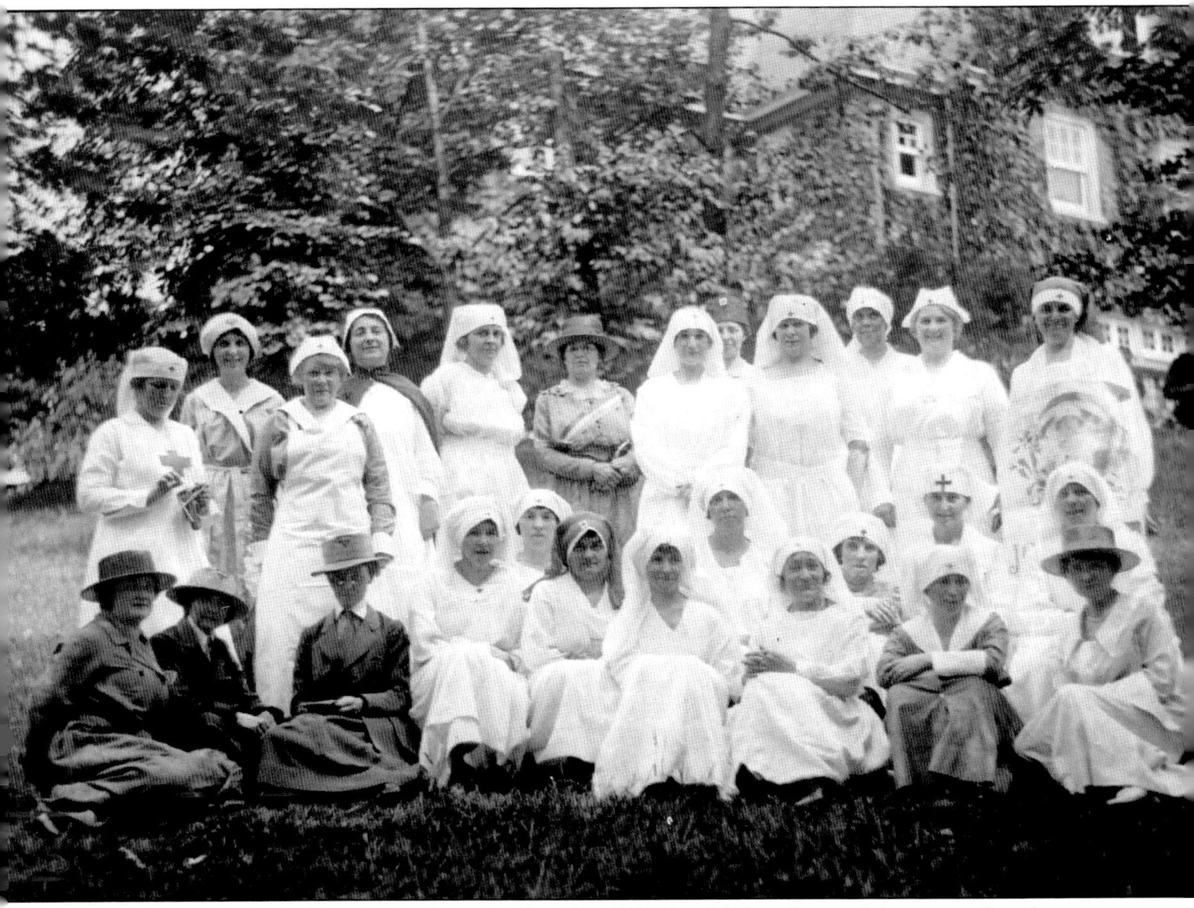

**MAY DAY PAGEANT, 1920.** During this World War I May Day celebration, the theme was "Victory Through Conflict." (Courtesy of the Chatham College Archives.)

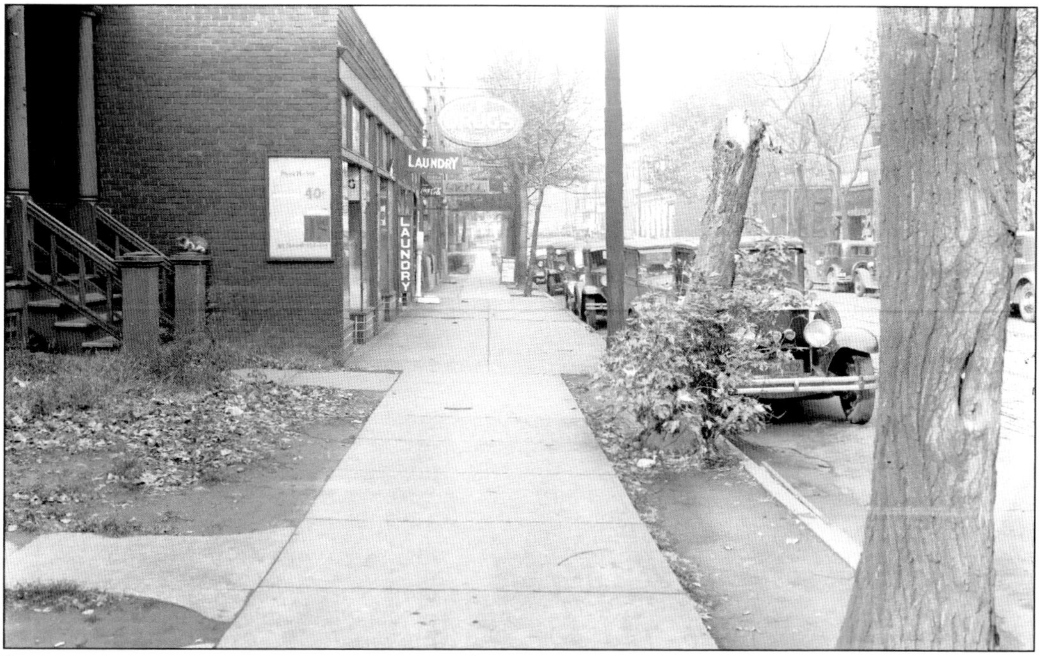


**SHADY AVENUE, NOVEMBER 2, 1934.** This is a view of the commercial district on Shady Avenue looking north from 236 Shady Avenue toward its intersection with Penn Avenue. A laundry, a grill, and a drugstore are clearly visible on the street. (Courtesy of the University of Pittsburgh Archives Service Center.)

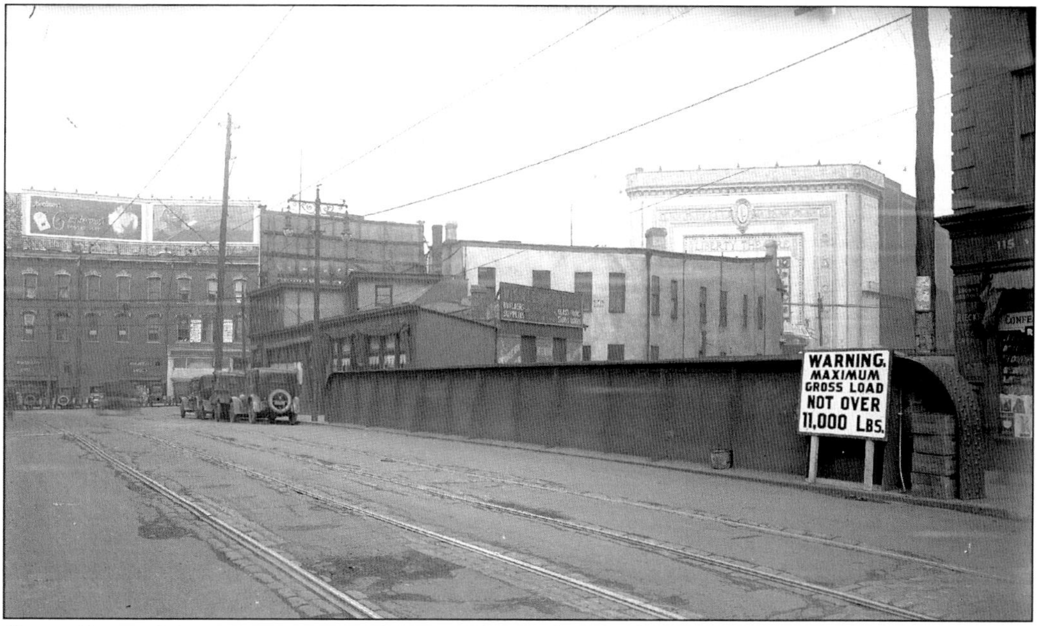


**GROSS LOAD, MARCH 14, 1924.** This view shows the Shady Avenue bridge looking toward East Liberty. Historically this was considered part of East Liberty, but currently Shadyside's border officially extends across the bridge to where Shady Avenue intersects with Penn Avenue. The Liberty Theatre is visible in the distance at right. (Courtesy of the University of Pittsburgh Archives Service Center.)

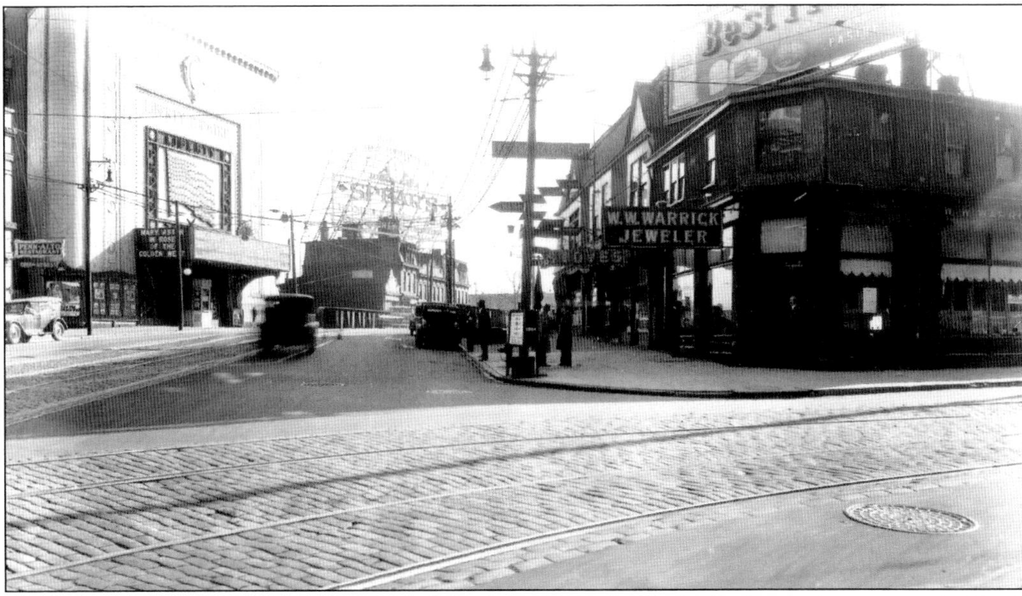


**Rose of the Golden West, 1927.** Historically looking down Penn Avenue with Shady Avenue veering off to the right the view was of East Liberty, which was an important shopping district for Shadyside residents. Today the official edge of Shadyside is defined by the center of Penn Avenue. The land right of center on Penn Avenue is considered Shadyside. (Courtesy of the University of Pittsburgh Archives Service Center.)

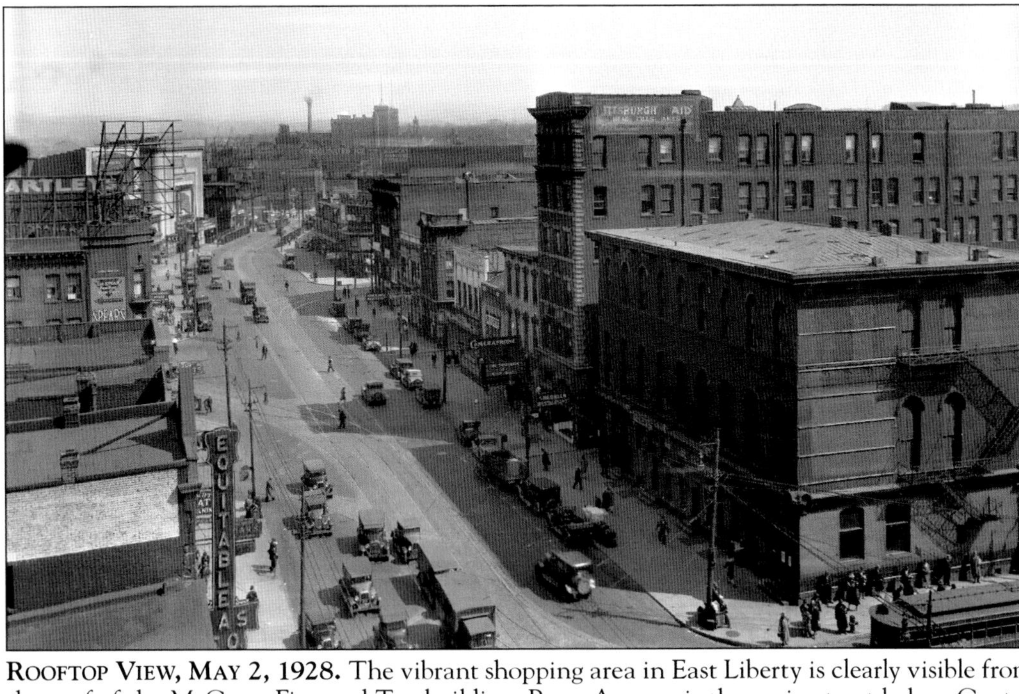


**Rooftop View, May 2, 1928.** The vibrant shopping area in East Liberty is clearly visible from the roof of the McCrory Five and Ten building. Penn Avenue is the main street below. Centre Avenue is the street visible at the lower right corner with the streetcar. Shady Avenue is the next street visible in the distance turning to the right from Penn Avenue. (Courtesy of the University of Pittsburgh Archives Service Center.)

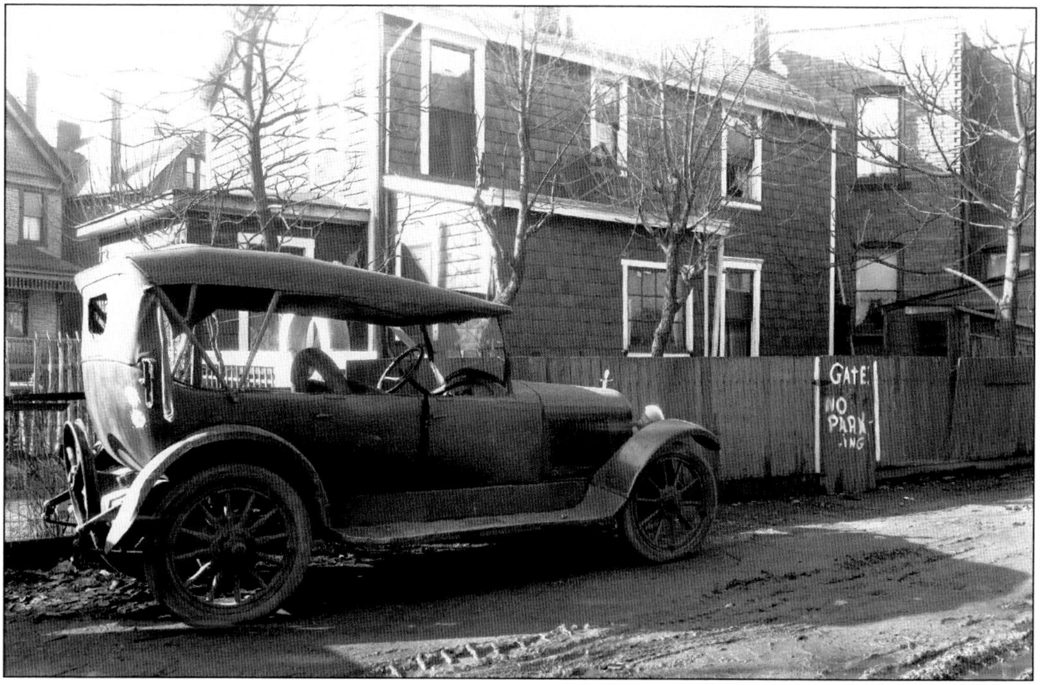


**NO PARKING, NOVEMBER 29, 1927.** Parking is a familiar problem today in Shadyside. This view is from 6383 Cassius Street looking west. (Courtesy of the University of Pittsburgh Archives Service Center.)

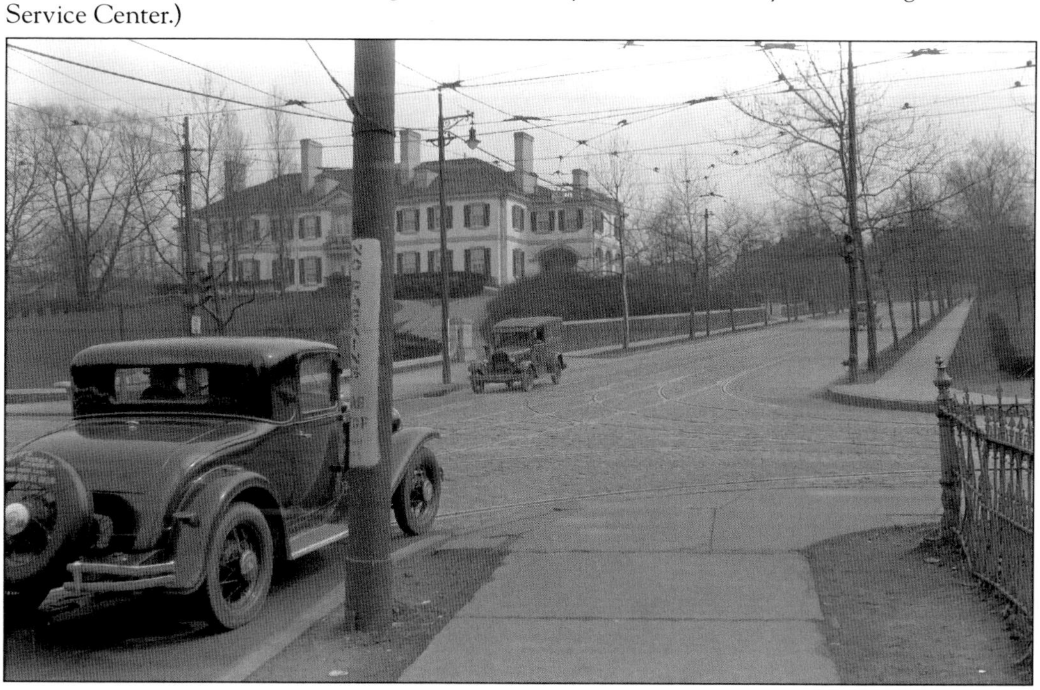

**MARSHALL HOUSE, MARCH 30, 1933.** Some prominent Pittsburgh people still choose to live in Shadyside even though many left the city for the suburbs. C. D. Marshall was the president of McClinitic-Marshall Construction Company and lived in this house at Fifth and Shady Avenues. (Courtesy of the University of Pittsburgh Archives Service Center.)